Networks, Terrorism and Global Insurgency

Post-9/11 we are living in a political climate characterised by fear of international terrorism and Global Insurgency. This book recognises the urgent need to assess the threat posed by international terrorism and consider how best it could be defeated. *Networks, Terrorism and Global Insurgency* brings together leading terrorism scholars and defence professionals to focus on the effect of networks on conflict and war.

This far-reaching book looks initially at the theoretical side of terrorism and global insurgency, before moving on to focus on networks themselves, with particular attention paid to the Al-Quaeda network. With eminent contributions including John Arquilla, David Ronfeldt, Stephen Sloan, Graham Turbiville Jr and Max Manwaring, this text makes vital reading for students and researchers of politics, and international relations.

This book was previously published as a special issue of the Journal *Low Intensity Conflict and Law Enforcement*.

Robert J. Bunker is a Counter-Terrorism and Less-Than-Lethal Weapons consultant to the National Law Enforcement and Corrections Center-West, a program of the National Institute of Justice. Dr. Bunker has written over one hundred works and essays for policy, military, and law enforcement publications.

Networks, Terrorism and Global Insurgency

Edited by
Robert J. Bunker

Routledge
Taylor & Francis Group

LONDON AND NEW YORK

First published 2005 by Routledge

This paperback edition published 2006 by Routledge
2 Park Square, Milton Park, Abingdon, Oxon, OX14 4RN

Simultaneously published in the USA and Canada
by Routledge
270 Madison Ave, New York, NY 10016

Transferred to Digital Printing 2006

Routledge is an imprint of the Taylor & Francis Group

© 2005, 2006 Edited by Robert J. Bunker

Typeset in Times 10/12pt by the Alden Group Oxford
Printed and bound in Great Britain by Antony Rowe Ltd., Chippenham,
Wiltshire

British Library Cataloguing in Publication Data
A catalogue record for this book is available from the British Library

Library of Congress Cataloging in Publication Data
A catalog record for this book has been requested

ISBN 0-415-38594-6 (pbk)
     0-415-34819-6 (Cased)

CONTENTS

Biographical Notes

Dr Sean K. Anderson is Professor of Political Science at Idaho State University. From 1980 to 1982, he worked as Chief Editor in the International Department of the Pars News Agency (now the Islamic Republic News Agency) in Tehran, Iran. In April 1990 he presented a paper, 'Iranian State Sponsorship of Terrorism', at the third annual Counter-Terror Study Center conference held at Winnipeg, Manitoba, which was later revised and published in *Conflict Quarterly*, Vol.11, No.4 (Fall 1991). He also wrote 'Warnings versus Alarms: Terrorist Threat Analysis Applied to the Iranian State-Run Media', *Studies in Conflict and Terrorism*, Vol.21 (Fall 1998), pp.277–303. Dr Anderson teaches courses on terrorism and comparative politics. He also works with state and local emergency planning and disaster relief agencies and participated in the April 2000 inaugural conference of the Oklahoma City Memorial Institute for the Prevention of Terrorism. He holds a PhD in Political Science from the University of Oklahoma.

Dr John Arquilla is a Professor of Defense Analysis at the US Naval Postgraduate School, and Co-Director of the Center on Terrorism & Irregular Warfare there. He has written several books and many articles on a variety of topics in military and security affairs; and is best known for his RAND studies with David Ronfeldt. Their joint research into cyberwar, networks and the concept of swarming has resulted in such studies as *Cyberwar Is Coming!* (1993); *In Athena's Camp* (1997); and *Networks and Netwars* (2001, Spanish and Chinese editions, 2003).

Lt Col. Matt Begert, USMC (Ret.) is Counter-OPFOR and Less-Than-Lethal Weapons programs manager, National Law Enforcement and Corrections Technology Center-West (NLECTC-West), a program of the National Institute of Justice (NIJ). He is a graduate of the Naval War College Senior Officers' course, has special operations experience with Thai, Korean and Japanese military forces and combat flight experience during the First Gulf War. He is a member of the Los Angeles Terrorism Early Warning Group and has counter-terrorism operational planning experience. His writings have appeared in many law enforcement and military publications.

Dr Robert J. Bunker is Counter-OPFOR and Less-Than-Lethal Weapons consultant, National Law Enforcement and Corrections Technology Center–West (NLECTC–West), a program of the National Institute of Justice (NIJ). He is a member of the Los Angeles Terrorism Early Warning Group and has counter-terrorism operational planning experience. He is a former Adjunct Professor, National Security Studies Program, California State University San Bernardino, past Fellow, Institute of Land Warfare, Association of the United States Army and former Professor, Unconventional Warfare, American Military University, Manassas Park, Virginia. He received his PhD from The Claremont Graduate University. He is the editor of *Non-State Threats and Future Wars* (Frank Cass 2003) and has written over one-hundred essays which have appeared in law enforcement, military, policy and military history publications.

Capt. Lisa J. Campbell, CA-ANG is an Intelligence Officer with the 146th Airlift Wing. She provides threat interpretation and recommendations to commanders and aircrews in the areas of airfield operations, flight planning and tactics for C-130 airlift missions. She has experience in readiness inspection exercises and has deployed to multiple theaters of operation, most recently CENTCOM, supporting aircrews flying missions for Operation Iraqi Freedom, Operation Enduring Freedom and the Horn Of Africa. She is a member of the Los Angeles Terrorism Early Warning Group.

Kimbra L. Fishel is Adjunct Professor of Political Science at George Washington University in Washington, DC. She teaches courses in International Politics, American Government and the American Presidency. She has published numerous articles and book chapters on US Foreign Policy and National Security, the United Nations, Conflict and Warfare, US Military Intervention and Terrorism. Her current research focuses on Al Qaeda's attempt to become a challenger to the existing international structure.

Dr Mark Galeotti is Director of ORECRU, the Organised Russian and Eurasian Crime Research Unit at Keele University, UK, the first such specialist centre in Europe. An acknowledged expert on post-Soviet security, crime and policing, he has written widely, including the recent edited work *Russian and Post-Soviet Organized Crime* and produces a monthly column on Russian security affairs for *Jane's Intelligence Review*. He is also the Managing Editor for the journal *Global Crime* and European Editor of *Low Intensity Conflict and Law Enforcement*. He has worked with many government and commercial agencies, including NATO, the US Department of Defense and the British National Criminal Intelligence Service. In 1996–97, he was seconded to the British Foreign Office in an advisory capacity.

Andrew Garfield serves as the European Director for the Terrorism Research Center, Inc. (TRC). In this capacity, Mr Garfield is responsible for TRC outreach and business initiatives within Europe. In addition, Mr Garfield provides direct support to US military and commercial customers wishing to utilize his extensive expertise on terrorism and security issues. Previously,

Mr Garfield served as a military then senior civilian intelligence officer, finishing his government service as a senior policy advisor in the UK Ministry of Defence. His specializations include Terrorism, Homeland Security, Psychological Warfare and Information Operations. He is currently the project leader for a major DoD funded study that is building a generic model of a terrorist organization and identifying common patterns of terrorist activity based on a detailed examination of recent terrorist campaigns. This model will also assess the various approaches adopted to combat terrorism determining the success and failure of each and identifying those tools and techniques that might be applicable to the current war. Mr Garfield is also Deputy Director of the International Policy Institute at King's College with special responsibility for North America.

Dr Max G. Manwaring holds the General Douglas MacArthur Chair of Research and is Professor of Military Strategy at the US Army War College. He is a retired US Army colonel and has served in various civilian and military positions, including the US Army War College, the United States Southern Command, and the Defense Intelligence Agency. Dr Manwaring holds a PhD in Political Science from the University of Illinois, and is a graduate of the US Army War College. He is the author and co-author of several articles, chapters and reports dealing with political-military affairs, and global and regional security concerns. He is the editor or coeditor of *El Salvador at War; Gray Area Phenomena: Confronting the New World Disorder; Beyond Declaring Victory and Coming Home: The Challenges of Peace and Stability Operations* and; *The Search for Security: A U.S. Grand Strategy for the Twenty-First Century*. Finally, Max Manwaring is co-author, with John Fishel, of *Uncomfortable Wars Revisited* (University of Oklahoma Press, forthcoming).

Neal A. Pollard is Vice President of Hicks & Associates, Inc., and co-founder of the Terrorism Research Center, Inc. He is a national security lawyer and counterterrorism planner, serving on the Board of Directors of the Terrorism Research Center, as an adjunct member of the Los Angeles Terrorism Early Warning Group, and on the adjunct faculty of the Georgetown University Walsh School of Foreign Service, where he developed and teaches courses on technology and homeland security. He holds degrees in mathematics and political science, a Master's degree in international security studies from the University of St Andrews, Scotland, and a Juris Doctor *cum laude* from the Georgetown University Law Center.

Dr David F. Ronfeldt has been a Senior Political Scientist in the International Security and Policy Group at RAND. During his 30 + years at RAND, he worked initially on US–Latin American security issues, then switched to work on information-age modes of conflict (e.g., cyberwar, netwar, swarming) and new principles for cooperation (e.g., guarded openness, noopolitik). He is co-author (mainly with John Arquilla) of *In Athena's Camp: Preparing for Conflict in the Information Age* (1997), *The Zapatista Social Netwar in Mexico* (1998), *Countering the New Terrorism* (1998), *The Emergence of Noopolitik: Toward an American Information Strategy* (1999), *Swarming and the Future of Conflict* (2000), and *Networks and Netwars: The Future of Terror, Crime, and Militancy* (2001). He is now working on a framework about the long-range evolution of societies, based on their ability to use and combine four major forms of organization (tribes, hierarchies, markets and networks).

Dr Stephen Sloan is Professor Emeritus at the University of Oklahoma and now a University Professor at the University of Central Florida. He formerly was associated with Booz-Allen & Hamilton, Inc., where he was in charge of the counter-terrorism practice and was a Senior Research Fellow at the Center for Aerospace Doctrine, Research, & Education at Air University, Maxwell AFB, Alabama. He is a recognized authority on terrorism with over 30 years of research experience, has written numerous publications including with Sean Anderson *The Historical Dictionary of Terrorism* and has conducted terrorism simulations for foreign and domestic police and military forces. He has also conducted crisis management exercises in the corporate and public sectors. Dr Sloan has also worked closely with state and local authorities in reference to developing their counter-terrorism intelligence capabilities.

John P. Sullivan is a researcher specializing in terrorism, conflict, urban operations, intelligence studies and the intersection between war and crime. He is currently a sergeant with the Los Angeles Sheriff's Department where he serves as officer-in-charge of the Los Angeles Terrorism Early Warning Group. His current research focus is the development of networked counter-terrorism and global security measures and military-police interaction in constabulary operations. He is the lead editor of *Jane's Unconventional Weapons Response Handbook* (2002) and has written for various law enforcement and military publications.

Graham H. Turbiville, Jr is a defense consultant with IAQ, Inc., Oakton, Virginia. He is the former director of the U.S. Army's Foreign Military Studies Office (FMSO) and the associated Fort Leavenworth Joint Reserve Intelligence Center, as well as past editor of *Low Intensity Conflict and Law Enforcement*. In addition to authoring many articles in military and law enforcement publications, he is the editor of *Global Dimensions of High Intensity Crime and Low Intensity Conflict* and the three-volume National Defense University Press series, *The Voroshilov Lectures*.

Preface: Future Trends in
Low Intensity Conflict

GRAHAM H. TURBIVILLE, JR

It has been a dozen years since the first issue of the journal *Low Intensity Conflict & Law Enforcement* was launched, an event that coincided with the demise of the faltering Soviet Union. The USSR's decline and essential end of the Cold War had already sparked a reexamination of fundamental military and security assumptions and especially the nature of future threats. The journal was intended to address a host of complex security problems around the world – some enduring and some strikingly new – that in terms of content, scale and impact seemed destined to define the international security environment in the years ahead. It was driven by perceived trends in a post-Cold War world where state institutions were increasingly being rendered ineffective by sweeping political and economic change, internal challenges or war – and where intensified ethno-national conflict, religious fundamentalism and more robust forms of terrorism and transnational crime joined traditional security problems.

Particular emphasis was placed on how these and associated issues interacted and blurred the distinctions among what had been seen as more clearly defined military and law enforcement challenges, and how 'national security' and 'public safety' were in some ways merging. In addressing these and associated issues, the journal focused on bringing together a wide range of practitioners and theorists, including international contributors. The identification of common elements and challenges despite a diversity of regions; the rising prominence of non-state actors and issues; the proliferation of non-traditional threats with ambiguous or shifting law enforcement and interagency content; and acute and simmering conflicts in global hotspots with an intermixing of ethno-national, political, ideological, religious and criminal and agendas have all been reflected in journal articles.

This special issue of the journal, ably edited by Dr Robert J. Bunker, illustrates how substantially our levels of analysis and understanding of these issues have progressed, and also how evolving, formerly exotic, or largely new phenomena have moved to center stage in the concern of security specialists. The post-11 September 2001 environment has consolidated their importance and centrality as urgent national and international security challenges that in many cases are linked in still-changing ways. In the articles contained here, terrorism in its various forms (including, of course, Al Qaeda and Islamic extremism); piracy and maritime violence; organized crime and criminal groupings; networks and linkages; perpetually troubled regions and vectors of conflict; technology and innovation; and new approaches, methods, tradecraft, and countermeasures have been treated excellently.

A number of the authors point to trends and likely developments ahead. There are two broad topics – among many that could be chosen – that this preface will underscore as well. These are the challenges posed by far more adaptive and innovative non-state actors, and a pressing need to better define and understand increasingly ambiguous opponents. These two broad issues are not new by any means, but they have gained new content and urgency illustrative of how other LIC and law enforcement-associated problems are evolving as well.

INCREASED THREAT OF ADAPTIVE, LEARNING ORGANIZATIONS WITH TERRORIST, INSURGENT AND CRIMINAL AGENDAS

Military assessments have for some years discussed the danger of adaptive enemies, most often in the context of national militaries at varying levels of development. The extent to which the context applies to non-state threats has become an even more pressing concern for the future. The extraordinary acquisition of Al Qaeda documents in Afghanistan and elsewhere – together with other revelations from around the world over the last few years – have highlighted the rapidly increasing adaptation and sophistication of non-state organizations. With ready access to information, the opportunities presented by globalization in its many forms, and an often deep appreciation of the role of perceptions management, this promises to be one of the most challenging aspects of LIC threat development in the years ahead.

The effective ways in which drug trafficking organizations collect intelligence; track law enforcement investigation, interdiction and seizure efforts; and effectively shift approaches and strategies to counter these efforts have been well known for many years. For at least a decade, terrorist and insurgent organizations – or their surrogates and representatives – have used the Internet and other computer and communications technologies in open and clandestine ways to advance their goals. Similarly, other technological innovations from ultra-light aircraft to advanced electronic equipment for surveillance, navigation and other uses have been procured and used with varying levels of success. The September 2000 discovery of a partially completed 100-foot submarine in a rural Colombian warehouse – together with Russian-language plans and instructions – defined for a brief while one of the more ambitious programs of illegal non-state actors (in this case narco-traffickers).[1]

But the level of systemized study, the incorporation of lessons learned and innovative approaches have today increased substantially, and point to an even more challenging future. At the lowest levels, law enforcement officers have been bemused by the dissemination of effective instructional material seized from well-organized criminal street gangs in and out of prison, to include tradecraft (e.g., lessons learned on weapons concealment, information gathering or survival) and rudimentary doctrines of self-justification. At the international security level, Al Qaeda clearly is one of the most innovative, and perhaps is a prototype for the kind of innovation and systematized planning that will evolve more generally with other groups in the years ahead. A notable illustration in this regard – and reportedly a pale reflection of other acquired materials not yet publicly available – is the Al Qaeda manual *Military Studies in the Jihad Against the Tyrants* that sets out approaches and tradecraft associated with target definition and preparation. The manual identifies, for example, the requirement to collect 'information about strategic buildings, important establishments, and military bases', including 'ministries such as those of Defense and Internal Security, airports, seaports, land border points, embassies, and radio and TV stations'. It defines personnel requirements, organizational techniques, security needs, the importance of analysis, funding approaches, and various kinds of tradecraft among other topics.[2] Other groups and sponsors have produced analogous, if less prominent and compelling, materials, but the state of the art has increased many-fold from a decade ago.[3]

The examination of non-state 'war-fighting' theory is also striking in its novelty. In February 2002, the Al Qaeda-associated Internet magazine *Al-Ansar: For The Struggle Against the Crusader War* published a piece written by Ubeid Al-Qurashi, identified as a close bin Laden aide.[4] The Western debates and discussions of the nature of future war – to include formulations like 'Fourth Generation Warfare', 'Preventive Strikes', 'Early Warning, Deterrence', and others – were incorporated into the article, which concluded that the apparent imbalance of forces between Islamic movements and America was far from an indicator of future success, and cited the need for Islam to 'internalize the rules of fourth generation warfare'. With a nice turn of the old and the new, of the Arab East and American-led West, the author noted: 'We pray to Allah to silence the cowards' crow-like calls, and to bring forth for this [Islamic] nation a new generation of preachers and clerics, who can meet the challenges posed by fourth-generation warfare.[5]

Nascent chemical and biological weapons development planning, carefully timed video releases and distribution, well-prepared news distortions and perceptions management, operational expansion into unlikely regions, new weapons and technology acquisition, the addition of maritime transportation and attack resources, and other analogous dimensions all mark now familiar, but accelerating trends for non-state actors.[6] The organization, training and capabilities of smaller and less developed armed groups have increased substantially as well, with notable examples appearing recently on both sides of the US southwest border.

In the wake of 11 September 2001 ('9/11'), the importance of border security and potential dangers to the US homeland have intensified, not only along the US–Mexican border but on the US–Canadian frontier as well. Certainly, the adaptability and learning abilities of drug trafficking and alien smuggling organizations had already become legendary along the 2,000-mile long southwest border. The constant struggle between criminal innovation and law enforcement countermeasures is instructive in itself. The new post-9/11 prominence of the border as a potential vector for terrorism, however, has been superimposed on other developing security challenges there.[7]

The US border has in recent years become an increasingly dangerous environment for law enforcement officers, with armed confrontations and planned or random shots frequently fired from across the border. High levels of border violence – including that directed at law enforcement – have been generated by increasingly well-organized and armed drug-trafficking organizations in Mexico and by other forms of cross-border criminality. Mexican military units and police patrols – in addition to drug traffickers, alien smugglers and illegal immigrants – cross into US territory by accident and design along the often unmarked border, raising concerns about risky, surprise encounters with the US Border Patrol, other law enforcement bodies, and even US military units.

In this milieu, the development and capabilities of some armed groupings supporting Mexican drug-trafficking organizations – including some operating in close proximity to the border – appear to be undergoing notable changes. A markedly different kind of armed group known as '*Los Zetas*' has engaged in fatal clashes between Mexican Police and Army units near the Mexican city of Nuevo Laredo on the US border. *Los Zetas* provide a principal means of firepower, security and coercion for the Mexican Gulf drug-trafficking cartel and underscore the near parity that such well-funded groups can achieve with law enforcement and the military. *Los Zetas* are judged by Mexican law enforcement and military officials to be composed of substantial numbers of former Mexican special forces soldiers and other military personnel. Such Mexican military special operations units as the GAFES (Airborne Special Forces Groups) have been used extensively in counter-drug operations, but have had problems in the past with corruption and human rights violations. It is disaffected members of the GAFES and other similar groups that have joined *Los Zetas* and turned their skills to murder, kidnapping and 'narco-military' actions.

They have developed an internal organization and improved skills in training camps whose description suggests an insurgent encampment rather than a criminal enterprise. Mexican officials have identified a farm equipped as a military training camp similar to a GAFE training site. Group members – possessing military training – are well armed and are judged to operate with more 'tactical' effectiveness than the Mexican authorities they have encountered. In addition to the standard automatic weapons (AK-47s and AR-15s), a 40-minute firefight in Nuevo Laredo in August 2003 revealed that they possessed grenade launchers and a 50-cal. machinegun ('from the war in the Middle East').[8] There are analogous organizations evidently appearing as well. In early 2004, a massive gunfight in Anáhuac was blamed on *Los Zetillas* – said to be children and nephews of *Los Zetas* members – that operate in Nuevo León and Tamaulipas.

It should be noted that the US side of the border is generating another entry into this mix that has shown considerable innovation and adoptability. The flood of illegal immigrants in some areas generated real concerns from US border ranchers and other residents, and sparked self-defense measures. While initially ad hoc efforts by individuals or small groups of ranchers and neighbors, efforts have gained organizational identity and visibility. Various local groups and coalitions have been established over the length of the border, including at least one formed by Native Americans on a reservation paralleling the Mexican border. These are not criminal or terrorist groups, of course, but they add arms and heat to a volatile non-state mix. One of the most prominent, vocal, and well-resourced of these groups is the American Border Patrol (ABP).[9] In addition to patrolling illegal immigrant crossing areas on foot, horseback and vehicle, performing occasional citizen arrests, and reporting crossers to authorities, the ABP has used technology in innovative ways. This includes the construction and use of video-equipped unmanned aerial vehicles (UAV) to record illegal crossing activities in real time. The so-called 'Border Hawk' UAV transmits live images including live feed via Mobile Internet Satellite Transmitter (MIST).

Overall, both sides of the southwest border on any day features a compelling and evolving mix of entities and agendas – patrolling law enforcement organizations, military personnel and units, organized criminal groupings, illegal immigrants including possible terrorists, and ordinary citizens pursuing their businesses and lives. To that mix has been added 'self-defense' groups and volunteer patrols in the United States, and south of the border increasingly organized, well-armed and criminal paramilitaries. How this politically charged volatile mix will evolve and interact in the months and years ahead is uncertain. But for those who believe that the United States has already lost control of this border, the prospect for increasing forms of 'low intensity conflict' by adaptive non-state organizations determined to increase their voice and effectiveness, seems all but certain.

DEFINING THE ENEMY – HISTORY AND DEEP CULTURAL ANALYSIS

An issue that continues to occupy specialists is identifying the nature of the unconventional enemy we are encountering – or may in the future encounter – on battlefields abroad and in our own backyards. There have been a number of notable and useful efforts over the last decade in this regard, that offer instructive generalizations and some specifics.[10] Certainly, the role of culture in understanding the causes and possible resolution of conflict has received greater, well-deserved attention in some analytical quarters, and has been further highlighted operationally by the successes of culturally trained and prepared special operations forces.[11]

Deep knowledge of a culture is instructive in many unanticipated ways. Could, for example, poetry be a dimension of LIC and a source of information? A peripheral issue, clearly, but discoveries of classically styled Arabic poems in 'abandoned safe houses, training camps, and trenches' in Afghanistan addressed the central causes, actions and consequences of Al Qaeda's war against infidels and suggested they had a strong mobilizing role as well as providing new insights to those who studied them.[12] Similarly, the efforts of government-sponsored Yemeni poets to counter extremism and terrorism – with at least some measure of success – highlight another aspect of a powerful cultural form that is at least worth knowing about.[13] There is a rich and growing body of scholarship – specialized and often less accessible to the general reader and even government security specialist because of its limited distribution – that underscores the importance of cultural issues and examining combatants in their regional, societal, and historical context.

In examining the spectrum of cultures, motives and methods by what are variously categorized as insurgents, terrorists, criminals, freedom fighters, etc., the value of looking back has proven – as is so often the case – to be instructive for better understanding the present and future. As one specialist put it well, 'a stronger grounding of culture and history with the power of imagination can serve as a bridge to preventing information gaps'.[14] Perhaps no research has been more instrumental as a catalyst for insightful research of this type than Marxist historian Eric J. Hobsbawm's two works *Primitive Rebels* and *Bandits*. In treating what he called 'social bandits' in their cultural context around the world, these two books sparked both controversy and immediately began to generate a superb body of research comprising books, monographs, and dozens of articles extending well beyond the original Hobsbawn model.

Whatever one may think of Hobsbawm's narrower original hypotheses and research, this continuing work is vastly expanding knowledge of mixed criminal, terrorist, insurgent and other violent non-state groups and the relationship of their actions to ideological, religious, tribal, kinship, cultural, criminal profiteering and other motivations. These informed assessments – many contained only in conference and seminar papers or in specialized, limited distribution journals – span many dimensions of historical low intensity conflict around the world that have contemporary relevance. They encompass, for example, mid-nineteenth-century Karbala (Iraq) mafia-rebels, Indian dacoits and their sometime political agendas, Kenyan Mau Mau, Western and US mercenaries, shifting Mexican and other Latin American rural and urban brigand-revolutionary activity, Chechen separatist-raiders, Zimbabwean and Mozambiquean criminal-revolutionaries, Cuban armed separatists, Malaysian White Flag Society members, and Chinese brigand-insurgents, among many others.[15]

Collectively they underscore what specialists writing in this volume well understand – that contemporary manifestations are not so new, and while they may be extraordinarily complex, they do not by any means defy understanding. As a previously cited specialist noted in regard to one security focus today that could be applied more broadly, 'like the roots of a tree, al Qaeda's cultural pedigree and those of the MILF [Moro Islamic Liberation Front] Laskar Jihad and Jemaah Islamiyah extend deep into historical obscurity in a web of associations'.[16] The point is that they do not need to be that obscure and careful study reveals not only instructive insights but potential solutions.

Piracy and intensified prospects of maritime terrorism provide an example of this 'historical parallelism' or at least strong echoes.[17] The Abu Sayyaf Group (ASG) – a terrorist-criminal group with links to Al Qaeda going back to Afghanistan – draws on the strong Moro maritime piracy heritage, operating as successful pirates in Philippine coastal waters and sometimes further from home. Filipino commentators draw parallels between the legendary Sulu pirate Jikiri of the early twentieth century and Abu Sayyaf. Branded a bandit and pirate by US authorities, Jikiri and up to 100 followers had led numerous successful depredations against Filipino, American, British and other national persons and interests before he was killed in a hand-to-hand battle with a US officer on the island of Patian.[18] Today, however, a more complex picture emerges of Jikiri, whose resistance and criminality was spurred by the authorities 'failure to respect the traditional rights of his people regarding the pearl beds of Sulu' as well as Moro history of Islam-based tradition of resistance, as a fighter for Moro rights.[19] In any event, the incident and others noted above point to the historical and cultural complexities surrounding so many areas of low intensity conflict today, and the potential value in sorting out motives and better defining problems as we seek to deal with them.

Overall, future requirements to deal with adaptive enemies and assessing motivations and aims of complex enemies addressed briefly above are only two of many issues facing security professionals concerned with issues of low intensity conflict. Evolved and perhaps quite different forms of terrorism, criminality, insurgency and other security threats will be generated by the experiences of the last years, and by the likely expanding access to information, availability of technology, and the interaction of political, economic and cultural forces in a 'globalized' environment. The contributions in this volume – for the understanding they bring to contemporary issues of 'networks, terrorism and global insurgency', and the insight they suggest for the future – will substantially advance the difficult job of quality assessment and effective action ahead.

NOTES

1. 'Colombian Drug Smugglers Built Sub', Associated Press, 8 September 2000; and 'Colombia Cops Find Submarines Big Enough for Tons of Drugs', Associated Press, 7 September 2000.
2. See *Military Studies in the Jihad Against the Tyrants* in 'Declaration of Jihad Against the Country's Tyrants Military Series', a document entered in evidence at the trial for the African Embassy bombings, Southern District Court, New York City Attorney General's Office, circa early to mid 1990s, in translation from Arabic. The 'Twelfth Lesson' dealing with espionage and information gathering is particularly applicable.
3. The French-based site ⟨http://stcom.net/⟩ is a case in point. Gaidz Miniassian, 'French Internet Site Offers Jihad Training Manual', *Le Monde*, 19 December 2002, available at ⟨http://www. lemonde.fr/⟩.
4. Middle East Media Research Institute, 'Bin Laden Lieutenant Admits to September 11 and Explains Al-Qa'ida's Combat Doctrine', Special Dispatch Series-No.134, 10 February 2002, available at ⟨http://memri.org/bin/articles.cgi?Page + archives&Area + sd&ID = SP34402⟩. See also the many other pertinent MEMRI media reports and Arabic, Farsi and Hebrew translations.
5. Ibid.
6. Jason Burke, 'Al-Qa'ida Launches Online Terrorist Manual', The *Observer*, 18 January 2004; 'Russia: Deputy FM Says Al-Qa'ida Trying to Expand to New Territories', *Interfax*, 20 January 2004, FBIS no. CEP20040120000253; Bob Newman, 'Terrorists Feared to Be Planning Sub-Surface Naval Attacks', *CNSNews.com*, 3 December 2003, at ⟨http://www. cnsnews.com⟩; Rohan Sullivan, 'Al-Qaida Program to Make Chemical, Biological Weapons Halted by Afghan War', *Cnews*, 26 January 2004, at ⟨http://cnews.canoe.ca/CNEWS/⟩
7. Much of federal border law enforcement – notably the Border Patrol, Immigration and Naturalization Service, and the Customs Service – have been subsumed by the Department of Homeland Security (DHS), and the new Northern Command incorporates a range of organizations performing support missions related to border security and civil authority support. Under DHS, the Border Patrol is continuing installation of monitoring devices along the borders to detect illegal activity and the growth initiated some years earlier has continued. According to The White House, 'Fair and Secure Immigration Reform', Fact Sheet, 7 January 2004, found at ⟨http://www.whitehouse.gov/news/releases/2004/01/20040107-1.html⟩, Border Patrol strength, for example, increased from 9,788 on 11 September 2001 to 10,835

on 1 December 2003. In addition, 'between ports of entry on the northern border, the size of the Border Patrol has tripled to more than 1,000 agents'.

8. Diego Enrique Osorno, 'Drug Trafficking Is Allowed', *Milenio Semanal*, 12 October 2003, as translated in FBIS LAP20031013000069.

9. The Website for this group is found at ⟨http://www.americanborderpatrol.com/⟩.

10. See, for a few examples, Ralph Peters, 'The New Warrior Class', *Parameters* (Summer 1994), pp.16–26; John Mueller, 'The Remnants of War: Thugs as Residual Combatants', paper delivered at the International Convention of the Central and Eastern European International Studies Association and the International Studies Association, Budapest, Hungary, 27 June 2003; and Raymond C. Finch III, 'A Face of Future Battle: Chechen Fighter Shamil Basayev', *Military Review*, (June–July 1997), available at ⟨http://fmso.leavenworth.army.mil/fmsopubs/issues/shamil/shamil.htm⟩.

11. Kevin Avruch, *Culture and Conflict Resolution* (Washington, DC: United States Institute of Peace, 1998) does a particularly good job in that regard.

12. Some of these may have been written by bin Laden himself. David Rohde, 'Verses Form bin Laden's War', *New York Times*, 7 April 2002.

13. An assessment of the program's success in Yemeni tribal areas by a government 'strategist' there had this take: 'It's been very effective ... It's not the American way, it's the Yemeni way.' Geoffrey York, 'Battling Terror With Verse: It's the Yemeni Way – Poetry the Solution in a Lawless Word of Violent Radicals', *The Globe and Mail*, 8 May 2003, p.A3, available at ⟨http://www.globeandmail.com/servlet/ArticleNews/TPStory/LAC/20030508/UYEMEN_2/International/Idx⟩.

14. Graham Gerard Oag, 'Pre-empting Maritime Terrorism in Southeast Asia', Institute of South East Asian Studies, 29 November 2002, available at ⟨http://www.iseas.edu.sg/viewpoint/ggonov02.pdf⟩.

15. These works are far too numerous to list here, but representatives of several illustrative regional works include, among others: Pierre Gilhodes, 'La Violence en Colombie, Banditisme et Guerre Sociale', *Cahiers du Monde Hispanique et Luso-Bresilien*, Vol.26 (1976), pp.70–81; Juan R.I. Cole and Moojan Momen, 'Mafia, Mob and Shiism in Iraq: The Rebellion of Ottoman Karbala, 1824–1843', *Past and Present*, Vol.112 (August 1986), pp.112–43; Vinita Damodaran, 'Azad Dastas and Dacoit Gangs: The Origins and Underground Activity in Bihar, 1942–1944', *Modern Asian Studies*, Vol.26, No.3 (1992), pp.417–50; Michael Watts, 'Banditry, Rebellion, and Social Protest in Africa: A Review,' *African Economic History*, Vol.16 (1987), pp.123–9; Richard W. Slatta, ed., *Bandidos: The Variety of Latin American Bandits* (Westport, CT: Greenwood Publishing Group, 1987); Gary R. Perlstein, 'The Mercenary as Social Bandit: A Preliminary Look', *International Journal of Offender Therapy and Comparative Criminology*, Vol.32 (December 1988), pp.201–207; 'Social Banditry: Hobsbawm's Model and the "Mau Mau"', *African Studies*, Vol.39 (January 1980), pp.77–97; 'Social Banditry in Zimbabwe (Rhodesia) and Mozambique, 1894–1907', *Journal of South African Studies*, Vol.4 (October 1977), pp.1–30. A frequent manifestation is the mix of criminal, political and ideological agendas. In Robert Cribb, *Gangsters and Revolutionaries: The Jakarta People's Militia and the Indonesian Revolution, 1945–1949* (Honolulu, HI: University of Hawaii Press, 1991), for example, the mix of criminal and revolutionary interests among post-Second World War Indonesia's people's militias seems quite contemporary in some ways.

16. Oag.

17. One of the recent book-length additions to this body of work, C.R. Pennell, ed., *Bandits at Sea: A Pirates Reader* (New York: New York University Press, 2001), addresses the phenomenon of piracy in its many regional and cultural forms.

18. Vic Hurley, *The Swish of the Kris* (New York: E.P. Dutton & Co., 1936), ch.21, 'Jikiri', p.223. This fine old book is also available on-line at ⟨http://www.bakbakan.com/swishkb.html⟩. See also Peter Jaymul V. Uckung, 'From Jikiri to *Abu Sayya*', *Philippines Inquirer*, 9 June 2001, available at ⟨http://www.inq7.net⟩.

19. Uchung.

Foreword: Responding to the Threat

STEPHEN SLOAN

Since the profound shock waves generated by the events of 11 September ('9/11'), governments and the public have essentially been reacting to threats and acts of terrorism. Whether there is the promulgation of a new color-coded threat level or a call for a global response to the latest acts of carnage, the mass audience often rides an emotional roller coaster characterized by chronic unstated fears of what could happen or by anger and intimidation after a particularly massive or graphic incident of terrorism. Governments in turn reflect the public mood and engage in heated rhetoric and establish commissions addressing what should have been done to prevent the carnage. In the cycle of under- and over-reaction, the official focus is primarily on 'crisis management', 'consequence management', and other techniques that address the response to incidents and these often take precedence over the need to develop long-term policies associated with strategies against adversaries who have long-term and often violent political and criminal agendas.

Internationally, regionally and domestically, and locally, authorities are primarily concerned with either 'putting out fires' or taking the precautions necessary to prevent an immediate threat. The focus on measures to counter a current threat is, of course, vital but until the often-fragmented counterterrorism community is engaged in strategic assessment and adopts a 'look over the horizon mentality', governments will essentially pursue short-term tactical reactions to what is ultimately a long-term, offensive, strategic threat. Such an assessment is not a luxury that can only take place in the relative quiet of academia. It is imperative that, despite the daily pressures policy makers and those in the operational arena face, they engage in a longer-term evaluation of future trends in line with the changing nature of terrorism and, more specifically, the intentions, capabilities and goals of those who have taken the initiative in their assault on the civil order. A failure to take the long-term offensive will continue to place authorities in an often ad hoc defensive and reactive position based on short-term requirements instead of long-term vision.

The editor of this volume has brought together an impressive group of contributors with academic, policy and operational experience. Each one provides an understanding based on their expertise that can assist present and future authorities who will have to address a continuing and enduring threat. The authors provide a series of themes that can help the international community to seize the initiative in that protracted conflict known as terrorism.

TERRORISM AS A MANIFESTATION OF THE TRANSFORMATION OF THE INTERNATIONAL SYSTEM AND THE RISE OF NON-STATE ACTORS

At the outset, it is vital to recognize that terrorism is ultimately a manifestation of the changing nature of the international political system. The end of the Cold War broke down the arbitrary order imposed by the United States and the Soviet Union through their competition and 'the balance of nuclear terror'. The disintegration of an old order led to the loss of coherence in global politics, the rise of new and often fragile states, as well as geographic areas of ungovernability where there was a total breakdown of state sovereignty and control. In a most profound manner, the way of conducting international politics that had its genesis in the Treaty of Westphalia and the Congress of Vienna is undergoing a profound transformation. What we are now witnessing is the increasingly potent challenge to the 'state-centric system' with the emergence of non-state actors. These actors take many forms including multinational corporations, non-governmental organizations, criminal enterprises and transnational guerilla and terrorist groups. The breakdown of the inter-state system has been marked by a very disorderly process where in more or less sovereign states have increasingly been supplanted by new non-state players in international affairs.

   This transition, is of course, not solely the result of the demise of the Cold War. Equally profound has been the impact of modern technology, particularly in the realm of transportation and communication, that has made the arbitrary boundaries of the classic nation-state increasingly porous and less significant in the face of a technological change heretofore undreamed of – in the form of the Internet and the transcendental nature of cyberspace. Yet, even as the information explosion outwardly creates the sense of a global community, there is a dialectic at work. In this expanding technological and information universe, there is a resurgence of traditional values and goals as a reaction to the technological revolution that is now taking place and will accelerate. In response to globalization, there has been the reassertion of the power of idealized traditional communities based on such factors as ethnicity, language and religious belief. The call for 'self-determination' through cyberspace challenges strong, weak and almost non-existent states; that is, states virtually in name only.

At the same time, those who reject what they perceive to be the secular, Western-centric aspects of globalization are quite willing to use the technology of globalization in their quest to go beyond the nation-state in the pursuit of their vision of transforming regions, and indeed the world, to meet ideals fueled by their interpretation of religion and deeply held tenets of their faith. These non-state actors believe that they transcend the traditional state system and, in a very real sense, wish to 'go back to the future' to fulfill a dream, by employing modern technology to return to their version of a golden age.

Finally, there are those non-state actors who – like the mercenaries that preceded them – are more than willing to be involved in criminal enterprises, to hire out to religious and secular transnational groups, and to also provide their services to states whose security is threatened. What we are now witnessing is what this author has called 'the privatization of public violence' where the mercenaries of the past who were in the service of the king have now been supplanted by their modern counterparts in the service of the corporation, the criminal cartel or the terrorists. In sum, contemporary mercenaries in the form of sub national or transnational organizations are new players in an environment where the classic concepts of sovereignty and physical and legalistic boundaries have been reshaped by criminal non-state actors in an international system under profound pressure and transformation.

TERRORISM AS A MANIFESTATION OF THE CHANGING NATURE OF WAR

If terrorism is one of the manifestations of the changing nature of the international system, it is particularly significant that, as a corollary, terrorism is a manifestation of the changing nature of war. Contemporary terrorism is very much a reflection of the new face of warfare. Brian Jenkins succinctly stated this reality when he noted that 'terrorism is warfare without territory'. It is very much the result of two interrelated phases in technological innovation along with the ability of terrorists to adopt them in the pursuit of their objectives. The first phase was the result of the revolution in transportation from the late 1950s to the 1970s. With the introduction of commercial jet aircraft, terrorists could literally strike at global targets in a matter of hours. In a very real sense, the world witnessed the emergence of what the author has called 'non-territorial terrorism', where the terrorists were not confined to engaging in a conflict within a clearly delineated geographical area. Whether holding hostages during a skyjacking at 30,000 feet or using an aircraft to transport them to a target thousands of miles away from their base of operations, terrorists used the medium of aerospace to engage in what could analytically be called low intensity aerospace warfare. The tragic culmination of such warfare took place on 11 September where terrorists used aircraft as a weapon delivery system, what was, for all intents and purposes, given the potential range of the aircraft, a low intensity inter-continental delivery system. One can note that the words 'low intensity' do not fully convey the repercussions of the acts, given the casualties and economic, social, political and psychological impacts on the global audience that witnessed it. In a very real sense, the yield of the attack rivaled that of a 'small' nuclear device.

The second element in this phase of technological innovation was, of course, the revolution in communications. With the massive introduction of communication and satellite technology, terrorists could literally spontaneously spread their message of fear and intimidation to a global audience. The Munich Massacre of 1972 is viewed as the initiation of what could in retrospect be called the prototype stage of global information warfare, now effectively utilized by a new generation of terrorists. It is often hard to believe that the second stage of the communication revolution is so recent. Essentially created in the 1980s, it has now, in the fullest sense, literally encompassed the globe. With the development of the Internet and the global net, terrorists could not only use the medium of aerospace but, more specifically, cyberspace to not only expand their capabilities and operations but also to engage in the organizational innovation that is and will continue to be a challenge to authorities – namely 'netwar'. The impact of this innovation will be addressed shortly.

The technological transformation of warfare that is now taking place is very much the product of new technology and it is a product that is and will continue to be a challenge to military thinking in both the near and long term for those who will have to both lead and fight in a new conflict environment. Contemporary warfare is indeed non-spatial and multidimensional. There is no territorial field or theaters of operations for today's terrorists and it will take time for conventional military strategists and policy makers to adapt to this reality. This does not mean to imply that territorially based conflicts will cease – the reality of containing border wars, expansion of nation-states, and the continued existence of tension areas where territorially based conflict is not only taking place but possibly expanding – cannot and should not be dismissed.

We are beginning to witness a global war where geographic, legalistic and jurisdictional fields of operations lose their meaning. In this conflict, a new adversary, who has often been motivated by the most traditional values, is waging a form of what one of the author aptly calls a 'global insurgency' where the object is not the use of terrorism as one aspect of a guerrilla war to seize state power, but which emphasizes terrorism as a means of fundamentally transforming entire regions. In this type of insurgency, the old techniques of counter-insurgency may not work. Whose 'hearts and minds' can be won over or what area can be 'pacified' when the battle is non-territorial? Perhaps even more ominous is that the battle is now over those 'hearts and souls'; a battle that, to the true believer, transcends not only territory but life itself with the promise of a version of eternal paradise.

NETWAR: THE ORGANIZATIONAL DIMENSIONS

If the introduction of jet aircraft and television marked the beginning of modern terrorism in the form of non-territorial terrorism, the development of the Internet has initiated yet a new chapter in the history of terrorism. With the emergence of social netwar, a wide variety of groups ranging from anarchists to territorially based insurgents to global terrorists can mobilize support for their cause and initiate operations through the medium of cyberspace. The Zapatista Movement may have initiated these techniques in its conflict with Mexican authorities but the operational art has expanded to any number of groups who seek to dramatize their cause, obtain support and seek to destabilize existing governments in the pursuit of their objectives. In so doing, they, as did the territorially based insurgents before them, engage in an 'indirect approach' to neutralize the strength of vastly superior enemies by converting the strength of an opponent in the form of its critical infrastructure, reliance on technology and interdependence of complex organizations. All these then become a liability to major powers and the post-industrial societies they govern. The modern terrorist is very effectively practicing asymmetric war where small is beautiful and simplicity of organization enables an outwardly weaker foe to seize the offensive against a cumbersome and outwardly far stronger adversary. By so doing, those who practice asymmetric warfare have utilized the classic cell-like organization, as do those who have engaged in 'small wars', enabling them to be difficult to detect or counteract. Moreover, through the use of the Internet, they can maintain their security even while planning or launching complex operations, given the anonymity of cyberspace. Where as before operations had to be largely localized to achieve security, now the new terrorists have a form of decentralized command and control that has enabled them to plan and execute complex global operations, as in the case of 9/11, the Madrid Bombings, the USS Cole, the embassy attacks and other operations, without compromising their security. Unfortunately, the targets of these operations, most notably the United States and other post-industrial societies, still often seek to utilize in the war on terrorism an organizational doctrine characterized by a ladder hierarchy, top-down command and control, bureaucratic layering and jurisdictional complexity, and stove pipes that are at best cumbersome and at worst lead to bureaucratic competition and immobilization. Using the United States response to 9/11 as an illustration, while the new Department of

Homeland Security may indeed be a necessity, the emphasis on creating more bureaucracy may not address the need to have the capacity to some degree to mirror the organizational doctrine of terrorist groups. That is, there needs to be some recognition of the requirement for appropriate decentralization of control and the development of counterterrorist cadres to challenge those who have used simplicity and clandestine actions in their 'War in the Shadows'. Admittedly, there is a vital need to reconcile the requirement in a democratic order to have accountability of actions on one hand and freedom of action on another for those in the operational arena but it remains a problem that must be addressed.

The development counterterrorist organizations that are small, flexible and innovative cannot be done in the context of a unilateral approach to combating terrorism. There must be a 'unity of action' on the regional and international level that breeches the jurisdictional battles among countries that often seems to take precedence over a integrated war against terrorism. Furthermore, such an approach will require that an emergent counterterrorism community also draw upon the resources of non-state actors, be they multinational corporations or non-governmental organizations, to also play a crucial role in an evolving international system. Ultimately, such organizations, acting in concert, must seek to preempt instead of primarily reacting to threats and acts of terrorism. The stakes are particularly high in an environment where, irrespective of the refinement of 'crisis management' and 'consequence management techniques', the potential for a government to be overwhelmed by terrorist's weapons of mass destruction cannot be dismissed.

THE PRIMACY OF THE PSYCHOLOGICAL

In the final analysis, terrorism has been and will continue to be a profound form of psychological warfare that is aimed at spreading fear and intimidation to a global audience. It is additionally, as noted earlier, a form of protracted warfare that will not be marked by decisive outcomes and unconditional victory. Ultimately, it is a test of resolve that transcends territorially based conflicts and encompasses a global area, a global battlefield. Therefore, governments and their populations must understand the nature of the war, its emphasis on psychological intimidation, and its protracted character. This is and will continue to be difficult to do in the face of continuing bloodshed and the call for immediate solutions.

Beyond the present and future mutations of terrorism, there should always be the desire to identify and seek to eliminate the causes of terrorism, be they underlying, precipitating or accelerating. One must also acknowledge than there are, among those who engage in terrorism, individuals and groups who reject out of hand any negotiation in their absolute war against all.

Furthermore, there unfortunately must be the recognition that terrorism and other forms of violence generate new dynamics that may have little relationship to the original causes that are used to justify the acts or campaigns directed at the global order.

CONCLUSION

The contributors to this collection provide very insightful analyses that are of importance to the academic who studies the subject, the policy maker who is responsible for meeting the threat to security, and to those in the operational arena who must take both the short- and long-term offensive against non-state actors who have unfortunately until now seized the initiative in the changing arena of international politics and conflict and warfare. It is a challenge that must be met in a global context where violence too often seems to have replaced diplomacy in resolving disputes not only between and among nation-states but perhaps more significantly in the disputes of organizations and cultures beyond the nation-state against the state-centric world.

Introduction and Overview:
Why Response Networks?

ROBERT J. BUNKER

INTRODUCTION

Few of us who were raised and spent most of our lives in the many decades spanned by the Cold War imagined at that time that the global security environment of 2004 would end up being so drastically different from that of its predecessor. The interwar years from the fall of the Soviet Union to the 11 September ('9/11') attack did not generate a clear consensus concerning where the security environment was heading. In retrospect, the interwar years represented a honeymoon period between the last of the great state-on-state wars and the rise of the non-state-on-state wars. Then 9/11 hit and it became clear to all, except to the most out of touch governmental bureaucrats, that warfare had changed and we had to change with it.

State-on-state warfare, represented by Clausewitzian thinking and coalitions of Westphalian states, has increasingly given way to failed states, intra-state conflict and the rise and proliferation of non-state threats. Even challengers to the state form itself, if Al Qaeda and some of the larger transnational organized crime organizations are taken into consideration, are now emerging. The global security environment is undergoing immense changes across the board. Some of the more significant of these changes tracked by Fourth Epoch War and cooperating theorists are as follows:

Crime and War Operational Environment

Military institutions are configured to operate in a state-on-state warfare environment while law enforcement institutions are configured to operate within a state against criminals to uphold the rule of law. Overlap between these two operational environments, as found in failed states and with the activities of non-state (criminal) soldiers such as terrorists, drug cartel enforcers, and private armies, represents a 'gray area' for which traditional military and law enforcement institutions are not well suited to operate. Over the last three decades, this crime and war operational environment has increased in size as more regions of the world have become threatened by non-state forces and seen their governments collapse.

Fifth-Dimensional Battlespace

The emergence of fifth-dimensional battlespace derived from traditional space–time; x, y and z (battlespace box) and t (time), with the addition of the fifth dimension, c (cyber). This form of battlespace is more sophisticated than modern four-dimensional battlespace and allows limitations in that battlespace to be overcome for advanced warfighting purposes. The fifth dimension is regularly exploited by non-state-based stealth masked forces such as terrorists and by state-based forms of advanced weapons platforms such as the stealth-fighter.

Non-Lethal (Directed Energy) Weapons

Mechanical-based weaponry (such as firearms, artillery and bombs) is over five hundred years old and is now giving way to new forms of post-mechanical-based weaponry. These advanced forms of non-lethal weapons are not to be mistaken with legacy systems such as bean bags, batons and other basic riot control devices. Rather, they are directed energy based and represent such systems as pulsed energy projectiles, acoustic and millimeter wave devices, laser rifles and microwave/radio frequency weapons. These weapons provide advanced operational capabilities to state and non-state forces alike.

Bond-Relationship (Disruptive) Targeting

Network-based forces possess disruptive rather than destructive forms of combat power. This form of targeting, known as bond-relationship targeting (BRT), is defined as follows: 'Rather than gross physical destruction or injury, the desired end state is tailored disruption within a thing, between it and other things or between it and its environment by degrading, severing or altering the bonds and relationships which define its existence.' During the Vietnam War, the Vietcong utilized BRT against the American military, government,and people. A prime example is the Tet Offensive which, while a crushing battlefield defeat for the Vietcong, resulted in the final severing of the American bonds and relationships which held the war effort together.

Non-State (Criminal) Soldiers and Mercenaries

Non-state forces have been proliferating and evolving as threats for decades now. Drug cartels, terrorists and heavily armed street gangs are a global concern, as are mafia enforcers, pirates and the foot soldiers of warlords and bandit chiefs. Private security groups have now also appeared, reminiscent of the great mercenary companies of the Renaissance, with the defunct South African firm Executive Outcomes representing an early example of this trend.

War Over Social and Political Organization

Conventional state-on-state warfare is based on the centuries-old idea of 'a struggle between nation-states or their coalitions over the preservation and extension of national sovereignty'. With wars being increasingly intra-state and non-state-on-state based, sovereignty and traditional politics are no longer of the same importance they once were. Issues concerning how people live and behave and what social and political forms will guide them are now of increasing importance. War then takes place between competing forms of social and political organization as a means to determine what state form type will guide humanity in the postmodern world. War thus takes on the character of nation-state and successor form against all non-state competitors: transnational organized crime groups, drug-cartels, third-generation street gangs, emergent city-states, sprawling warlord-controlled slums, free-booter corporations, Al Qaeda and descendent networks, and ghost and criminal-states.

Network Organizational Forms

Non-state OPFOR groups are building themselves around the basic forms of stars, chains and all-channel networks. This gives them an operational edge over hierarchical state-based military and law enforcement institutions. The Netwar concept provides the means to understand this category of change and provides us with the accurate perception that it takes a network to fight a network.

These broad areas of change suggest we are seeing a more encompassing epochal change underway. This level of change is equivalent to that which took place during the transition from the classical to the medieval world and from the medieval to the modern world. During these great transitions, the military (and police) institutions of the then dominant state form were unable to reconfigure themselves to meet the new demands required of them in the emergent battlespace (operational space) which was forming. This resulted in the military (and police) institutions of the then dominant state form ultimately being unable to protect their people. An eventual outcome of this process is the failure of the dominant state form.

These historical lessons drawn from Fourth Epoch War theory can be applied to the postmodern transition now underway. If the military and law enforcement institutions of the state should fail in their mission of protecting the people, then the nation-state as we understand it will also eventually fail as a social and political form of organization. Liberal employment of private security groups and other war outsourcing and privatization schemes, such as the creation of gated communities, may stave off state failure but it does not address the fundamental problem.

This leads us to the question of response networks. Why do we need them? The answer is both simple and blunt. If the military and law enforcement institutions of the state are to remain viable and protect the public they will be required to change their organizational form. This new organizational form will be based upon networks and not upon traditional hierarchies. Trends indicate that non-state OPFORs will increasingly embrace networks as their dominant organizational form and gain more advanced operational capabilities. Military and law enforcement institutions will either embrace networks as the organizational foundation with which to conduct counter-non-state OPFOR operations or they will become irrelevant. Irrelevant institutions will result in private security and mercenary take over of this state function and in time help to undermine the nation-state as we recognize it today.

SPECIAL ISSUE OVERVIEW

This special issue of *Low Intensity Conflict and Law Enforcement* draws upon an 'Alpha Team' of terrorism, low intensity conflict, guerilla warfare, military and defense, transnational organized crime and netwar researchers. In addition, intelligence and counter-terrorism specialists are represented in these pages.

The vision promoted by this special issue is to gain a deeper understanding of the topic of 'Networks, Terrorism and Global Insurgency'. Non-state threats are evolving at a rapid pace and to keep pace with ever-changing attributes of conflict and war, as touched upon in the introductory section, directed research is required. From this directed research, it is thought that lessons learned and insights gained will aid us in our counter-OPFOR planning. The special issue is divided into four thematic sections and is conceptually linked to an earlier work, *Non-State Threats and Future Wars*.[1]

The initial section concerns theory and international law. The first contribution represents the most recent update of the seminal netwar concept originally published in 1993. This concept has gone on to have immense impact in both military and law enforcement circles and represents one of the most useful conceptual tools today in our understanding of network-based non-state threats. The second contribution addresses the new global security landscape. This landscape is filled with failed and failing states and armed non-state groups that are challenging the nation-state's physical and moral right to govern. Generations of war and conflict, signposts of change, and challenges and tasks facing us are also discussed. The third contribution looks at 'Globalization's Bastards', criminal entities such as organized crime syndicates and transnational terrorist networks, from the legal perspective. It details how international law views illegitimate non-state actors, states that support them, and the resulting challenges this entails for our besieged state-centric world.

The second section addresses broad issues of terrorism and global insurgency. The first contribution focuses on the phenomena of terrorism, crime and private armies. The latter topic is one the United States is now fully facing in an occupied Iraq with upwards of 20,000 US and allied private security contractors and mercenaries. This condition has existed for years in a fragmented Colombian state containing tens of thousands of guerillas, cartel-armies, criminal bands and private militias and has been seen repeatedly throughout the globe in countries such as Lebanon, Somalia, Chechnya and Bosnia.

The second contribution views the effectiveness of US counter-insurgency efforts against Iranian-sponsored terrorism in the 1980s. It provides insights into how to deter states that seek to sponsor or ally with terrorist groups. The relevancy of this contribution has further increased with the recent news that 'Iranian sources and media asserted that the Iranian Revolutionary Guard Corps has established a center to train suicide attackers throughout the world. The sources identified the center as the World Islamic Martyrs and Fighters Staff Headquarters.'[2] The third contribution discusses Provisional Irish Republication Army (PIRA) leadership evolutionary patterns. Two leadership generations are evident with a projected third generation emerging. This form of analysis has cross-over utility to the current global war against terrorism. Such analysis will not tell us whom the new and emerging leaders of Al Qaeda actually are but it may help us to frame the right questions to ask our intelligence collectors.

The third section provides an Al Qaeda network focus. Al Qaeda, a new warmaking entity, exists within an operational environment that fully blurs the traditional crime and war and domestic and international axes created by our state-centric system (see Figure 1). For nation-states to properly counter this new entity current analytical tools will need to be applied against it as well as new tools developed. The first contribution takes concepts of global revolutionary or imperial powers, formerly applied to states, and merges them with a modified Manwaring paradigm, also used for threat analysis within the international system, to analyze Al Qaeda's challenge to the state-based international system. The second contribution takes current military order of battle concepts, normally applied only to the military forces of states, and applies them to Al Qaeda force structure and operations.

The fourth section provides perspectives on networks and response networks. The first contribution represents a hybrid analysis overlapping the third and fourth sections of this collection of writings. It analyzes the operational combat capability of networks as applied to Al Qaeda. Networks, typically non-state based, are viewed as having offensive, defense, speed and

FIGURE 1

AL QAEDA IN STATE-CENTRIC SECURITY ENVIRONMENT

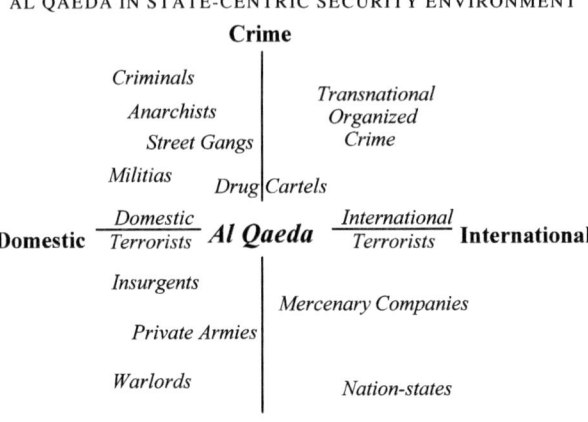

Counter-OPFOR Program, NLECTC-West © 2004

combat-multiplier advantages over hierarchical organizational forms, which are typically state based. The second contribution spotlights the structure and functioning of traditional Chechen networks of crime and resistance and discusses how they are being supplemented by separate networks of Islamic extremists which are devoted to guerilla and terrorist operations. The third contribution discusses multilateral counter-insurgency networks based on the Los Angeles Terrorism Early Warning (TEW) Group model developed in 1996. These types of networks are viewed as allowing states to gain competitive operational capabilities against network-based non-state forces. As mentioned in the introductory section, unwillingness and/or inability to embrace these networks will result in catastrophic failure for the nation-state form.

The special issue also contains a preface and a foreword by world-recognized terrorism and low intensity conflict scholars respectively. These contributions discuss how better to respond to the threats that we face and look at emergent trends taking place. In addition, a selected bibliography highlights many of the works cited by the various contributions found in this special issue.

I would like to offer special thanks to John T. Fishel, editor of *Low Intensity Conflict and Law Enforcement*, for his backing of this special issue and the guidance he has provided during its preparation. In addition, I would like to thank the Counter-OPFOR Program, National Law Enforcement and Corrections Technology Center-West for its support of this project along with the support provided by the center director Dr Robert J. Waldron. While none of the writings in this collection represent official Counter-OPFOR Program,

National Law Enforcement and Corrections Technology Center-West or National Institute of Justice policies, this venue of publication promotes the continued mission of that program by seeking to support US law enforcement against non-state threat forces.

Finally, I would like to thank the many contributors to this special issue for their professionalism, dedication to this project, and their creation of the works it contains. These are, by name, Graham H. Turbiville, Jr., Stephen Sloan, John Arquilla, David F. Ronfeldt, Max G. Manwaring, Neal A. Pollard, John P. Sullivan, Sean K. Anderson, Andrew Garfield, Kimbra L. Fishel, Lisa J. Campbell, Matt Begert and Mark Galeotti.

NOTES

1. That earlier work was published by Frank Cass in 2003, and originally appeared as a special issue of *Small Wars & Insurgencies*, Vol.13, No.3 (Summer 2002).
2. 'Suicide U.: Iran registers volunteers for martyrdom', *World Tribune.com.* 28 May 2004; Also see 'Mullahs of Iran to recruit suicide bombers', *Persian Journal*, 28 May 2004.

Netwar Revisited: The Fight for the Future Continues

JOHN ARQUILLA and DAVID F. RONFELDT

Both the violent and the peaceful proponents of *netwar* – a term we coined to call attention to the rise of a new mode of conflict that relies on network forms of organization, strategy and technology attuned to the information age – have grown stronger and spread farther since we first published *Networks and Netwars* at RAND in 2001. That book develops more fully the netwar concept that we fielded initially in 1993 and expanded upon in our 1996 RAND monograph, *The Advent of Netwar*. Today, in 2004, sprawling networks of non-state actors are assailing US policies on multiple fronts. One major front consists of Al Qaeda and its affiliates, which keep striving to mount catastrophic terrorist attacks. Another front features civic-action networks around the world that have banded together in (mostly) peaceful efforts to constrain US power – particularly the application of American military power. Both types of netwar actors pose serious challenges to US policy and strategy, and to US–European relations. The former – the terrorists – continue to endanger US and European security. But, over the long term, the emergence of a globally networked civil society should prove the more powerful, enduring, and transformative development. These are the themes we emphasize in this article, which updates some of the key points that we made in the 2001 edition of our book and in the foreword to the 2003 Spanish edition of *Networks and Netwars (Redes y Guerras en Red)*.

THE TERROR FRONT

As to the terror war, our predictions from 2001 have been borne out. The early weeks of the American military attack on Al Qaeda at its hub in Afghanistan relied on strategic bombing and a hunt for Osama bin Laden. These measures did not work very well, so US leaders turned to the use of special forces teams. The skillful networking of these few hundred commandos with attack aircraft and unmanned drones, as well as with indigenous soldiers of the Northern Alliance, then led to battlefield swarming tactics that drove the Taliban and Al Qaeda from power and made the Afghan campaign a 'war to change all wars'.[1]

Besides innovative military operations, the terror war has also brought the creation of a large multinational network of some 90 nations to counter the radical networks. The hallmark of this counterterror network is a widespread sharing of information among military, law enforcement and intelligence officials in all participating countries. Because of this unusual information exchange, hundreds of Al Qaeda operatives have been rounded up, all around the world, over the past few years. Many attacks have been preempted – from truck-bombings in Singapore to assaults on ships moving through the Straits of Gibraltar.

Al Qaeda has been further disrupted by the discovery and capture of pieces of its financial, logistical and recruiting cells throughout Europe. Damaging losses have been inflicted by Spain, France and Germany – all of whom are attuned to the need to operate in a networked fashion. Perhaps this has come more naturally to these three countries than it has to the United States, since each has had to deal with earlier forms of networked terror – e.g., Spain vs Basque separatists; France vs Algerian radical Islamists; and Germany vs domestic terrorists since the Baader-Meinhof Gang's heyday in the 1970s. These past experiences may have helped prime our allies for effective networking against terrorism.

Meanwhile, Al Qaeda has been busily adapting, apparently bearing out another of our hypotheses – that it would evolve away from a mainly hub-and-spokes design centered on Osama bin Laden into a more distributed design characterized by dispersed small zones of all-channel connectivity linked loosely by chains. This organizational redesign continues the terrorists' trend toward more decentralized operations, and it could enable them to increase the tempo of their attacks. If they are willing to emphasize smaller actions (like, e.g., the synagogue bombing in Tunisia), the number of operations they can mount may grow. This may correct a deficiency in their original design, whose reliance on a centralized vetting of all planned attacks restrained their operational tempo. The apparently Al Qaeda-inspired terror campaigns in Turkey and Saudi Arabia in 2003 – which consisted of more but smaller attacks – indicate that the terrorists are learning how to pick up and sustain the pace of their operations. It remains an open question, however, to what extent an extremely decentralized 'leaderless resistance' doctrine appeals to these terrorists.[2] But Al Qaeda-linked jihadis infiltrating into Iraq during the American occupation do appear to be guided by this notion, developing a capacity for mounting attacks on a daily basis, from the Kurdish north to the Shia south of Iraq.

Defeating Al Qaeda will not end the plague of networked terror. Osama bin Laden may long be remembered, and emulated, as an organizational and doctrinal pioneer who showed that network designs offer a cheap and effective new approach to war. Extremist groups and rogue elements in governments elsewhere are sure to notice that developing their own commando terror networks is an attractive, cost-effective option. Indeed, a new kind of arms race may ensue, in which rogue states and terrorists build networks for their dark purposes, while those who would defend against and defeat them strive to cobble together their own counterterror networks.

THE ACTIVIST FRONT

As for peaceable social netwar, over the past year or so the world has watched the rise of a remarkable network of civil-society actors devoted to constraining the emerging 'Bush Doctrine', which calls for using military force preventively.[3] Greatly enabled by the Internet, dispersed anti-war activists have organized into sprawling realms of all-channel connectivity – and from there, have coordinated and mounted synchronized demonstrations around the world. This bears out a prediction made in 1996 in our first study about the dynamics of netwar:

> In the years ahead, the possibility should not be overlooked that a major new global peace and disarmament movement may eventually arise from a grand alliance among diverse NGOs (nongovernmental organizations) and other civil-society actors who are attuned to the doctrinal elements of netwar. They will increasingly have the organizational, technological and social infrastructures to fight against recalcitrant governments, as well as to operate in tandem with governments and supranational bodies that may favor the movement.[4]

The anti-war movement played an influential role in encouraging the diplomatic effort in the United Nations that preceded the American-led invasion of Iraq. And from September 2002 to March 2003, these peace networks demonstrated their nimbleness by building strong links with like-minded nation-states – France in particular. That they failed in the end to prevent an attack on Iraq shows that their influence is limited. Yet the anti-war activism obliged US leaders to become sensitive to the importance of the 'story' that would be told by and about the campaign, and they resolved to do as little physical damage as possible in the upcoming war. Thus, even in the wake of diplomatic failure, the burgeoning peace networks motivated some circumspection in US behavior. At this writing (February 2004), the failure to find any weapons of mass destruction in Iraq – the stated justification for the war – can only revitalize anti-war networking in the event of any contemplated future applications of the Bush doctrine.

Lately, within the United States, civil-society networks, as well as independent actors working on cyberspace issues, have helped warn about negative aspects of the USA Patriot Act and other post-9/11 laws and government practices that, though meant to fight terrorism, could infringe on American privacy and freedom concerns in the name of security.[5] The influence of these networks too has been quite limited, but they provide further instances of the unfolding nature of social netwar – as does the set of transnational NGOs and networks comprising the anti-globalization movement.

While NGOs and other non-state actors around the world have played roles in the anti-war and anti-globalization networks, the most salient cases of social netwars these past few years have come from Asia's various pro-democracy movements. For example, in the Philippines, the political demonstrators who helped overthrow President Joseph Estrada and install Gloria Macapagal Arroyo in January 2001 included many working-class voters mobilized by text messaging. In 2003, young voters mobilized by an election-day get-out-the-vote blitz helped carry South Korean presidential candidate Roh Muh-hyun to victory. In this case, Roh's campaign workers made explicit use of 'swarm tactics' on election day, by converging first on one district then another as the turn-out monitors reported their observations on an hourly basis. Elsewhere, civil networks have put increasing pressure on corporations doing business with the Burmese military junta. In this case, however, Burma's military rulers have shown an aptitude for networking as well. They continue to attract corporate support for their continuance in power, and oddly aspire to persuade civil-society actors – by means of articulate propaganda posted on pro-government web sites – that the junta is acting in Burma's best interests.

Meanwhile, new studies have appeared since 2001 that add to our understanding of the rise of networks, the dynamics of social activism, the prospects for a Web/Net-based global civil society, and the implications for the spread of democracy around the world.[6] We hope that global civil-society networks will grow swiftly and strongly enough to impose constraints on dictatorial states, and that all types of states will learn to work with civil-society networks in ways that amplify democracy, transparency and the protection of human rights. The fresh energies being released by these networks may even serve to constrain antagonistic states where insiders may be contemplating the development of dark new netwar doctrines. Yet this is just a cautious hope, precisely because of these darker possibilities – which we discuss further in the last section of this article.

For now, members of the international community in Europe and Asia seem more attuned to positive social networking trends than do Americans, and may prove more adept at using network dynamics to increase both their 'hard' and 'soft' power in the coming years. One of the best examples of international networking in recent years is the successful, principally Asian-led effort to stem the spread of the SARS virus. Rapid, all-channel information sharing made all the difference in achieving containment in this crisis. Yet in the United States, difficulties persist in grasping the network concept; and the American capacity for coercive hard power keeps relegating suasive and cooperative soft power to the background – at least for the present.

LOOKING ACROSS FIVE LEVELS OF ANALYSIS

Some of the difficulties the United States is having with network dynamics can be understood by briefly updating our view of US performance across the five levels that we noted for measuring network strengths and weaknesses: the organizational, narrative, doctrinal, social and technological levels. Many analysts and practitioners, especially in the United States, tend to emphasize the technological level – the area of greatest innate strength. But the other levels are equally important. Analyzing all five levels in detail is necessary for drawing 'net assessments' of networked adversaries, and of state capacities to respond and fight back.

Netwar is essentially an organizational phenomenon. The civil and uncivil society networks discussed above maneuver by using variants and hybrids of three basic network forms: chains, in which there is very limited communication with fellow network members; hubs (or stars), which radiate out a series of spokes from a central (but not centralizing) node; and all-channel networks, in which every member is linked directly with every other. A number of new theoretical and practical studies of networks have tended to bear out our general conceptions and opened up new terrain as well.[7] Nonetheless, for many analysts it remains unclear, and debatable, whether it is better to view networks as the most basic form of all (i.e., 'the mother of all forms'), or as a particular, distinctive type of form (hierarchies and markets being other major types).

In any case, new progress is being made in analyzing how the topology of a network system may change as it grows (or erodes) over time. One insightful analysis posits a four-stage progression in which a network system emerges as a set of scattered, barely connected clusters, then grows interconnections to form into a single hub-and-spoke design, then becomes more complex and disperses into a multi-hub 'small world' network, finally to grow so extensive, inclusive and sprawling it becomes a complex core/periphery network.[8] The pressures put on the Al Qaeda network have evidently decreased it from a hub-and-spoke back to a scattered-cluster design – still a dangerous, adaptable design. Meanwhile, some of the civil-society networks, which extend way beyond just the anti-war movement, are growing large and complex enough to amount to a set of small-world if not core/periphery networks.

It is an important step to discern whether a particular adversary is organized as a flat, relatively leaderless, non-hierarchical network – but only an initial step. Exactly what kind of network is it: hub, multi-hub, all-channel, core/periphery, or what? And where are the bridges and holes that may connect to outside actors? Such questions must be addressed, for each design may have different strengths, weaknesses and implications. Some may be vulnerable to leadership targeting, though networks may be generally less vulnerable than hierarchies in this respect. As research proceeds on how to disrupt, destabilize and dismantle networks, analysts are finding that in some cases it may be best to focus on key nodes and in other cases on key links, in some cases on middling rather than central nodes or links, and in other cases on nodes or links on the periphery.[9] But so far, much less is understood about how to analyze the capacity of networks to recover and reassemble after a disruption, possibly by morphing into a different design.

Governments around the world are learning to fight terrorist networks by assembling their own networks. At the organizational level, the international situation is improving mainly because, as noted above, a network of nations remains actively involved in countering terrorism, despite the divisive infighting that accompanied the run-up to the war with Iraq. A major organizational problem continues to be an American attachment to hierarchical domestic security institutions. The creation of a cabinet-level department of homeland security is evidence of this; the building of civil–military, federal–local, and public–private networks remains a stern challenge facing the United States, organizationally.

Perhaps the civilian departments of the US government should look at the military services. They have begun to network their forces skillfully and are now reaping unexpected dividends from networked field operations. Indeed, the US military has made revolutionary advances in the use of communications and sensing technologies, and its forces have learned how to 'swarm' opponents – i.e., to strike simultaneously from many directions. This occurred first in Afghanistan, where a few hundred commandos working with the Northern Alliance won a major campaign, then in Iraq, where America's second Gulf war saw operations more than twice the scope of the first war undertaken by less than half the number of expeditionary forces. In these military aspects of networking and swarming, the United States is making full and effective use of its advanced information technologies, its area of greatest comparative advantage in the terror war. Yet Al Qaeda continues to swarm, too, at a slower but increasing tempo. Technology alone will not prove decisive in this war.

It is in the narrative dimension, where the 'battle of the story' is waged, that the United States has gone furthest off course. In the immediate wake of the 9/11 attacks on America, the story was quite clear – Al Qaeda was trying to foment a 'clash of civilizations', but the United States responded effectively by proclaiming it was a 'fight for civilization' based on liberal values. The world greeted the American narrative with acclaim, and 16 countries went so far as to send troops to Afghanistan – and many are still sending contingents to serve in the International Security Assistance Force. But in the wake of Operation Enduring Freedom in Afghanistan, the US government formulated an unusual doctrine calling for the early resort to preventive military force – with or without allies. This doctrine, though embraced in the US Congress, rekindled global anxieties that had surfaced at the end of the Cold War about America wanting to consolidate some form of world-wide primacy.

This shift in US policy altered the narrative dimension of the terror war, and has had an impact in the social realm as well. It has made much harder the task of holding together a multinational world coalition, because the limitations of existing social and cultural ties are no longer compensated for by a compelling story that sustains world support against terror. Evidence of the seriousness of this problem can be found in the fact that the United States went to war against Iraq with significant allied forces being provided only by other English-speaking countries – Great Britain and Australia, two nations with whom America enjoys deep sociocultural bonds.[10]

In our netwar-oriented view, it is advisable for US policy to keep working to improve on advances in the organizational dimension, so that broader and deeper networking is achieved. But the challenge is not solely organizational; greater energy should also be devoted to the narrative level, where the fight against terror has begun to founder. Selectively shifting US strategy away from assertive, unilateral stances, toward more consultative, multilateral, networked approaches in a range of policy areas around the world – from the Palestinian intifada to the North Korean nuclear proliferation crisis – could elevate US capacities to engage at the narrative level with increased hopes of success. Table 1 below summarizes our foregoing discussion of American performance across the five levels of analysis by which network strength can be measured.

All this implies a strategic principle for the network age: the advisable way to out-compete is to out-cooperate.[11] This notion applies well to the terror war, where the United States and its allies must form cooperative

TABLE 1
AMERICAN NETWORKING IN THE TERROR WAR

Level of analysis	American performance
Organizational	Improving international networking. Continued attachment to hierarchy at the domestic level.
Narrative	Effective 'fight for civilization' based on universal liberal values gave way to parochial interest in Iraq.
Doctrinal	US military shows great and growing aptitude both for networking and swarming. Intelligence and law enforcement not yet as fully developed.
Social	The weakest aspect of American-led counterterror networking efforts, showing drift toward Anglo-American *dirigisme* in the wake of Iraq war.
Technological	Area of greatest comparative advantage, especially in military realm. But tendency to focus closely on technological edge slows advances at other levels.

networks to defeat the terrorists' networks. But this principle also applies beyond the security and military crises of the moment, to issues of global environmental protection and global health, as well as to possible future matters of humanitarian interventions in failed and failing states where human-rights abuses abound. Building information-age cooperation networks to address such problems is probably the best hope for the United States to tell a compelling story that will attract states and NGOs to join together in striving for a world that will leave less room for disaster and terror to flourish.

NETWAR AND THE RETURN OF FASCISM?

But we shall not end this chapter on such a hopeful note. All is not well for the forces of freedom and democracy. Today's world situation is instructive not only about the spread of bright new civil-society networks, but also about the resilience and recurrence of old, dark systems of rule. Closed regimes are learning to use the information age to suit themselves while fending off outside forces.[12] Worse, the world may be moving into an era when major dangers to the West will stem from a new round of fascism in far-off places.

The great twentieth-century war against fascism – the Second World War – ended its rise for decades to come. But two recent wars have already been waged against fascism: first against Slobodan Milosevic's quasi-fascist regime in Serbia, and next against Saddam Hussein's Baathist regime in Iraq, which, despite the comparisons of Saddam to Stalin, had much more in common with the western European fascist systems of the 1930s.

People usually like being liberated from dictatorships, but not necessarily from fascism. What's the difference? What is fascism? Fascism is no mere dictatorship – it is more than a subjugation by one leader, his cohorts and their coercive apparatuses. Yes, it imposes a centralized, organic, if not totalitarian, organizational structure, with a single party, secret police, and para-military thugs. But that is not what keeps fascism in power and explains its appeal.

Fascism is a total system of existence that willingly engages a broad spectrum, even a majority, of elites and masses. At its core, fascism has a deeply mythic appeal; it offers a quest to overcome dystopian times and achieve a utopian rebirth, a restoration, of a nation's greatness. Thus fascism rules the mind as well as the body – and both the mind and the body accept that rule and participate in it. In this quest, fascism is terribly anti-liberal; for it values order far more than freedom, and it brooks no boundaries between public and private, or between state and society. Yet fascism is also anti-conservative; for it seeks to transform the status quo on behalf of all, not to preserve it for the sake of a few. Furthermore, while fascism is fundamentally secular in its methods and goals, it has a messianic quality, in that it promises national redemption and progress to break through to a new millennium.[13]

Where and why does fascism take hold? It cannot happen just anywhere – its tendencies may, perhaps, but not fascism as a system. To take hold, fascism requires, first, a developed society, one that has entered the modern era and has a serious state, a significant private business sector, and a complex civil society. The ultra-nationalism that is characteristic of fascism resembles extreme tribalism – but societies that turn fascist are far too advanced to be considered tribal. Moreover, while studies of totalitarianism typically view communism and fascism as having many similarities, they have a crucial difference that often gets downplayed: the presence of a private sector and a market system, however weak. Communism must be rid of them; but fascism needs them and proposes to strengthen them, albeit in a suborned way.

Second, to take hold fascism requires that this modernizing society be suffering from deep disturbances and grievances. There should be a widespread sense of social disaster and disarray – stemming, say, from a lost war, severe inflation and depression, pervasive corruption scandals, or humiliating foreign interference. And these should motivate a gripping longing for national rebirth – not to mention a great charismatic leader to show the way. This does not make fascism inevitable, and there may be various directions such a society could go in. But if somehow fascism gains sway, it does so partly because it promises to unite people, overcome the obstacles, and purge society of its ills – of all that is weak, wayward and deviant.

Fascism further promises to create not only a new order but also a new kind of man who can assure that the rebirth works and stays in place. People at large are so fed up, furious, divided and fearful about the condition of their nation that, if fascism's exponents manage to seize office through election or by force (e.g., a coup), it is not all that hard to make people become complicit, compromised, convinced and accommodative to fascism's ways. Meanwhile, a leadership cult and grandiose expressions of national solidarity, identity, sovereignty and independence build up fascism's mythic appeal, just as its intelligence-gathering and coercive apparatus expand to assure compliance.[14]

Why remind ourselves of this? Because fascism is far from dead or obsolete. The spread of the capitalist market system, the unleashing of democratic forces, and other aspects of globalization are having ambivalent effects around the world. The early effects seem positive; there are new signs of upward progress in many societies. But not in all of them. Some nations – their states, business sectors, and civil societies – are having wrenching, grievous difficulties adapting to and benefiting from globalization and from related pressures to create open market systems in societies whose regimes may prefer rigged, protected ways of doing things.

Thus, the conditions for fascism, which were centered in Europe many decades ago, seem likely to recur in new places and regions. We are not sure where or in what variety and numbers, but some could prove much riskier for the West than others. For example, Russia's travails since the dissolution of the Soviet Union in 1991 suggest the possibility of a neo-fascist drift – e.g., see Vladimir Putin's re-election in 2004 against virtually no serious opposition. Such a great nation – which still retains a sizeable military and several thousand strategic nuclear warheads – could surely unbalance global politics if it emerged as fascist from its recent 'time of troubles'. Equally worrisome, if terrorism induces the creation of a new Islamic caliphate in the Middle East, it will likely have a fascist nature.

If fascism does enjoy an information-age revival, it may also extend the double-edged nature of netwar. For popular new fascist regimes will surely want to block activist transnational civil-society networks from intruding into their nations for many reasons, even as those regimes seek to develop covert commando units and networks that they could deploy abroad for asymmetrical defense – and perhaps for aggression as well. If a 'Napoleon of netwar' ever emerges, he may well be a fascist.

We have in our other writings likened the netwar concept to Janus, the Roman god of changes, who had two faces – one light and forward-looking, the other darker, older and looking to the past. Both of these natures can clearly be seen in this emerging age of networks. A global civil society to integrate us all is possible, but new incarnations of terror, transnational crime, and fascism may also emerge. Both visions will likely co-exist for some time, though ever more uneasily as the fight for the future continues. Yet, in the end, we believe that the darker face of Janus, and thus the darker side of netwar, can be reduced to a shadow, far outshone by the peace, social progress and prosperity that come with the brighter side of networking.

ACKNOWLEDGEMENTS

© RAND Corporation, Santa Monica, CA, reproduced by kind permission.

NOTES

1. Our view differs sharply from a leading US Army assessment. Stephen Biddle, *Afghanistan and the Future of Warfare: Implications for Army and Defense Policy* (Carlisle Barracks, PA: Strategic Studies Institute, 2002), argues that Operation Enduring Freedom represented nothing new – it was just another fight between two ground forces, in which air power greatly aided one side.
2. Recent writings on this topic include Jessica Stern, *Terror in the Name of God: Why Religious Militants Kill* (New York: Ecco Press, 2003), and Simson L. Garfinkel, 'Leaderless Resistance Today,' *First Monday*, Vol.8, No.3 (March 2003), online only at ⟨http://firstmonday.org/issues/issue8_3/garfinkel/index.html⟩.
3. Technically, 'preemption' occurs when one is under imminent threat of attack. The Bush doctrine, which envisions using force to head off the rise of new threats, falls under what ethicists call 'preventive war'. On the ethical dimensions of this approach to conflict, see Michael Howard et al., *The Laws of War: Constraints on Warfare in the Western World* (New Haven, CT: Yale University Press, 1994); James Turner Johnson, *Just War Tradition and the Restraint of War* (Princeton, NJ: Princeton University Press, 1981); and Michael Walzer, *Just and Unjust Wars* (New York: Basic Books, 1977). Note that adherence to a preventive war doctrine could fuel nation- and network-based opposition to American policies in the future.
4. From John Arquilla and David Ronfeldt, *The Advent of Netwar* (Santa Monica, CA: RAND, 1996), p.76.
5. One significant expression of these concerns is the report of the Markle Foundation Task Force on National Security in the Information Age, *Protecting America's Freedom in the Information Age* (New York: Markle Foundation, 2002), available online at ⟨http://www.markletaskforce.org/⟩.
6. Recent US-published studies include David Bollier, *The Rise of Netpolitik* (Washington, DC: The Aspen Institute, 2003); Howard Rheingold, *Smart Mobs: The Next Social Revolution* (Cambridge, MA: Perseus Publishing, 2003); Starhawk, *Webs of Power: Notes from the Global Uprising* (Gabriola Island, BC: New Society Publishers, 2002); and David Weinberger, *Small Pieces Loosely Joined: A Unified Theory of the Web* (Cambridge, MA: Perseus Publishing, 2002). Important studies by various authors (notably Thomas Carothers, Ann Fiorini and Marina Ottaway) have been issued by the two think-tanks that are on the cutting edge for tracking and analyzing the phenomena at hand: the Carnegie Endowment for International Peace (www.ceip.org), and the United States Institute for Peace (www.usip.org).
7. Insightful new network studies include Albert-László Barabási, *Linked: The New Science of Networks* (Cambridge, MA: Perseus Publishing, 2002); Mark Buchanan, *Nexus: Small Worlds and the Groundbreaking Science of Networks* (New York: Norton & Company, 2002); Fritjof Capra, *The Hidden Connections* (New York: Doubleday, 2002), Peter Monge and Noshir Contractor, *Theories of Communication Networks* (New York: Oxford University Press, 2003), and various pieces by Valdis Krebs posted since 9/11 on his website at ⟨www.orgnet.com⟩.
8. From Valdis Krebs and June Holley, 'Building Sustainable Communities Through Network Building,' 2002, at http://www.orgnet.com/Buildingnetworks.pdf
9. See Kathleen M. Carley, Jeffrey Reminga and Natasha Kanmeva, 'Destabilizing Terrorist Networks,' NAACSOS conference proceedings, Pittsburgh, PA, 2003, posted at ⟨http://www.casos.ece.cmu.edu/casos_working_paper/Carley-NAACSOS-03.pdf⟩.

10. Japan agreed to send only humanitarian forces, while a few central European countries agreed to send troops trained to cope with the consequences of chemical and biological attack. The Poles eventually sent a small combat contingent of several hundred soldiers, and in February 2004 South Korea agreed to send 3,000 troops principally to help with reconstruction. Before the war broke out, France also promised to send combat forces if the Iraqis resorted to the use of weapons of mass destruction – which never happened, but which would have decisively shifted the narrative aspect of the conflict back to one of being a 'fight for civilization'.

11. For a sporting source of this principle see David Ronfeldt, 'Social Science at 190 MPH on NASCAR's Biggest Superspeedways', *First Monday* (February 2000), online only at ⟨http://firstmonday.org/issues/issue5_2/index.html⟩.

12. See Shanthi Kalathil and Taylor C. Boas, *Open Networks, Closed Regimes: The Impact of the Internet on Authoritarian Rule* (Washington, DC: Carnegie Endowment for International Peace, 2003).

13. On the idea of progress and its millennialist aspects, see Robert Nisbet, *History of the Idea of Progress* (New Brunswick, NJ: Transaction Publishers, 1994), and Arthur Herman, *The Idea of Decline in Western History* (New York: The Free Press, 1997).

14. Sources include Roger Griffin, ed., *Fascism* (New York: Oxford University Press, 1996), and Stanley G. Payne, *A History of Fascism, 1914–1945* (Madison, WI: The University of Wisconsin Press, 1995), and Robert O. Paxton, The Anatomy of Fascism (New York: Alfred A. Knopf, 2004). On the prospect of 'friendly fascism' in advanced democratic societies, see Bertram Gross, *Friendly Fascism: The New Face of Power in America* (Boston, MA: South End Press, 1980).

The New Global Security Landscape: The Road Ahead

MAX G. MANWARING

Before the Second World War, especially in the English-speaking countries, security was almost exclusively the province of soldiers. National security was a term primarily associated with possible or probable military threats from other nation-states concerning strategic access or denial of raw materials, markets, lines of communication, choke points or the national territory. As a corollary, strategy was generally limited in its application to the use of military means to achieve the objectives (ends) of national security policy.[1]

The current international security dialogue goes beyond traditional national policy objectives and focuses on relative well-being. The United Nations (UN), for example, has made human security an explicit condition warranting intervention with or without the concurrence of the so-called 'sovereign' state whose population is at risk.[2] Now, more frequently, national security implies protection – through a variety of military and nonmilitary means – of more ambiguous political, economic, social, cultural, ideological and environmental interests.[3] Additionally, the contemporary security dialogue stresses that challenges to the national well-being are generated by a lack of development and resultant chronic poverty, violence and instability.[4] As a consequence, security can no longer be considered only in terms of protecting national territory and interests against outside military aggressors. Rather, security is being redefined more broadly, to encompass stability – and stability is dependent on the legitimate political, economic and social development (well-being) of the global community. Thus, the redefinition of security calls for a wider concept of what constitutes threat. First, a deeper look at the new global security arena is required.

A LOOK THROUGH A MAGICAL MICROSCOPE INTO THE CONTEMPORARY GLOBAL SECURITY ARENA

If the appropriate magic could be conjured and one could look down through the familiar artificial political lines and colors of a current world map into the twenty-first century's strategic reality, one could see a complex new security arena. A deeper look into that picture would provide snapshots that show several types of ambiguous and asymmetric conflicts as well as state failure – and their causes and consequences. The following examples should suffice:

- A vision of 79 low-intensity conflicts, 32 complex emergencies and 18 ethnic (genocidal) wars overlapping with 175 small-scale internal wars throughout the world today. This picture would also show unspeakable human destruction and misery involving refugee flows, modern plagues, food and water scarcity, and resource conflicts. In this connection, a magical snapshot would show that during the period since the first Persian Gulf War, anywhere from 80 to 210 million people have lost their hopes, their property and their lives. The resultant political alienation – sufficiently reinforced by significant governmental corruption, criminal activity and social violence – tends to direct the survivors and their advocates toward more and more violence, terrorism and the asymmetrical tactics of despair.[5]
- A view of a vicious downward spiral that manifests itself in diminished levels of popular and institutional acceptance and support for weak and ineffectual governments and generates further disorder, violent internal conflicts and mushrooming demands by various groups for political autonomy. These governance issues translate themselves into constant subtle and not so subtle struggles for power that dominate life in much of the contemporary world. Results of these dynamics can be seen not so much in the proliferation of new countries, but in an ironic explosion of

weak, incompetent, misguided, insensitive and/or corrupt governments throughout the globe.[6]

• In that connection, one can see a broken pattern of emerging city-states, shanty-states, amorphous warlord-controlled regions, criminal anarchist controlled regions,[7] and a 'steady run of uncivil wars sundering fragile but functioning nation-states and gnawing at the well-being of stable nations'.[8] Ultimately, this instability – along with the human destabilizers who exploit instability for their own self-determined objectives – leads to crises of governance and another downward spiral into failing and failed state status.[9] Indeed, it has become evident that humanitarian assistance, if not managed in the context of restoring the legitimacy of the failed state, actually nurtures warlords by providing additional bases for illicit power and wealth, and corruption.[10]

This takes us back to where we began – to the fact that armed non-state groups are challenging the nation-state's physical and moral right to govern. This almost chronic political chaos can been seen propagating its respective forms of instability and violence in large parts of Africa, Eastern Europe, the Middle East, Asia and Latin America. In many of these cases, governments are waging war on their citizens, fighting to survive assaults from their citizens or have become mere factions among other competing political factions claiming the right to govern all or part of a given destabilized national territory. It is in this context that international organizations, such as the UN, and individual national powers, such as the United States, confront a succession of failing and failed states.[11]

Then, with some additional adjustments of focus on our microscope, we can discern a number of issues that cannot be shown in two-dimensional space. First and most important, we can get a better idea of the complex threat situation and the ultimate threat – state failure. Second, an even deeper examination of the vision of contemporary wars reveals the shadows of things that have been and of those that will be on the road ahead. Third, a closer look at the familiar and troubling world map exposes some signposts on the road ahead that identify the most significant changes in the landscape. Finally, our magical microscope reveals a short list of the challenges and tasks that will help discerning civilian and military leaders negotiate the road through the new global security landscape.

THE DEEPER, MORE COMPLEX, MULTIDIMENSIONAL THREAT SITUATION, AND THE ULTIMATE THREAT – STATE FAILURE

The traditional international problem of conventional external aggression retains a certain credibility, but not the urgency it once had. For sovereignty to be meaningful today, the state and its associated governmental institutions, working under the rule of law, must be the only source of authority empowered to make and enforce laws and conduct the business of the people within the national territory. The violent, intimidating and corrupting activities of illegal internal and transnational non-state actors can abridge or negate these powers. In this connection, probably the most insidious security problem facing the world and the nations in it today centers on the threats to a given nation-state's ability and willingness to do the following: (1) control the national territory and the people in it fairly and justly and (2) control internal factions or non-state actors seeking illegal violent change *within* the borders of the nation-state. Ultimately, this kind of instability – along with the human destabilizers who exploit it – lead to a final downward spiral into failing and failed state status.[12] In that context, instability and the people who create and/or exploit it are tactical-operational level threats in their own right. However, the ultimate political – strategic threat is that of state failure. This takes us directly to the following questions:

1. What is a failed state; and why do states fail?
2. Why does state failure matter?
3. At what point in a state's disintegration should state failure be dealt with; how should state failure be handled; and what entities should deal with state failure?

What is a Failed State, and Why Do States Fail?

First, state failure is a process, not an outcome. It is a process by which the state loses the capacity and/or the will to perform its essential governance and security functions. At the same time, it may be a process by which the state never sufficiently developed those capabilities in the first place. The logic behind this distinction is simply that it is impossible to lose that which never existed. At the same time, however, if we focus only on the capacity to govern, we may lose sight of the fact that a state and its institutions may lack effective legitimacy. Haiti, North Korea, Afghanistan under the Taliban, and former President Saddam Hussein's Iraq are cases in point. History demonstrates that individuals and groups (including security forces) can prop up the capacity of the state to govern through the use of sheer force and 'state terrorism'.

Nevertheless, over time, the weaknesses inherent in the lack of legitimacy can lead to the eventual erosion of governmental authority and to a process of state failure.[13]

In *The Constant Gardener*, John le Carré outlines the answer to the associated questions of 'What is a failed state?' and 'Why do states fail?' from the point of view of a common-sense practitioner:

> I would suggest to you that, these days, very roughly, the qualifications for being a civilized state amount to – electoral suffrage, ah – protection

of life and property – um, justice, health and education for all, at least to a certain level – then the maintenance of a sound administrative infrastructure – and roads, transport, drains, et cetera – and – what else is there? – ah yes, the equitable collection of taxes. If a state fails to deliver on at least a quorum of the above – then one has to say the contract between state and citizen begins to look pretty shaky – and if it fails on all of the above, then it's a failed state, as we say these days.[14]

And, as Figure 1 and Table 1 indicate, this state of affairs is normally the result of an evolutionary process brought on by poor and irresponsible governance and leads to two other very fundamental reasons why states fail. First, state failure can be a process that is exacerbated by non-state groups that, for whatever reason, want to take down or exercise illicit control over a given government. Colombia is a good example of this. The narco-terrorist nexus in that country represents an unconventional, asymmetric threat to the authority of the central government. Through murder, kidnapping, corruption, intimidation and other means of coercion and persuasion, these violent internal non-state actors compromise the exercise of the state's authority. The government and its institutions become progressively less and less capable of performing the tasks of governance and exercising the effective sovereignty of the state. As a result, the narco-terrorists become increasingly wealthy and powerful, and the country deteriorates further and further toward failed state status.[15]

At the same time, Figure 1 and Table 1 also trace the patterns through which the many specific links between security and sovereignty may be targeted and broken by the use of nonmilitary and non-lethal information warfare and sophisticated technology. In this context, the state collapses under a process of knowledge-based technology, manipulated by those self-proclaimed leaders who wish to destroy 'bond-relationships' that unite a government, its security forces, and a people, and to erode governmental authority. Their intent is to weaken or control government or to replace it with their own regime.[16] Clearly, there are different paths or processes that lead to state failure.

Why Does State Failure Matter?

The argument is, generally, that failing or failed states comprise the most dangerous long-term security challenge facing the global community today. More specifically, failed states become breeding grounds for instability and terrorism. They breed massive humanitarian disasters and major refugee flows. They can host 'evil' networks of all kinds, whether they involve criminal business enterprises, narco-trafficking, and/or some form of ideological or religious crusade. They spawn a variety of pernicious

FIGURE 1

CAUSAL LINKS BETWEEN ENVIRONMENTAL DEGRADATION, SECURITY
PROBLEMS, VIOLENCE, AND EVENTUAL STATE FAILURE

Stage One: The Beginnings of the Threat

Resource Shortages
Over exploitation of land,
forest, and water resources.
Production of industrial
Contaminants of land, Forest
and water resources. Results
in land, forest, water, and
industrial slowing, etc.
Generating rising wealth
differentials.

**Resource and Environmental Stress,
and governmental stresses.**
results in rising wealth differentials, societal
and governmental stresses taking advantage
of shortages for own advantages, and boosting
capital demand faced by the state and the
economy. In turn increases susceptibility of
government, economy, and society to sudden
shocks like floods, draughts, and sharp downward
changes in the economy, political system, and
security environment.

**Dealing effectively with these
problems demands strong,
competent,** resilient, and
uncorrupted governmental action
at all levels of economy and
society, e.g., legitimate governance. Also requires strong
uncorrupted inter-National
coordination and cooperation.
Otherwise, the environmental
situation can move into Stage Two

Population Stresses
Reduction of standard of
living and increased social
violence. Results in internal
and external migration, and
social segmentation. In turn
generates capital shortfalls
and susceptibility to sharp
changes in the economy,
the political system, and
the security environment.

Stage Two: Moving Closer to the Threat

Phase III – Second Level Threat

Inadequate reforms and adherence
to Rule of law **results in** further
social, economic, and political
degradation, and more widespread
and better organized social
violence. **Requires** medium to
long-term deep reforms to deal
with poverty and other root
causes of instability; and the
prudent applica tion of force to
enforce reforms and law and
order.

Phase I – Precursors

Resource and environmental
stresses, and governmental
stresses incompetently or
insensitively managed.
Resulting in structural
degradation and economic
scarcity.

Phase II – Third Level Threat

Constrained economic production, disease,
migration, expulsion, elite rent-seeking
(greed), and power-grabbing. **Results in**
personal violence, strikes, kidnappings,
bank robberies, bombings, criminal anarchy
and death squads, and refugee flows. **Requires**
short-term political, social, and economic
reforms; and minimum force to help ensure
personal security.

Stage Three: Violent Conflict

Phase IV – First Level Threat

Regime unwillingness or inability to promulgate and enforce
necessary reforms, and provide personal and national security
results in further weakening of institutions, group identity
crises and ethnic conflicts, more internal and external
migration, terrorism, *coups d'etat*, insurgency, and possible
external intervention. **Requires** continuation of reforms and
development of deep regime legitimacy; as well as development of superior organization, unity of effort, and ability
to exert deadly force against violent internal foe(s).

Phase V – Failing or Failed State Syndrome

Failure to achieve legitimacy and deal effectively
with progressively worsening internal social,
economic, and security problems **results in**
virtually complete turmoil and generally ineffective institutions. **Thus, intervention to preclude
state failure, or state failure.**

and lethal activities and outcomes, such as human rights violations, including
torture and murder; poverty, starvation and disease; the recruitment and use of
child soldiers; illegal drug trafficking; trafficking in women and body parts;
trafficking and proliferation of conventional weapons systems and weapons of

TABLE 1
THREAT DIMENSIONS

Level of threat	Type of threat	Civil–military actions to confront these threats
Third	Instability; e.g., personal violence, increased strikes, kidnappings, bank robberies, violent takeovers, death squads, bombings, murders/ assassinations, criminal anarchy, and the beginnings of insurgency, ethnic cleansing and refugee flows	Short-term political, economic and social reform; and minimum force to guarantee personal security
Second	Widespread social violence; e.g., increases in third-level instability	Medium-to long-term deep reforms to deal with poverty and other root causes of instability; and the careful application of force to enforce reforms and law and order.
First	Regime unwillingness or inability to promulgate and enforce second- and third-level reforms and provide personal and national security	Long-term deeper reforms to create changes in mind-set; and development of political, military/police competence under an umbrella of legitimacy
Fourth	Completely entrenched violent 'revolutionaries'	Continuation of reforms and development of deep regime legitimacy; plus development of superior organization, unity of effort and ability to exert deadly force against a violent internal foe

mass destruction; genocide, ethnic cleansing and warlordism; and criminal anarchy and insurgency. At the same time, they usually are unconfined and 'spill over' into regional syndromes of destabilization and Conflict.[17]

Additionally, failing and failed states simply do not fade away. Ample evidence demonstrates that failing and failed states become dysfunctional states, 'rogue states', criminal states, narco-states, or new 'people's democracies'. Moreover, failing and failed states tend not to buy US and other Western-made products; tend not to be interested in developing democratic and free market institutions and human rights; and tend not to cooperate to solve shared problems, such as illegal drugs, illicit arms flows, debilitating refugee flows and potentially dangerous environmental problems. In short, failing and failed states tend to linger and go from bad to worse. The longer they persist, the more they and their problems endanger global peace and security.[18]

Where, When, and How Should State Failure Be Dealt With?

Perhaps the most relevant questions in this section are 'Where, when, and how should failing or failed states be dealt with?' The realist answer to the first question is that attempts must be undertaken where they matter the most.

Not all individual cases of potential or actual state failure matter equally. Some states matter more than others. Thus, the primary implication is that the United States and its Western partners should consider a grand strategy that adopts state failure as a core focus and combines it with a 'pivotal states' approach to global security.[19]

Likewise, as implied in Figure 1, the realist answer to the second question is that heading off the problems of a failing state must be attempted as early as possible in the state failure process. If the global community waits to deal with a failed state, it will be dealing with the hardest and the most expensive cases. The rule of thumb would be, then, that when it is mutually agreed that a case is clearly of vital interest to a community – the sooner the better. The presumption is that governments choose to do nothing or something as a result of having weighed the various costs and benefits of a specific course of action.

Finally, the realist answer to the third question is that the United States and its Western partners should look to other key actors within regions who can play larger roles in monitoring, preventing, and addressing the challenges of state failure. Again, as Figure 1 indicates, an international and multilateral coordinated, regionally based multidimensional framework for action – rather than a unilateral military approach – is essential for political-strategic success now and for the future.

Conclusions

Admittedly, putting the already large humanitarian 'root causes' issue of the state failure process into an even larger global stability-security context generates such a complex problem that many leaders and scholars are tempted to disregard this approach as 'too big', 'too hard', or 'impossible'. However, looking at the grand strategic picture of cause and effect allows one to understand better that 'humanitarian/environmental problems can no longer be thought of as ancillary', [20] 'substantially more sophisticated policy structures will be required to define and manage the interests of nations-states',[21] and the United States and the West need 'an overarching campaign plan to operationalize strategic [shaping and engagement] guidance'.[22]

Attacking the foreign internal development or reconstruction causes and consequences of instability and violence is no longer a matter of grace, charity or patronizing kindness. Because of the very real threat to peace and prosperity, it is a matter of intense national and global self-interest. The conscious choices that the international community and individual intervening powers make about how to conduct national stability and reconstruction efforts now and in the future will define the processes of national reform, regeneration and well-being – and, thus, relative internal and global security, stability, peace and prosperity.

A VISION OF CONFLICT ON THE ROAD AHEAD: SHADOWS OF THINGS
THAT HAVE BEEN AND THOSE THAT WILL BE [23]

The United States and the parts of the global community most integrated into
the interdependent world economy are embroiled in a security arena in which
time-honored concepts of national security and the classical military means to
attain it, while still necessary, are no longer sufficient. Now, in addition to
traditional regional security issues, an array of nontraditional threats challenge
the West at home and abroad:

Military Threats

These include the proliferation of weapons of mass destruction, regional
ethnic and religious conflicts, myriad varieties of terrorism, and criminal
anarchy.

Nonmilitary Threats

These include trade wars, financial wars, cyber wars, and new terror wars,
involving improved and more sophisticated use of chemical and biological
agents.

At the same time, these 'new' traditional and nontraditional threats blur the
old dividing lines among military, political, and economic security affairs.
Clearly, effective involvement in the contemporary global security
environment requires some serious conceptual adjustments. They center on
understanding the transformation of conflict.

The Transformation of Conflict

Carl von Clausewitz reminds us:

> It is possible to increase the likelihood of success without defeating the
> enemy's forces. I refer to operations that have direct political [and
> psychological] repercussions, that are designed in the first place to
> disrupt the opposing alliance, or to paralyze it, that gain us new allies,
> favorably affect the political scene, etc. If such operations are possible,
> it is obvious that they can greatly improve our prospects and that they
> can form a much shorter route to the goal than the destruction of the
> opposing armies.[24]

In these terms, there is only one governing rule for contemporary conflict,
that is, 'there are no rules'. Nothing is forbidden.[25] This is warfare in the age of
globalization and, while possibly less bloody, it is no less brutal. We can see
these characteristics in a brief outline of what is more frequently being called
first-through sixth-generation warfare methods.[26] It is important to note, also,
that each generation or method of warfare is not completely different and
separate from the others. Each successive methodology builds on the previous

one, and all overlap with each other. Finally, there is the 'mix and match' of the past that can produce what we call a 'Chinese Cocktail'.

First-Generation War. Low-technology *attrition war* has been a means of conducting conflict from the beginning of time. The basic idea is that the more opponents that are killed or incapacitated – relative to one's own side – the better. And, the last man or military unit left standing is the winner. Historically, attrition warfare appears to serve only those protagonists with 'the largest battalions'. When facing a numerically superior opponent, thus, it has been important to find other means to compensate for military inferiority.[27]

Second-Generation Warfare Methods. Relatively higher technology-led *maneuver warfare* was intended to provide the proverbial 'equalizer' to compete against sheer numbers. The basic concept is to utilize better and/or faster weaponry against an opponent. That is to say, the military force that can move, shoot and communicate more effectively, relative to the opponent, has the advantage and is more likely to prevail. Over 2,500 years ago, Sun Tzu warned, 'In war, numbers alone confer no advantage. Do not advance relying on sheer military power.'[28] The German 'Blitzkrieg' of the Second World War II and the US 'shock and awe' of the recent Iraqi War are examples of effective maneuver war and take us to the next generation or method of warfare.

Third-Generation Conflict Methods. At this point, the concept is to move from the blatant use of force toward the employment of 'brainpower'. That is, *movement from 'hard' toward 'soft' power*. In addition to using transport (movement), weaponry (shoot) and speed involving command and control (communication), third generation methodology tends to take advantage of intelligence, psychological operations and more knowledge-based technology as 'force multipliers'. The addition of 'soft' power to the military equation provides an efficient and effective means by which to paralyze enemy action – rather than simply to crush enemy forces.[29] It should also be noted that while intelligence, psychology and other forms of 'soft' power are less bloody than the 'hard power' of infantry, tanks and artillery, the ultimate objective of war remains the same: to compel the enemy to serve one's own interests.[30]

Fourth-Generation Methods. The primary characteristic of this methodology is that of *asymmetry*. This is the methodology of the weak against the strong. It is the use of disparity between contending parties to gain advantage. Strategic asymmetry is defined as 'acting, organizing, and thinking differently than opponents in order to maximize one's own advantages, exploit an opponent's weaknesses, attain the initiative, or gain greater freedom of action. ... It can have both psychological and physical dimensions'.[31] This is a concept as old as war itself, but some military officers and political leaders do not like it. They argue that asymmetry is not the way 'real soldiers' fight because they are not fighting fair. This view is unfortunate. What many military and political leaders seem not to have learned about contemporary conflict is that terrorists, insurgents, drug traffickers, paramilitaries, and so on (the 'weak') can be what Ralph Peters calls 'wise competitors'. He argues, 'Wise competitors will not even attempt to defeat us on our terms; rather, they will seek to shift the playing field away from conventional military confrontations or turn to terrorism and other nontraditional forms of assault on our national integrity. Only the foolish will fight fair'.[32] Thus, what is required more than weaponry and technology is lucid and incisive thinking, resourcefulness, determination and a certain disregard for convention.

Fifth-Generation Conflict. This methodology tends to emphasize the use of *information (that is, propaganda) and high technology* and is aimed at both civilian and military organizations. On one level, it involves the propaganda-oriented strategy derived from Maoist insurgency doctrine against a vulnerable government or set of targeted institutions. As an example, Peru's Sendero Luminoso calls activities that facilitate the process of state failure and generate greater insurgent freedom of movement 'armed propaganda'. Additionally, Colombia's narco-terrorists call the same type of activities 'business incentives'.[33] Those organizations operate with psychological, political and military objectives – in that order. On a more sophisticated information and technology level, fifth-generation conflict includes but is not restricted to financial war, trade war, economic warfare, media war, cyber war, net war and bond-relationship targeting.[34] As one example, Chancellor Helmut Kohl used the powerful German deutsche mark to breach the Berlin Wall – not tanks, artillery or aircraft. The point in fifth-generation conflict, according to Qiao Liang and Wang Xiangsui, is to 'fight the fight that fits one's weapons, and make [asymmetric] weapons to fit the fight'. In these terms, one uses 'all means, including armed force or non-armed force, military and nonmilitary, and lethal and nonlethal means to compel the enemy to accept one's interests'.[35]

Sixth-Generation Warfare. This type of conflict is sometimes called new terror war. It elaborates on all the previous generations, but *emphasizes biological and informational methods* to achieve desired ends.[36] We can see this in many ways – a single computer virus invasion, a single man-made stock market crash, and/or a single rumor or the exposing of a single scandal that leads to the fall of a government. Additionally, we can see the introduction of biological weapons, as in the poisoning of a water system of a major metropolitan area, poisoning the air in a given subway system, and/or the imposition of a single biological virus (such as 'mad cow disease') – into a specific country. The mix of possibilities is only limited by the imagination and willingness to use 'unethical' bio-informational technology to disrupt, control or destroy an enemy. Thus, the lines between civilian and military and lethal and nonlethal are eliminated, and the 'battlefield' is extended to everyone, everything and everywhere.[37]

An Example of a 'Chinese Cocktail'.   Liang and Xiangsui explain that any number of completely different scenarios and actions can occur using a mix of the various generations or methods of conflict. As an example:

> If the attacking side secretly musters large amounts of capital without the enemy nation being aware of this at all and launches a sneak attack against its financial markets, then after causing a financial crisis, buries a computer virus and hacker detachment in the opponent's computer system in advance, while at the same time carrying out a network attack against the enemy so that the civilian electricity network, traffic dispatching network, financial transaction network, telephone communications network, and mass media network are completely paralyzed, this win cause the enemy nation to fan into social panic, street riots, and a political crisis. There is finally the forceful bearing down by the army, and military means are utilized in gradual stages until the enemy is forced to sign a dishonorable peace treaty.[38]

Conclusions

War has changed. Today, war is no longer limited to using military violence to force desired change. Today, *all means* that can be brought to bear on a given situation must be used to compel the enemy to do one's will. Technology is no panacea. Technology may not dominate knowledge or information; however, it is the principle of the 'scissors, rock, and paper game' applied to the 'Great [Geopolitical] Game'. This represents a sea change in warfare and requires nothing less than a paradigm change. The direction of change may be seen in some signposts on the road ahead.

SOME SIGNPOSTS ON THE ROAD THROUGH
THE SECUIRTY LANDSCAPE

In protecting one's interests and confronting and influencing an adversary today, the proverbial road ahead is not easy. There are curves and bumps, and, perhaps, detours. We can see these supplementary deviations in the conflict situation in several different ways.

Ambiguity

First, the definitions of 'enemy' and 'victor' are elusive, and there is a lack of consensus on the use of 'power' to secure, maintain and enhance vital interests. Underlying these ambiguities is the fact that contemporary conflict is more often than not an intrastate affair that international law and convention are only beginning to address. Generally, a part of one society is pitted against another. In these so-called 'teacup' wars, clear-cut conditions do not apply or are not present; therefore, there are (1) normally no formal declarations or terminations of conflict, (2) no easily identified human foe to attack and defeat, (3) no specific territory to take and hold, (4) no single credible government or political actor with which to deal, (5) no legal niceties such as mutually recognized national borders and Geneva Conventions to help control the situation, (6) no guarantee that any agreement between or among contending authorities will be honored, and (7) no specific rules to guide leadership in a given 'engagement' process.

These aspects of the global security environment in general and any given specific context in particular are not only complex – they are political – psychological, and they are very ambiguous.[39]

The Need to Redefine 'Enemy'. 'Power' and 'Victory'

As a consequence, there is a need to redefine some standard conflict terminology. The enemy is no longer a recognizable military entity or an industrial capability to make traditional war. The enemy now becomes 'violence' and the causes of violence. Thus, the purposes of power have changed. Power is not simply 'hard' combat firepower directed at a traditional enemy military formation or industrial complex. Power is multi-layered, combining 'hard' and 'soft' political, psychological, moral, informational, economic, societal, military, police and civil bureaucratic activities that can be brought to bear appropriately on the causes as well as the perpetrators of violence. And victory is no longer the acknowledged destruction of an enemy's military capability. Victory (or success) is now – more frequently, and perhaps with a bit of 'spin control' – defined as the achievement of stability and the possibility of a 'sustainable peace'.[40]

'New' Centers of Gravity

These ambiguities intrude on the comfortable vision of war in which the assumed center of gravity has been enemy military formations and the physical capability to conduct conventional war. Clausewitz reminds us, however, that 'in countries subject to domestic strife ... and popular uprisings, the [center of gravity] is the personalities of the leaders and public opinion. It is against these that our energies should be directed.'[41] Thus, the primary center of gravity changes from a familiar military concept to an ambiguous and uncomfortable multidimensional political – psychological paradigm. A major implication that is often ignored is the fact that centers of gravity must not only be attacked but also defended. It is as important for an attacker to take the necessary measures to defend his own centers of gravity as it is for him to deal with those of his opponent. For example, during the Vietnam War, US leadership failed to defend American public opinion against the full-scale 'propaganda war' that was conducted by North Vietnam and its allies throughout the world. At that time and since then, US leadership seems to have failed to understand that the 'streets of Peoria' and the 'halls of Congress' are probably more decisive in determining the outcome of a given war than a battlefield thousands of miles away.[42]

Conflict Has Become Multidimensional, Multilateral and Multiorganizational

As examples, the conflicts in Colombia and Iraq are not simple military-to-military confrontations. These conflicts involve the entire population of the countries, as well as a large number of national civilian, military and police agencies, other national civilian organizations, international organizations, nongovernmental organizations (NGOs) and subnational indigenous actors who must work together to deal with complex internal and transnational threats to security, peace and well-being. As a result, a viable unity of effort is required to coordinate the multilateral, multidimensional and multiorganizational effort necessary to play effectively in a given security arena.[43]

Deterrence

Deterrence is not necessarily nuclear or military – although both are important. It is not necessarily negative or directly coercive – although these aspects, too, are important. Deterrence is broader than these descriptions. Deterrence is the creation of a state of mind among opponents that either encourages one thing or discourages something else. Under these terms, motives and culture, as well as weapons and tactics, become crucial. As a consequence, the deterrence task is straightforward. Culturally effective ways and means must be found to convince traditional as well as nontraditional external and internal players that it is not in their best interests to continue perceived negative and destructive behavior.[44]

Linkages

Clausewitz's 'Holy Trinity' of government, security forces and population depicts the crucial activities of the major players in any given conflict situation. It portrays the allegiance of a population as the primary center of gravity. Persuasive and coercive measures will determine success or failure in the achievement of 'victory' and peace. In these terms, both the government and its external allies and the internal illegal opposition and its external allies can coerce and persuade the populace into actions on behalf of either side.[45] This takes us to the implications for the modem knowledge-based use of information and communication technology to manipulate political leadership and public opinion.[46] The intent, again, is to break the bonds that unite a government, its security forces and a people – or those of an adversary and its supporters. Whichever side that wins the 'bond-relationship' targeting battle will require a superior organization, a unified civil – military strategy and the careful application of soft and hard power.

Contemporary Conflict is Not Limited: It is Total

Finally, contemporary nontraditional war is not a kind of appendage (a lesser or limited thing) to the more comfortable conventional military attrition and maneuver warfare paradigm. It is a great deal more. As long as opposition exists that is willing to risk illegal violence to control or take down a government, there is war. Again, it may be military or nonmilitary, lethal or nonlethal, or a Chinese mix of everything in an unrestricted arsenal. This is a zero-sum game in which there is only one winner or, in a worst-case scenario, no winners. It is, thus, total. This is the case with other governments, rogue states, Maoist insurgents, Osama bin Laden's terrorists, the Japanese Aum Shinrikyo cult, Mafia families, Southeast Asian warlords, or any group's ethnic cleansers, among others. It is also the case with the deliberate financial attack or hacker attack, among others, that that can impair the security of a nation as effectively as a nuclear bomb.[47]

Conclusions

Over the Years, national security has been viewed largely in terms of military defenses against external military threats. Given the opportunities and threats inherent in the predominantly interdependent global security environment, that is clearly too narrow a conception. The historical record demonstrates that the better a power or government is at conducting the military aspects of conventional war near the top of the conflict ladder, the more a potential external enemy or internal enemy is inclined to move asymmetrically toward the predominantly political-psychological conflict at the lower part of the conflict spectrum. As a consequence, this conclusion espouses a forward-looking, proactive, unified civil-military approach to 'protect against our asymmetric vulnerabilities to sustain our strategic position...'.[48] It would combine the potent virtues of the proverbial military-police 'iron fist' within the political-diplomatic 'velvet glove'. According to General Sir Frank Kitson, 'Thus, instead of thinking of the various manifestations of war as being singularly military, it is imperative to regard them as steps in the ladder of warfare as a whole.'[49]

In sum, these are the basic political-psychological realities of conflict for now and the future. These realities must inform the development of a conceptual framework – or filter mechanism – that can support issue identification, deal with changes in center of gravity, and establish priorities for efforts and actions to deal with the constellation of human and more traditional security issues that threaten the well-being of myriad peoples, societies and countries. The consequences of failing to do this are clear. Unless thinking and actions are reoriented to deal with these asymmetric, knowledge-based information and technology realities, the problems of global, regional and subregional stability and security will resolve themselves – none will remain.

THE CHALLENGES AND TASKS FOR THE ROAD AHEAD

Even though prudent armies must prepare for high-risk, low-probability conventional war, there is a high probability that the US president and Congress and the UN's Security Council will continue to require military participation in horrible new dilemmas that arise from the chaos engendered by the contemporary global security environment. They center on the traditional threat that stems from current and potential nuclear powers and the many smaller – but equally deadly – nontraditional threats that are generated out of the unevenness of global economic integration.[50] Moreover, these threats to national and international stability will be gravely complicated by the processes of state failure that they will trigger.[51] In this security environment, governments, military and police forces, and other related agencies have little choice but to rethink security as it applies to nontraditional threats that many political and military leaders have tended to ignore or wish away.

The Challenge

The primary challenge, then, is to come to terms with the fact that contemporary security, at whatever level, is at its base a holistic political – diplomatic, socioeconomic, psychological – moral and military – police effort. The corollary is to change from a singular military approach to a multidimensional, multiorganizational, multicultural and multinational paradigm. That, in turn, requires a conceptual framework and an organizational structure to promulgate unified civil – military planning and implementation of the multidimensional concept.

Associated Tasks

The study of the fundamental nature of conflict has always been the philosophical cornerstone for understanding conventional war. It is no less relevant to nontraditional war.[52] In the past, some wars, such as the Vietnam War, tended to be unrealistically viewed as providing military solutions to military problems.[53] In the twenty-first century, the complex realities of contemporary wars must be understood as holistic processes that rely on various civilian and military agencies and contingents working together in an integrated fashion to achieve common, workable and reasonable political-strategic ends.[54]

Given today's realities, failure to prepare adequately for present and future contingencies is unconscionable. At a minimum, there are five fundamental educational and organizational imperatives needed to implement the tasks noted above and deal effectively with contemporary conflict situations. They are the following:

- Civilian and military leaders at all levels must learn the fundamental nature of subversion and insurgency with particular reference to the way in which military and nonmilitary and lethal and nonlethal force can be employed to achieve political ends, and the way in which political considerations affect the use of force. Additionally, leaders need to understand the strategic and political – psychological implications of operational and tactical actions.
- Civilian and military personnel are expected to be able to operate effectively and collegially in coalitions or multinational contingents. They must also acquire the ability to deal collegially with civilian populations and local and global media. As a consequence, efforts that enhance interagency as well as international cultural awareness, such as civilian and military exchange programs, language training programs, and combined (multinational) exercises must be revitalized and expanded.
- Leaders must learn that an intelligence capability several steps beyond the usual is required for small internal wars. This capability involves active utilization of intelligence operations as a dominant element of both strategy and tactics. Thus, commanders at all levels must be responsible for collecting and exploiting timely intelligence. The lowest echelon where adequate intelligence assets have been generally concentrated is the division or brigade. Yet, such operations in most contemporary wars are normally conducted independently by battalion and smaller units.
- Non-state political actors in any kind of intrastate conflict are likely to have at their disposal an awesome array of conventional and unconventional weaponry. The 'savage wars of peace' have and will continue to place military forces and civilian support contingents into harm's way. Thus, leadership development must prepare peacekeepers (that is, peace enforcers) to be effective war fighters.
- Governments must restructure themselves to the extent necessary to establish the appropriate political mechanisms to achieve effective unity of effort. The intent is to ensure that the application of the various civilian and military instruments of power *directly* contribute to a mutually agreed

political end-state. Generating a more complete unity of effort will require contributions at the international and multilateral levels, as well.

FINAL CONCLUSIONS

These challenges and tasks are not radical. They are only the logical extensions of basic security strategy and national and international asset management. By accepting these challenges and tasks, the United States and the West can help to replace conflict with cooperation and to harvest the hope and fulfill the promise that a new multidimensional paradigm for a more peaceful and prosperous tomorrow offers. These cooperative efforts may not be easy to establish; however, they should prove in the medium to long term to be far less demanding and costly in political, economic, military, and ethical terms than to continue a 'business as usual', crisis-management approach to contemporary global security.

ACKNOWLEDGEMENTS

The views expressed in this report are those of the author and do not necessarily reflect the official policy or position of the Department of the Army, the Department of Defense or the US Government.

NOTES

1. Russell F. Weigley, 'The Evolution of Strategic Thought', in B. Thomas Trent and James E. Harf (eds), *National Security Affairs: Theoretical Perspectives and Contemporary Issues* (New Brunswick, NJ: Transaction Books, 1982), pp. 69–71.
2. This point is noted in Jessica Mathews, 'Power Shift', *Foreign Affairs* January/February 1997, pp.58–60.
3. Amos A. Jordan, William J. Taylor, Jr and Lawrence J. Korb, *American National Security: Policy and Process*, 3d ed. (Baltimore, MD: The Johns Hopkins University Press, 1988), p.3.
4. *A National Security Strategy of Engagement and Enlargement* (Washington, DC: The White House, February 1966); *A National Security Strategy for a New Century* (Washington, DC: The White House, May 1997); *A National Security Strategy for a New Century* (Washington, DC: The, White House, October 1999); and annual editions to date.
5. Robert David Steele, *The New Craft of Intelligence: Personal, Public & Political* (Oakton, VA: OSS International Press, 2002), which draws on 'World Conflict and Human Rights Map' prepared by Berto Jongman with the support of the Goals for Americans Foundation, St Louis (2002); *The State of the World Atlas* (1997); and website for Genocide Watch.com (Dr Greg Stanton), among other sources.
6. William J. Olson, 'International Organized Crime: The Silent Threat to Sovereignty', *The Fletcher Forum of World Affairs*, Summer/Fall 1997, pp.66–80; and Roy Godson and William J. Olson, 'International Organized Crime', Society, January/February 1995, pp. 18–29.
7. Robert D. Kaplan, 'The Coming Anarchy', *Atlantic Monthly*, February 1994, pp.72–6; idem, *The Coming Anarchy* (New York: Random House, 2000), pp.3–57.
8. Leslie H. Gelb, 'Quelling the Teacup Wars', *Foreign Affairs*, November/December 1994, pp.5–6.

9. Daniel C. Esty et al., 'The State Failure Projects: Early Warning Research for U.S. Foreign Policy Planning', in John L. Davies and Ted Robert Gurr (eds), *Preventive Measures: Building Risk Assessment and Crisis Early Warning Systems* (New York: Rowman & Littlefield, 1998), pp.27–38. See also Thomas F. Homer-Dixon, *Environment, Scarcity, and Violence* (Princeton, NJ: Princeton University Press, 1999), pp. 133–68.
10. William Shawcross, *Deliver Us from Evil: Warlords, Peacekeepers, and a World of Endless Conflict* (New York: Simon & Schuster, 2000). Also see John Mackinlay, 'Beyond the Logjam: A Doctrine for Complex Emergencies', in Max Manwaring and John T. Fishel (eds), *Toward Responsibility in the New World Disorder: Challenges and Lessons of Peace Operations* (London: Frank Cass, 1998), pp. 120–22; and John Mackinlay, 'War Lords', *Defense and International Security* (April 1998), pp.24–32.
11. Edwin G. Corr and Max G. Manwaring, 'Some Final Thoughts', in Max G. Manwaring and Anthony James (eds), *Beyond Declaring Victory and Coming Home* (Westport, CT: Praeger, 2000), pp.248–52.
12. Ibid.; Homer-Dixon.
13. Robert H. Dorff, 'Strategy, Grand Strategy, and the Search for Strategy', in Max G. Manwaring, Edwin G. Corr and Robert H. Dorff (eds), *The Search for Security: A U.S. Grand Strategy for the Twenty-First Century* (Westport, CT: Praeger, 2003), pp. 131–7.
14. John le Carré, *The Constant Gardener* (New York: Charles Scribner's Sons, 2001), p. 137.
15. See Max Manwaring, 'U.S. Too Narrowly Focused on Drug War in Colombia', *The Miami Herald*, 15 August 2001.
16. Dorff. Also see David C. Jordan, *Drug Politics: Dirty Money and Democracies* (Norman, OK: University of Oklahoma Press, 1999); Ana Maria Bejarano and Eduardo Pizarro, 'The Crisis of Democracy in Colombia: From "Restricted" Democracy to "Besieged" Democracy', unpublished manuscript, 2001. Also see: Eduardo Pizarro and Ana Maria Bejarano, 'Colombia: A Failing State?', *Re Vista: Harvard Review of Latin America*, Spring 2003, pp. 1–6.
17. Ibid.; Esty et al.
18. Ibid.
19. For a good discussion of this approach, see Robert S. Chase, Emily B. Hill and Paul Kennedy, 'Pivotal States and U.S. Strategy', *Foreign Affairs*, January/February 1996, pp.33–51.
20. Braden R. Allenby, 'Environmental Security: Concept and Implementation', *International Political Science Review* (2000), pp.6–7.
21. Ibid.
22. Author interview with General Charles E. Wilhelm, USMC (Ret.), former Commander-in-Chief, US Southern Command, USMC, 9 February 2001, in Reston, VA.
23. This phrase was used to good effect by Ian Beckett, 'Forward to the Past: Insurgency in Our Midst', *Harvard International Review*, Summer 2001, p.63.
24. Carl von Clausewitz, *On War*, ed. Michael Howard and trans. Peter Paret (Princeton, NJ: Princeton University Press, 1976), pp.92–3.
25. Qiao Liang and Wang Xiangsui, *Unrestricted Warfare* (Beijing: PLA Literature and Arts Publishing House, 1999), p.2. The term, 'cocktail mixture' is first used on p.48 and elaborated in more detail on pp. 116–23.
26. The terms, 'first, second, and third wave war' were popularized by Alvin and Heidi Toffler, *War and Anti-War: Survival at the Dawn of the 21st Century* (New York: Little, Brown and Company, 1993).
27. Ibid., pp.33–37. Also see Michael Howard, *The Lessons of History* (New Haven: CT: Yale University Press, 1991).
28. Sun Tzu, *The Art of War*, trans. Samuel B. Griffith (London: Oxford University Press, 1963), p.122.
29. B.H. Liddell-Hart, *Strategy*, 2nd rev. ed. (New York: Signet, 1974), p.333.
30. Liang and Xiangsui, p.48.
31. Steven Metz and Douglas V. Johnson II, *Asymmetry and U.S. Military Strategy: Definition, Background, and Strategic Concepts* (Carlisle Barracks, PA: Strategic Studies Institute, 2001), pp.5–6.

32. Ralph Peters, 'Constant Conflict', *Parameters*, Summer 1997, p.10. See also 'The Culture of Future Conflict', *Parameters*, Winter 1995–96, pp. 18–27.
33. Simon Strong, *Shining Path: A Case Study in Ideological Terrorism*, No.260 (London: Research Institute for the Study of Conflict and Terrorism, 1993), pp. 1–2, 23–6; Max G. Manwaring, 'Peru's Sendero Luminoso: The Shining Path Beckons', *The Annals of the American Academy of Political and Social Science*, September 1995, pp. 157–66; idem, 'Guerrillas, Narcotics, and Terrorism: Old Menaces in a New World', in Richard L. Millett and Michael Gold-Biss (eds), *Beyond Praetorianism: The Latin American Military in Transition* (Coral Gables, FL: North–South Center Press, 1996), pp.37–57.
34. Robert J. Bunker, 'Battlespace Dynamics, Information Warfare to Netwar, and Bond-Relationship Targeting', in Robert J. Bunker (ed.), *Non-State Threats and Future War* (London: Frank Cass, 2003), pp.97–107.
35. Liang and Xiangsui, pp.6, 17.
36. Walter Laquer, 'Post-Modern Terrorism', *Foreign Affairs*, September/October 1996, p.36; idem, *The New Terrorism* (Oxford: Oxford University Press), 1999.
37. Liang and Xiangsui, p.109.
38. Ibid., p.123.
39. Author interviews with General John R. Galvin, USA (Ret.), Boston, MA, 6 August 1997; Lieutenant General William G. Carter, III, USA (Ret.), Washington, DC, 30 November 1998 and 2 March 1999; General Anthony Zinni, USMC, Commander-in-Chief, United States Central Command, Washington, DC, 2 June 1999 and 6 October 2000; and General Charles E. Wilhelm. These observations were also made by former Secretary of State George P. Shultz in an address before the Low-intensity Warfare Conference at the National Defense University on 15 January 1986, in Washington, DC.
40. Ibid. Also see Boutros Boutros-Ghali, 'Global Leadership After the Cold War', *Foreign Affairs*, March/April 1996, pp.86–98; idem, *An Agenda for Peace* (New York: United Nations, 1992), pp.11, 32–4.
41. Clausewitz.
42. General Vo Nguyen Giap, 'The Factors of Success', *in People's War, People's Army* (New York: Frederick A. Praeger, 1962), pp. 36–7. Also see David K. Shipler, 'Robert McNamara Meets the Enemy', *New York Times Magazine*, 10 August 1997, p.50.
43. For an elaboration of this idea, see David Last, 'Winning the Savage Wars of Peace: What the Manwaring Paradigm Tells Us', in John T. Fishel (ed.), *The Savage Wars of Peace* (Boulder, CO: Westview Press, 1998), pp.211–39.
44. For excellent discussions regarding this topic, see Colin S. Gray, 'Deterrence and the Nature of Strategy,' in Max Manwaring (ed.), *Deterrence in the 21st Century* (London: Frank Cass, 2000), pp. 17–26; Colin S. Gray, *Defining and Achieving Decisive Victory* (Carlisle Barracks, PA: Strategic Studies Institute, 2002); Colin S. Gray, *Modern Strategy* (London: Oxford University Press, 1999).
45. Clausewitz, p.89.
46. Bunker, pp.104–107.
47. Liang and Xiangsui.
48. US Department of Defense, *Transformation Planning Guidance* (Washington, DC: Department of Defense, 2003).
49. General Sir Frank Kitson, *Warfare as a Whole* (London: Faber and Faber, 1987).
50. Mathews.
51. Esty et al.
52. Kitson.
53. Giap; Shipler.
54. Liang and Xiangsui.

Globalization's Bastards: Illegitimate Non-State Actors in International Law

NEAL A. POLLARD

"They are the enemies of the whole world. If you ask where their country is, they point to the far-off horizon."

> British agent Herbert Edwardes,
> on inhabitants of Pakistan's tribal
> lands, 1847,

"It wasn't until after September 11 that most of us realized that, for the first time in human history, a non-state actor, a group of religious extremists at the very bottom of the international system, had the capability to inflict devastating damage on the very pinnacle of the international system."

> Dr. Coit Blacker, Director
> Stanford Institute for International Studies
> *New York Times*, Apr. 5, 2004

PREFACE

Some argued that the terrorism of 11 September 2001 was the death knell for globalization. With some distance from that date, others have argued that terrorism has hijacked or otherwise co-opted globalization, as though terrorism were an external force. Neither argument is totally accurate: modern terrorism *is* globalization, albeit a parasitic (and paradoxical) dark side of it, and we in the midst of the first war of globalization. International law has an important role to play in this war, but it will be ineffectual until it is adapted to the nature of this war and the enemy of globalization: transnational agendas of extremist religious authoritarianism, such as propagated by Al Qaeda.

A transnational terrorist group such as Al Qaeda is the quintessential illegal non-state actor in the international system. But despite a clear consensus among states on the desirability to eradicate illegal non-state actors and their influences, the international system has great difficulty in dealing with illegitimate non-state actors. This is due to two main factors: the quality and quantity of power these illegitimate actors have obtained in an era of globalization, and the fact that international law considers only individual criminals and terrorists as subjects, rather than the entire illegitimate enterprise, and does not adequately link individuals and enterprises to more nuanced and complex forms of state sponsorship.

These factors might be mitigated by considering insights from how international law deals with 'globalized' multi-national corporations and non-governmental organizations as subjects, and applying these insights to international procedures that deal with their illegitimate counterparts as entire enterprises rather than specific individuals. However, insights alone will not prepare the international system better to deal with illegal non-state actors. Rather, these insights must be a foundation, built upon to inform and equip international law with new tools to counter the influence of illegal non-state actors on the international system.

These new tools of international law should reflect a more sophisticated understanding of modern terrorism as an enterprise, as well as its influence on the international system. These tools should also embrace a more complex (and courageous) understanding of state sponsorship of terrorism. Finally, these tools must be embedded in the fabric of globalization: that is, in the world's international agreements and legal instruments, used as part of the incentive structure that gives meaning, force and accountability to the words of international law.

INTRODUCTION

International actors – states, non-governmental organizations, multi-national corporations and transnational terrorist groups – seek to influence outcomes in the international system, by wielding economic, political, diplomatic, social and occasionally military tools. The use of these tools in the international system is governed by international law, an amorphous corpus of normative expressions, standards, principles, institutions, procedures and written agreements by which states agree to abide (in theory, if not in practice).

International law today is seeking to accommodate the forces and actors behind globalization and their influence on the international system. Traditionally, international law has been seen as the law made by states to govern relations between and among them. Non-state actors are not governed by international law unless states have explicitly made them the subject of law between states. Nevertheless, an undeniable characteristic of globalization has been the effects that non-state actors on the international system, and the recognition among states that international law must understand the actions and interactions of non-state actors, if not explicitly recognize them as subject of international law. This recognition is especially apparent in the field of human rights, and indeed, international law even accords individual human beings status and standing before some international institutions, offering them protection before courts of human rights, or punishment before international tribunals.

Modern political violence presents perhaps the greatest challenge of globalization for international law to accommodate. This challenge is primarily one of understanding the relationship between power and violence, and the use of both by international actors. To be sure, war predates the modern international system, which traces its origins to the end of the Thirty Years' War in 1648. But even war itself has been affected by globalization. This was apparent on 11 September 2001, as transnational terrorism manifested itself as the dark side of globalization, prompting the United States to wage war against a non-state entity.[1]

War is still a continuation of politics by other means, to paraphrase Clausewitz. But globalization has changed the global distribution of effective power that underlies, among other things, the ability to wage war effectively. If international law is to moderate the behavior of actors within the international system, it must be able to identify and affect how actors wield power – including political violence – to influence outcomes in the international system. If international law seeks to have some beneficial influence over political violence – an objective that lies at the very heart of the most important international institutions, including the United Nations – then it must understand the relationship among power, violence, and the pursuit of interests in the international system.

Many authors have described a 'power shift' occurring, in which the role and authority of the sovereign state is being challenged by non-state actors – multi-national corporations, non-governmental organizations, etc. – and effective power to influence outcomes in the international system is 'shifting' to these non-state actors.[2] A 'power shift' in the international system is not a new notion: its modern characterization was well described at least as far back as 1977 by the noted scholar Hedley Bull, and it has been a general but recurrent theme of international political discourse since 1648, with the rise of the sovereign state, and its evolution as the dominant arbiter of power in the world political system. Since the concept of private property was invented, the balance, exchange and even currency of 'power' in the international system have never been particularly stable. 'Power' is a slippery concept to qualify or quantify, even when a state has the unqualified power to destroy the world.

Some observers have noted that the very character of 'power' itself – the ability and means to impose one's will upon others (to paraphrase a Clausewitzian definition) – is changing, in addition to a 'shifting' distribution of it. The general debate over the extent and types of power and influence of non-state actors in international relations begs other important questions such as: Is this necessarily a bad thing? Are there more benefits than drawbacks from non-state actors wielding influence in the international arena? How can balances be struck in international law to regulate non-state actors and hold them accountable for negative consequences? And, how can states craft international law to maximize benefits of non-state actors' participation in international relations, while minimizing negative benefits?

These questions are fairly one-sided with respect to illegitimate non-state actors. Reasonable people disagree about the benefits or desirable limits of legitimate non-state actors' participation in the international system (e.g. the ability or extent of multi-national corporations or non-governmental organization to influence outcomes in the international system). However, reasonable people, by definition, stand against the extremist agendas espoused by illegitimate non-state actors such as global organized crime syndicates or transnational terrorist campaigns. Nevertheless, international law has no easier time addressing illegitimate non-state actors and minimizing their influence on the international system.

Terrorists are murderers, but as non-state actors, they are also a paradox. A hallmark of globalization has been for non-state actors to seek participatory roles in the international system, in order to influence outcomes in the system that benefit their interests (e.g. trade or investment agreements, tariff adjustments, international human rights policies, participatory status in UN bodies, treaties and international agreements, etc.). Terrorists such as Al Qaeda, as non-state actors, similarly seek to participate in the international system, but for the purposes of destroying it. Ironically, much of the potential power terrorists have to disrupt the international system is directly derived from that very system. It is at this nexus of both reliance and hostility that international law can minimize the influence terrorists have on the international system.

THE DARK SIDE OF GLOBALIZATION: MODERN TERRORISM

Globalization has changed the character of potential power in the international system, to include the quality and 'quantity' of power that terrorists wield. The body of scholarship researching 'power shifts' in international relations has a pedigree spanning decades. So does scholarship researching the role of terrorism in international relations. The study of terrorism cohered into a field of inquiry in political science in the late 1960s and early 1970s, when Palestinian airline hijackings, terrorist bombings and assassinations, and a keen international media guaranteed publicity for extremist agendas.[3] Terrorism had 'globalized' in a sense, if for no other reason, because terrorism in Germany could be viewed in American living rooms. However, terrorism was a phenomenon of political violence long before the 1970s, going back millennia. Sun Tzu, a Chinese military strategist living in the fourth century BCE, said 'kill one, frighten ten thousand'. 'Thug', 'assassin', and 'zealot' are examples of names derived from terrorist movements from centuries ago. When people's expectations are disappointed, the most extreme reaction can be violent. Today, dashed expectations can have dire effects on the international political system.

The phenomenon of modern terrorism finds an intellectual place in the scholarship examining the influence of non-state actors (NSAs) on the international system. This scholarship generally separates NSAs into two types. The first type is comprised of corporate and financial actors with wealth considerations as a primary objective (e.g. multi-national corporations, or MNCs). These are the corporate entities whose operations span continents, and although their identity might seem peculiarly specific to one country (e.g. McDonalds or Sony), they are responsible for much of the international flow of capital; 'in terms of economic power, transnational companies operate on a scale that is larger than that of most countries. At least a dozen transnational corporations have annual sales that are larger than the gross national products of more than half the states in the world.'[4]

The second type is comprised of groups such as non-governmental organizations (NGOs, i.e. human rights, environmental or multi-national political organizations) that seek as a primary objective to influence political decisions of other actors in international relations. Joseph Nye described some of these groups as claiming to act as:

> a 'global conscience' representing broad public interests beyond the purview of individual states, or interests that states are wont to ignore. They develop new norms by directly pressing governments and business leaders to change policies, and indirectly by altering public perceptions of what governments and firms should be doing.[5]

These two types of non-state actors do not represent a sharp distinction of classes, but rather a continuum.[6] On one end of the continuum are actors with self-serving motivations to promote the well-being of the group on one end of the continuum (e.g. financial growth and profits), while at the other end are epistemic communities and advocacy networks motivated by shared values and a perceived 'common good'.[7] There are also two schools of thought regarding the impact of NSAs on world politics: some 'praise the emergence of a global transnational civil society ... while others denounce an increasing transnational capitalist hegemony'.[8] Both views agree that NSAs exert an 'extraordinary influence' on outcomes in international politics.[9]

Every civil society has criminals, even a global transnational one. The two general types of NSAs described above also have analogous illegitimate elements: transnational criminal organizations focused on self-interest and financial gain (such as drug producers and traffickers, arms smugglers, racketeers, pirates and international money launderers) and transnational terrorist groups and movements that act as radical 'epistemic communities' seeking to propagate by force a common version of extremist politics on behalf of a constituency that extends beyond the perpetrators themselves (e.g. Al Qaeda, Hizb'allah, Aum Shinrikyo, etc.).

Transnational organized crime groups and terrorist movements are obviously non-state actors. They wield a considerable amount of power and influence international relations. Through activities including smuggling, bribery, robbery, coercion and violent attack on massive scales, they are able to negatively influence international politics. They foster corruption that results in market inefficiencies and decreases in free trade; proliferation of arms and weapons of mass destruction that results in regional instability and insurgency; destruction that causes humanitarian disasters, massive economic damage and capital flight; and money laundering and smuggling to finance and support all of these activities. The death, destruction and intimidation on such a massive scale causes governments fearful of more destruction to capitulate in foreign or domestic policy changes. In the worst case, such as Afghanistan, Iran or Russia, illegitimate NSAs can be instruments or directors of state policy themselves, thus making, if not influencing, state decisions.

The engines of globalization – the information revolution, cheap and open intercontinental transportation, global 24-hour media, electronic finance infrastructure, increasing participation in international organizations, and liberalized trade and investment – have benefited legal and illegal non-state actors alike across the spectrum. Table 1 illustrates the continuum of international actors, their illegal counterparts and

TABLE 1
INTERNATIONAL ACTORS IN THE GLOBALIZATION AGE

Type of actor	Legal actor	Illegal actor
State	United Nations member	'Rogue state'
Profit	Multi-national corporation	Transnational organized crime syndicate
Policy	Non-governmental organization	Transnational terrorist group
Technology/ globalization nexus	Information revolution	Cyber-terror/crime
	Global media	Propaganda, al Jazeera
	Scientific collaboration and development	Proliferation
	Electronic finance	Money laundering
	Increased foreign investment	Terror sponsorship and fundraising
	Cheap intercontinental travel and transportation of goods	Smuggling
	Greater productivity	11 September 2001, Russian organized crime

the technological nexus that provides them with resources to influence the international system.

The forces behind globalization provide power to transnational terrorist and criminal organizations, and enable them to influence the international system. This has been a long time coming. Scholars have argued that the thirteenth-century equivalent of sovereign rulers authorized the use of force by private armies and mercenaries, in order to accumulate power and wealth.[10] The unintended consequences of this privatization of international violence were the ancestors of today's terrorist movements, private liberation armies, and pirates, against which thirteenth-century rulers struggled to regain their monopoly over violence.[11] The Information Revolution is accelerating and exacerbating this 800-year-old trend, however: 'Governments of all kinds will find their control slipping during the twenty-first century as information technology gradually spreads to the large majority of the world that still lacks phones, computers, and electricity.'[12]

The modern state retains this monopoly today (for now), but in 1977, the scholar Hedley Bull recognized the same shift in power that has pervaded international politics for centuries. More interesting, Bull foresaw the unprecedented convergence of a number of factors today that redefine the meaning, quality and global distribution of power and ability to influence outcomes. Bull described this shift as 'new medievalism', an alternative to a state-centric ordering of world politics (and arguably evidence of the decline of the state system) defined by five characteristics:

- regional integration of states (e.g. the European Union or Organization of American States);
- the disintegration of states (e.g. the Soviet Union, Yugoslavia, and even the United Kingdom with political power in Northern Ireland and Scottish devolution);
- the restoration of private international violence (in both terrorist movements, insurgencies, and private military companies and defense contractors representing major powers);
- transnational organizations (MNCs, NGOs, the UN, etc.); and
- the technological unification of the world (facilitated through advances in transportation, communications, financial structures, trade, etc.).[13]

Bull posits that the five elements of his 'new medievalism' world order model as evidence of the decline of states, in that they are 'other associations' (to use the medievalists' expression) that are making inroads on the sovereignty and supremacy of a state over its territory, its citizens and its ability to decisively influence world politics.[14] That is, these five elements are evidence of a fundamental shift in power toward NSAs, enabling to move to the 'formal plane'. Although it is cliché (and of questionable causality) that these elements are the result of globalization, it is nonetheless clear that they are enabled and accelerated by the forces of globalization. It is the globalization of forces that have likewise resulted in power changing and shifting to illegitimate by-products of the 'new medievalism', especially in the privatization of violence and transnational organizations. If the threshold for something as profoundly expensive and dangerous as global war has been lowered sufficiently that non-state actors can meaningfully participate, then it stands to reason that the threshold has been similarly lowered for participation in other less expensive or dangerous international activities. Globalization has made this possible, and provides the engine for such participation.

Globalization has been described and characterized variously as removal of national borders as a hindrance to, and increase in, the free flow among nations of economic trade and integration, personal contact and mass international communications, technology development and exchange, and political engagement and subscription to international organizations.[15] For example, the US Defense Science Board defined globalization as 'integration of the political, economic and cultural activities of geographically and/or nationally separated peoples.'[16] Ironically, that definition could easily have come from a list of Al Qaeda's objectives. It is ironic, because many scholars see terrorism such as Al Qaeda, as well as less violent activism such as that displayed in Seattle and Genoa coinciding with WTO meetings, as negative reactions to the forces of globalizations, yet it is these forces that enable these malcontents to be so effective at influencing outcomes.

Not all terrorist groups exploit globalization to influence the international system, nor have all terrorists sought this objective. Indeed, terrorism is a weapon of the weak, used by marginalized political elites who have (relatively) modest means, with traditionally modest (though extreme and violent) goals. Terrorism has generally consisted of predominantly strategic attacks by militant extremists who want to gain political relevance by exploiting a feeling of discontent among a larger population, but who feel unable to achieve their political goals through ordinary political, social, economic or conventional military means.

From the First World War to the post-Cold War, after the dismantling of empires, anti-colonialist separatists exploited ethnic and nationalist discontent and dashed expectations, seething in repressive or impoverished conditions, to foment armed struggle that was geographically oriented toward a 'homeland' that had been colonized. This violence was mainly directed against the colonial powers. Indigenous extremists in former colonies, from Algeria to Palestine to Indochina, engaged in guerrilla campaigns for independence that, while still largely centered on geography that marked a 'homeland', also included urban terrorist attacks that sought to frighten a larger population beyond the immediate victims of the attacks, and even beyond the borders of the geographic locus. Thus, these groups demonstrated the publicity value of low-level violence aimed at noncombatants.

Most of these groups calibrated their violence not to inflict too many casualties, so as not to undermine attempts to gain sympathy for their cause in the homeland and abroad. That apparent tendency persisted through the Cold War. Terrorist groups such as the Japanese Red Army, the Italian Red Brigades and the German Red Army Faction, supported by the Soviet Union, sought to spread Communist revolution beyond the borders of both the Soviet Union and the countries from which they came.[17] These groups found sympathetic, and often active, supporters with Communist and USSR-allied states as well as other terrorist groups in North Africa, Latin America, the Middle East and Southeast Asia – groups often engaged in ethno-nationalist or guerrilla campaigns that had taken on an ideological aspect to their manifestos (for example, the Marxist–Leninist Armenian Secret Army for the Liberation of Armenia, the Maoist Shining Path in Peru, or the Marxist–Leninist Popular Front for the Liberation of Palestine operating in the Middle East).[18] However, casualties were still usually measured in ones or tens of victims, not hundreds. To paraphrase Brian Jenkins's famous dictum, terrorists wanted a lot of people watching, not a lot of people dead.[19]

Modern terrorism's blend of globalized operations and religious extremism has yielded a trend of increasing lethality, well beyond the effects of the ideological terrorist groups of the Cold War. Terrorism became truly global, both in agenda and operations, during the 1970s and 1980s, at height of the Cold War, driven by the advent of cheap commercial intercontinental airline travel and international communications.[20] Not coincidentally, cheap intercontinental travel and international communications are two of the engines driving globalization. Bruce Hoffman has argued that these two engines of globalization gave birth to the modern age of terrorism on 22 July 1968. On that date, terrorists of the Popular Front for the Liberation of Palestine (PFLP) hijacked an El Al flight from Rome to Tel Aviv. Although this was not the first hijacking, it was unprecedented because of a number of its purposes, including trading the hostages for Palestinian prisoners, specifically targeting an Israeli air carrier, forcing Israel to communicate directly with a terrorist organization (to the contrary of Israeli policy), and with the specific aim to create an international media event.[21] As Hoffman notes, Zehdi LabibTerzi, the Palestine Liberation Organization's chief observer at the UN, said in a 1976 interview, 'The first several hijackings aroused the consciousness of the world and awakened the media and world opinion much more – and more effectively – than 20 years of pleading at the United Nations.'[22] Terrorist groups that were concerned with more than territorial influence found international air travel and the global media as effective means to spread a message of political violence beyond the borders of their home countries.

'Transnationality' has proved to be a powerful enabler of a lethal terrorist campaign. Modern terrorism has evolved to be transnational in scope, reach and presence, and this gives it much of its power. Terrorism has a transnational scope, meaning its agenda and goals focus far beyond a parcel of land in a former colony. Animal rights activists coordinate across continents to disrupt or attack multinational corporations that deal in some way with animals. Al Qaeda and Osama bin Laden seem to want nothing less than a global holy war against the West, or at very least, the disruption of several Islamic states from North Africa to the Pacific Rim. This breadth of scope enables terrorists to justify – and plan – international operations wherever they see an opportunity, in support of an agenda that spans (and finds adherents across) continents, cultures and even generations.

Terrorism is transnational in reach, meaning its organizations and operations are dispersed across several continents, in 'networks' of cells rather than in hierarchical divisions with clear chains of command. Members of an international group can cross borders fluidly from one cell of the organization to another on a different continent, sometimes directed by a single coordinating leader or cell (in the case of Osama bin Laden or Shoko Asahara of Aum Shinrikyo), or sometimes organized by cells closer to the operations (in the case of Mohammed Atta, thought to be the mastermind of the airplane attacks of 11 September). This transnational reach gives terrorists access to targets worldwide, rather than limiting terrorists to targets in one geographical location where security forces can mass. Furthermore, transnational reach enables several decisions to be made at different levels and nodes across the world, and makes for a more robust and adaptable planning system – if counterterrorism forces act in a way that disrupts an organization's planned operations, both the figurehead of the group and the dispersed operational cells can independently adjust to react to security forces without disrupting the overall campaign plan (for example, if it becomes impossible to bomb an embassy in Country X, then bomb one in Country Y). Operational security is further enhanced by the possibility that many terrorists know of the existence only of very few other cells with which they directly interact. Arrests and disrupted plots in April 2004 in Canada, London, France and Madrid illustrate that there are probably several efforts, parallel to the Madrid rail bombings of 11 March 2004, that are independent of any 'central command' or common tactical planning, but which espouse the same Al Qaeda agenda and robust operational code.

Modern terrorism is transnational in presence, meaning it has a support structure anywhere a modicum of 'safe harbor' can be found, whether it be a state that supports training camps within its borders (as with Libya and south Lebanon), or networks of transnational organized crime or narcotics traffickers who offer secure transshipment routes (used profitably and thus securely for smuggling, communications or money laundering and transferring) in exchange for money, arms or security from terrorists (as is often seen in regions such as the Presevo Valley of Kosovo, where local governments lack the power or will to prevent transnational organized crime and trafficking). Transnational presence means terrorists can procure resources or secure logistics wherever there is a vacuum of law and order, or linkages with transnational criminal networks.

Religious extremism is the second ingredient in modern terrorism; the growth and virulence of religious terrorism in recent years has been a driving force behind the increasing lethality of terrorism.[23] In the 1980s and 1990s, the bipolar ideological struggle of the Cold War began to dissolve.[24] In its wake came a multi-polar cacophony of religious extremism that provided increasingly radical motivations for terrorism.[25] Many of the terrorist groups that dominated the headlines during the 1970s and 1980s, including the Palestine Liberation Organization (PLO) and Irish Republican Army (IRA), had agendas with strong religious components. However, these groups were driven more by ethno-nationalist, geographically oriented motivations, of which religion was one defining factor; similar to the ethno-nationalist separatists, ideological groups demonstrated a desire to calibrate their violence so as not to alienate potential sympathizers to the international Communist cause.[26] The 1979 Islamic revolution in Iran was the herald of an evolving extremism that sought religious goals for the sake of religion, and was not confined to geographic loci.[27] Indeed, much as the Soviet Union sought to export Communist revolution worldwide, the Iranian Islamic government adopted as a pillar of foreign policy the global export of Islamic revolution. Terrorist groups like Hizb'allah in Lebanon, which arguably began with geographic goals, became tools of states' foreign policy operating (and attacking) worldwide.[28]

Religious extremism has combined with globalized operations and increasing lethality to bring us to where we are today: engaged in a war of globalization. It is important to note that the virulence of religious extremism derives from an extremist reaction to globalization, rather than any element unique to Islam or any other specific religion. Although modern terrorism is dominated by religion; it has never been restricted to Islamic extremists. Today, all of the world's major religions have provided motivations for purely religious terrorism: from the Christian Identity movement in the United States to the right-wing Jewish fundamentalism that took the life of Israeli Prime Minister Yitzhak Rabin.[29] Indeed, until the nineteenth century, religion provided the only justification for terrorism.[30] In addition, cults espousing obscure religious practices have embarked on terrorist campaigns: notably, the Bhagwan Shree Rajneesh cult in Oregon in 1984,[31] and Aum Shinrikyo, the terrorist group responsible for the first major act of 'apocalyptic' terrorism using sarin nerve gas.[32] Al Qaeda's brand of anti-globalization apocalyptic fundamentalism – which probably has more in common with Aum Shinrikyo's agenda than that of Hamas – combined with the modern non-state actor's ability to exploit globalization, has plunged the world into war.

Former Director of Central Intelligence R. James Woolsey and Professor Elliot Cohen of the Johns Hopkins School of Advanced International Studies have described this war of globalization as World War IV:[33] a more appropriate description of the current war than 'war against terrorism'.[34] Woolsey characterized this as a war against ideals – freedom of speech, freedom of religion, economic freedom, equal treatment of women – 'these people don't hate us for what we've done wrong. They hate us for what we've done right.'[35]

As all three previous world wars were about ideals – freedom and progress versus tyranny and authoritarianism – so is this war about ideals. It is different from the Cold War in that it is not capitalist democracy vs totalitarian communism, but rather democracy, free trade and cultural openness vs authoritarianism, fundamentalism and insular societies. John Arquilla and David Ronfeldt, referring to this war as a 'netwar', draw the cleavage of ideals in this struggle, quoting Jeremy Rifkin's description as a war 'between an emerging global civilization of the 21st century and a xenophobic religious fanaticism of the 14th century (or earlier). Osama bin Laden and his cohorts are tribal, medieval, absolutist, and messianic.'[36]

At heart, this war of globalization is a fight for credibility. Consistent with a war of ideals, the war against terrorism has been characterized as a 'war of ideas'. This implies then the war is a fight to gain adherents to ideas. Ideas are spread through various modes of communication: this is the essence of terrorism, which has been described as 'propaganda of the deed'.[37] In his book *The Paradox of American Power*, Joseph Nye describes the relation of information to power ('soft' and 'hard' power) in world politics and the 'paradox of plenty':[38]

> A plentitude of information leads to a poverty of attention. When we are overwhelmed with the volume of information confronting us, it is hard to know what to focus on. Attention rather than information becomes the scarce resource, and those who can distinguish valuable signals from white noise gain power. Editors, filters, and cue givers become more in demand, and this is a source of power for those who can tell us where to focus our attention...Among editors and cue givers, credibility is the crucial resource and an important source of power.

As Nye argues, politics is now a contest of competitive credibility. This presents a formidable struggle for those who would fight against terrorists that exploit globalization. Terrorism was born as a violent way to focus attention on issues to which the world's elite were otherwise not paying attention: this is the point of 'propaganda by the deed'[39] and the essence of Terzi's statement above. Terrorists have always been masters at information, information technology is at the heart of both modern terrorism and globalization, and the current war of globalization is about focusing attention on (and forcing) the choice between two ideal systems: globalization and 'xenophobic religious fanaticism'. Masters of information such as editors and terrorists increase in importance because they have (or least fight violently for the impression of) credibility, and 'soft' power rests on credibility. Soft power is becoming more important with respect to 'hard' coercive power as credibility becomes a key power resource for both governments and non-state actors.[40] The challenge to globalizing states is this: 'as soft power becomes more important in an information age, it is the domain where nongovernmental organizations and networks are poised to compete because it is their major power resource'.[41]

This has the potential to conjoin the levels at which states and terrorist movements influence the international system:

> foreign policy will not be the sole province of governments. Both individuals and private organizations ... will be empowered to play direct roles in world politics. The spread of information will mean that power will be more widely distributed ... The speed of Internet time means that all governments ... will enjoy fewer degrees of freedom before they must respond to events, and then will have to share the stage with more actors.[42]

Arguably, the next evolutionary stage of transnational terrorism – and the next defeat in the war of globalization – is the ability of terrorist campaigns to influence the international system by participating on a more formal plane of international politics. Professor Philippe Sands has argued that the influence of NSAs is nothing new. What is a critical change, in his opinion, is

> the involvement of non-state actors...moving from the informal plane to the formal plane. There is a tremendous struggle currently taking place to find ways in which non-state actors can find ways to express their views formally whether through participation in international ... negotiations, or through access to international courts and tribunals.[43]

Terrorists sought this kind of formal participation for at least the past thirty years, from Yasir Arafat addressing the world from the floor of the UN General Assembly (wearing an empty gun holster), to political parties evolving into political powerholders (e.g. IRA to Sinn Féin or PLO to the Palestinian Authority).

Soft power derived from globalization might provide terrorists with the tools and capabilities to force their own access to the 'formal plane' of international politics. The wardens of this 'formal plane' (i.e., states, through the international system) must proactively adapt to this potential eventuality, before it becomes a fait accompli. Both soft power and international law rest on credibility, and international law and international agreements offer a potential mechanism to counter apparent shifts in the aggregation and use of soft power in the hands of illegitimate non-state actors.

INFLUENCING INTERNATIONAL OUTCOMES: BATTLES OF CREDIBILITY IN THE WAR OF GLOBALIZATION

Probably the most 'formal' plane of international relations at which NSAs and states can interact is the international legal plane: that level of norms and customs as described in the introduction to this article. At this level, the war of globalization is still a struggle for credibility. Credibility is still a struggle to serve as the most authoritative 'cue giver' of information to constituencies. However, credibility at this level of interaction is also translating that credibility into political affirmation and support from those constituencies: in other words, legitimacy, as a political expression of a constituency's consent (or lack of power to object) to governance.

Scholars have worked to explain how NSAs influence outcomes in world politics. In the context of international conditions, there is an argument that the ability to influence world politics is not contingent on the cooperation or complacency of states, even for legitimate NSAs. This is clearly argued in Nye's theory of the aggregation of soft power among NSAs in the information age. Furthermore, scholars have argued that the history of human rights non-governmental organizations does not provide evidence that NSAs must first convince and gain the advocacy of states before they can influence international outcomes and decisions.[44]

The international system and component states consider transnational terrorist and criminal networks as illegitimate. These illegitimate NSAs generally do not take issue with this perspective: on the contrary, illegitimate NSAs such as terrorist groups a priori acknowledge their hostile relationship with legitimate powers and states, and do not expect to gain their advocacy through normal, legitimate means. Terrorist groups outright reject the status quo of the international system – and thus, *its* very claim to legitimacy – and seek to replace it with political structures they deem are more legitimate and consistent with their worldview and values. On the other hand, transnational criminal groups enjoy the world order status quo, thriving in its weaknesses and seeking to exploit and expand those weaknesses. Both types of networks do seek to influence world politics to further their objectives, and they do so by engaging states as well as international institutions.

Transnational criminal networks seek to influence outcomes in order to maximize their bottom lines, similar in purpose (and sometime means) to multinational corporations. This affects international politics to the extent these groups view and use political influence as a capital asset. These groups, the multi-national corporations of the illegitimate world, have their legal analogies. There are numerous examples of multinational corporate or financial actors that have wielded political influence as a capital asset to further the financial (and possibly, but coincidentally, political) objectives of their shareholders.[45] The illegitimate modern-day equivalents to this are transnational criminal networks such as the Triads, Yakuza, Balkan smugglers and slave-traders, pirates and drug runners in the Pacific Rim, the Russian organized crime establishment, etc.

A significant asset of criminal networks is access through official corruption. Corruption is the domestic problem it has always been for many countries. However, governments that are more corrupt or less transparent to participants of globalization (e.g. foreign direct investment, migration of workers, technological development, etc.) are less credible in the international system, hobbling them from taking equal advantage of globalization. In addition to hindering the participation of host states in globalization, some transnational criminal networks command such vast resources that they can purchase political power and use it as a capital asset to affect directly the policies of nations and international organizations toward their interests. However, this is done subtly: as in political lobbying, to call outright attention to such influence is to lessen its effect.

On the other hand, terrorism seeks to call attention to itself, but also directly engages states and international institutions, whether it is Yasir Arafat on the floor of the UN, Carlos the Jackal holding OPEC ministers hostage, Osama bin Laden using al Jazeera to solicit transnational networks of insurgency, or the Italian Red Brigades 'striking at the heart of the state' to effect international Communist revolution. Terrorist campaigns reject the legitimacy of the existing state order, and directly target states and legitimate international institutions (especially trade-oriented entities like the World Trade Organization, the World Bank and OPEC) in order to gain currency in world politics and change the international order.

Terrorists conduct international discourse with a mind to domestic conditions, and vice versa. Even global movements such as Al Qaeda work to influence international outcomes through domestic conditions. Scholars have characterized this phenomenon: 'In order to affect policies, transnational actors have to overcome two hurdles. First, they have to gain access to the political system of their 'target state'. Second, they must generate and/or contribute to 'winning' policy coalitions in order to change decisions in the desired direction.'[46] Terrorist organizations, who use the term 'target state' literally, operate to force both access and subscription to a coalition, mainly through the use of fear caused by violence. This has been conclusively demonstrated – in both cause and effect – by the rail bombings in Madrid in March 2004, and the subsequent change in the Spanish government and its announced withdrawal from the military coalition in Iraq.

Terrorist movements are also playing to another domestic audience: their perceived constituency, which can range from the simple set of cult members to the entire world membership of a specific religion. In this constituency terrorist elites find their pretense for political leadership, rationale for violence, source of recruits, and quite often, significant sponsorship in the form of succor, financial support, weapons and even real estate for training camps. Across the various types of potential support (even real estate), state assent is neither presumed nor necessary for groups to be effective in exploiting these resources, and even affecting the state host of a constituency by provoking political pressure on a state, if not posing the threat of gaining more 'credibility' than the state government itself.

The use of fear and violence in such a strategy implies an objective that the state will 'act' on behalf of the non-state actor to influence outcomes in the international system. There are different forms of 'action', from direct sponsorship to acquiescence in the face of fear or political pressure. However, despite their means, terrorist groups seek to influence international outcomes much in the same way as human rights groups and other NGOs. Scholars such as Aryeh Neier do not think of NGOs as

> alternatives to state actors because ... they try to ... influence state actors. They are not competitors [to states], but can only prevail in their cause if the can persuade or influence the states to act in a certain way ... They are a force acting in what they presumably consider to be the public interest, rather than in their own self-interest.[47]

Similarly, nationalist terrorist groups such as Hizb'allah, Hamas, the PLO, the IRA, Basque separatists, Colombian narco-terrorists, etc., all purport to represent some kind of constituency, and seek to influence states and gain political power and eventually legitimacy, sometimes at a zero-sum expense of a particular state. Even transcendental groups like Aum Shinrikyo and Al Qaeda – that is, groups whose agenda and objectives transcend a geographic area like Northern Ireland, Spain, or Palestine – purport to represent a constituency, even if that constituency is defined and united by common values and beliefs (however bizarre or alien to the 'mainstream'). Indeed, until the advent of these transcendental terrorist groups, the common belief was – as stated above – that terrorists moderated their violence out of concern of alienating members of their constituency. This phenomenon contributes to the façade of credibility, and indeed does provide tools to 'give cues' by focusing attention through violence.

The concern today is that a global transcendental jihad can still focus on domestic conditions (regardless of whether the jihad appeals to bored Saudi youths, impoverished Palestinian refugees, Kosovar orphans, Indonesian insurgents or disaffected American prison youth), thus gain credibility by appealing across cultures and generations. This phenomenon can in effect co-opt the role of the state, allowing an international sub-system in which terrorist groups eventually gain access to more formal planes of international relations.

To minimize the influence of illegitimate NSAs on the international system, the international system must certainly promote the role of the state in countering transnational terrorism, preventing such a role from being co-opted. This strategy can be undermined by state sponsors themselves. Certain (rogue) states have also played negative roles in the promotion of transnational terrorism. To minimize the influence of terrorism, the international system also must better recognize the role of the transnational terrorist enterprise and its constituent participants and processes within international politics. One of these constituent participants is the state sponsor – a term far too simplified in international law and diplomacy. Thus, a key to minimizing the influence of terrorism is not more bilateral international agreements on what to do with Carlos the Jackal or Osama bin Laden. The key is accountability for sponsorship embedded in international law.

OBJECTS OF INTERNATIONAL LAWLESSNESS: ACCOUNTABILITY IN THE WAR OF GLOBALIZATION

Since the earliest international conventions against hijacking, international agreements have notoriously been weak in combating terrorism, and the law enforcement and intelligence services of multiple countries collaborate at best in an ad hoc, event-driven fashion. International agreements have not realistically increased in strength against modern terrorism, but the influence of illegitimate NSAs has increased over the past few decades. This underscores the need for international law to consider illegitimate NSAs differently. The current shortcoming in international law is two-dimensional: first, it ought to consider networks of illegitimate operators as a transnational enterprise, rather than loosely affiliated individuals. Second, it ought to couple this consideration with measures to reduce states' support to, and influences by, these networks (e.g. the state as supporter of terrorism, or the state as dominated or corrupted by criminal networks). These measures include embedding tools for accountability into the fabric of international law and agreements, as well as exploiting opportunities to use international law to counter attempts at legitimacy and credibility by illegal non-state actors.

Transnational terrorism first evolved by taking advantage of two main engines of globalization: cheap intercontinental travel, and advances in information and communication technology. In addition to the advantages of globalization, transnationalism empowers terrorism and criminal networks in that states *are not* transnational. Criminal and terrorist networks cross several borders and jurisdictions, frustrating international agreements, bureaucratic boundaries, and institutional philosophies, all of which are much slower to adapt than is a distributed, networked entity like a terrorist group. Similarly, international law is having enough trouble catching up with legal NSAs' accession to the 'formal plane'. International law is struggling to accommodate the international influence of *legitimate* non-state actors as *enterprises*, (not individual CEOs or non-profit directors). Yet legally, the illegitimate counterparts of NSAs are still considered to be individual criminals, rather than transnational networked enterprises of various participants and processes.

If they are not subjects of international law, transnational terrorist enterprises certainly implicate it. Transnational terrorists and criminals can be acting in violation of customary law, or they can be committing crimes defined in treaty. Crimes such as piracy and slave trading have long been recognized under customary international law, as have war crimes (certainly the Bush administration views some terrorists as unlawful combatants). Some acts of international terrorism arguably would fall under such crimes as to be subject to universal jurisdiction. Furthermore, many of the crimes that support terrorism – hijacking, kidnapping, hostage-taking and attacks on diplomats – are defined and proscribed by a variety international antiterrorism conventions. Many of these treaty crimes enjoy such widespread acceptance and *opinion juris* that they are considered to be part of customary law.[48] However, critical support activities such as financing, weapons proliferation, recruitment or providing real estate for training camps at best implicate different areas of customary law, if any.

Terrorism's proximity to armed conflict might bring it conceptually closer to the law of nations, in that nations traditionally have enjoyed an absolute supremacy on the use of armed force. On the other hand, the crimes committed by transnational criminal networks – theft, smuggling, narcotics, etc. – would not raise the attention of the international community were it not for their transnational scope, the massive amount of resources involved and the resulting effect on international politics. This is reflected in an increasingly important area of international criminal law: the extent to which it can prosecute crimes under municipal law that have transnational implications, and what this means for the institutions and procedures involved in enforcement and prosecution of these crimes when municipal courts are too weak, corrupt or unavailable. Although this is analytically distinct from international law that rests on customary law or treaty, there is a considerable overlap, especially when international institutions such as Interpol are involved in their enforcement, or when domestic officers are deployed internationally to enforce laws (such as FBI legal attachés conducting investigations abroad).

The result of this nature of international law is that terrorist and criminal networks are prosecuted as individuals acting in violation of municipal and (only occasionally) international law proscribing specific terrorist acts (usually the violent acts themselves, rather than support activities). This would probably be sufficient, except that terrorism networks are clearly greater, and have more influence, than the sum of their parts. Furthermore, the role of state support is dealt with separately in both customary law and treaty. Thus, efforts to target individuals in law are not as effective as efforts to target the enterprise as a whole, and do not reach their sponsor states. This weakness is confirmed in discussions of how international law should regard and accommodate legal NSAs: multinational corporations and non-governmental organizations are not considered as individuals acting in tandem, but rather as enterprises and aggregate actions of individuals.

Even to the extent international law can reach an individual, crimes under international customary law or treaty placed responsibility on the individual, but were prosecuted in national courts in the absence of an international court with jurisdiction. The advent of the International Criminal Court may change this historical fact, certainly for crimes of terrorism, and possibly for financially oriented organized crime when its networks and effects are of sufficient transnational scope. This would go far toward overcoming obstacles in prosecuting illegitimate NSAs and reducing their influence. These obstacles have historically included corruption in national legal systems for punishing organized crime, 'political offense' exceptions for extraditing terrorists, and the element of fear in prosecuting both. It would not, however, bring international law any further toward considering transnational terrorist and criminal networks as enterprises that systemically affect international outcomes, nor would it touch on accountability for state sponsors.

The illegitimacy of terrorist and criminal networks is illustrated by international efforts in law and agreements among states to minimize these actors' influence in international relations. They are illegitimate because states' consensus casts them as such in the international domain (which is governed by law made by states). It is a genuine point of debate the extent to which lawful NSAs ought to be seen as partners alongside states in international politics, and the debate frequently focuses on the amount and methods of access NSAs actually, and ought to, have on international outcomes. By contrast, the normative discussion of illegitimate NSAs' role in international politics is not subject to dispute: the overwhelming consensus among states is that they should have no role. Both normative and positivist principles of international law would agree that illegitimate NSAs are to be eliminated from international politics. The real issue of illegitimate NSAs as objects of international law is what tools and effect can international law have in reaching illegitimate NSAs and reducing their influence. This is especially important if one considers international law as a necessary compensation for weaknesses in respective states' municipal law for prosecuting illegitimate NSAs. One reason underlying past failures of municipal law is the role the state plays in supporting terrorist campaigns, from acquiescence in fear to direct sponsorship.

If the international system is to minimize the influence of illegitimate NSAs more effectively, international law must more adequately link individual terrorists to the whole enterprise, including other critical participants and processes such as sponsorship and resources. States are limited in their ability to influence non-state actors, or to limit those actors' influence on the behavior of states. The primary way states try to do this is through municipal law and international agreements to counter the effects of crime and terrorism. This is what casts such actors as 'illegal' non-state actors. But that designation begs the question, illegal according to whose law or definition? If a terrorist group gains power and subsidy from a rogue state, or a criminal group pressures a host state to legalize its activities, the notion of 'legal' becomes murky from a municipal law perspective. Notions of legitimacy are perhaps easier to grasp.

The legitimacy of a non-state actor in the international system (especially the international legal system) turns on accountability. As discussed earlier, illegal NSAs seek access and influence in different modes than via legitimacy, e.g. through credibility and coercion. Accountability – that is, the ability of legal or other controlling authorities to hold them responsible for the negative consequences of their actions and force them to absorb the costs themselves – is what indeed defines illegal NSAs. Accountability is central to addressing the influence and activities of illegal NSAs.

Loss of accountability and control over NSAs has direct implications for international law: once accountability over a legal NSA reaches zero and states lose the ability to control the operations of NSAs, 'the only way to effectively control these non-state actors is through coordinated efforts in multilateral fora'.[49] This, however, has not worked very well for illegal NSAs, primarily because holding an individual accountable does not hold the enterprise accountable, nor does it necessarily diminish its influence, especially when that enterprise is a network greater than the sum of its parts, and might even directly involve state support.

This is not to say accountability is impossible, however. To consider the enterprise of a non-state actor (criminal or legit), one must begin by considering the underlying organizational processes and participants – leadership, management, recruitment, training, planning, resources, sponsorship, etc. This enterprise-wide approach is applied in law to legitimate non-state actors, but not as well to their illegitimate counterparts. The development, coordination and application of resources and leadership described above are the products of decisions. Thus, there are a number of decision points in a terrorist campaign at which leaders and sponsors can be credibly held accountable, for example, for decisions to escalate the lethality or scope of a given terrorist campaign, or to provide specific types of support.

To wit: when considering the impact of multinational corporations or nongovernmental organizations, international law considers the influences from the various relationships among capital investments and transfers, market strategies, interaction or advocacy with trade pacts or agreements, lobbying efforts, nationality of the corporate headquarters and principal places of business, revenues, cultural influences, policy positions, etc. – i.e. factors well beyond Microsoft chairman Bill Gates or Amnesty International Secretary General Irene Khan. Yet it is usually individuals (especially terrorist leaders or crime bosses) that are sought as the 'heads' of organizations whose prosecution would bring about the fall of the organization. However, it is also the 'foot soldier' who is arrested as he is caught traveling across borders with contraband or explosives, and who have actually been responsible for planning the operation. It is the *individual* involved in illegitimate NSAs that is the primary object of international law. This is in contrast to legal NSAs, over which the debate focuses on how they *as enterprises* (not individuals) influence the international system, and thus ought to be considered in international law.

The strength of municipal law, and the role of international law and agreements, all can be strengthened by ingraining in these laws and agreements a more refined notion of sponsorship, and linking these notions directly to tools of accountability and enforcement. Notions of state sponsorship are hopelessly outdated, do not reflect the sponsorship needs of modern terrorism, and lack an appreciation of the complexity of sponsorship available to terrorist campaigns. The US State Department still maintains a list of seven state sponsors of terrorism: Cuba, Iran, Iraq, Libya, North Korea, Sudan and Syria.[50] Al Qaeda's patron state Afghanistan, which provided Al Qaeda with the real estate necessary to develop its effective training capability, has never been on the list of terrorism sponsors. Iraq is currently under control of the same state that controls the above list. The sponsorship (and clients) of Cuba are trivial. The financial support for extremists coming from Saudi Arabia is murky and controversial. Before a terrorist enterprise can be adequately considered in international law, the notion of sponsorship must be refined, in international law, and in the laws and foreign policies of nations.

Notions of sponsorship can be refined by considering what terrorists require to sustain a campaign, and where they can meet their requirements. A transnational terrorist campaign such as Al Qaeda requires three common requirements to transition from a group to a movement: a cadre of marginalized elites that rise to terrorism leadership, a discontented population that the elites can exploit, and weak or rogue states and sponsors that provide some kind of passive or active support.[51] A terrorist campaign uses the human terrorist as its primary weapons platform, and this platform goes through four general phases of 'development' in its use: recruitment, training and indoctrination, planning and resources, and operational preparation and execution. Underlying all of these phases are common activities such as communications, security, financing, propaganda and ideology, weapons development, and even social support. For terrorism to develop into a lethal campaign (as opposed to a 'one-off' terrorist attack), these various components of terrorism – agenda and goals, strategies and organization, and tools – must be supported by resources, and developed, coordinated and applied by terrorist leaders and sponsors. Resources include:

- Rhetoric
- Finances and financial systems or instruments
- Territory or safe haven
- Logistics and transportation of materiel or personnel
- Weapons and explosives
- High technology including weapons of mass destruction
- Diplomatic assets and protection
- Specialized training and training bases
- Intelligence support
- Command and control with direct tasking for missions.[52]

These resources come from sponsors, state or non-state. Sponsors can be private individuals or leaders such as Osama bin Laden, corporate-type organizations such as Aum Shinrikyo or Al Qaeda, or states. With some notable exceptions, the most dangerous and lethal terrorist campaigns cannot be conducted without increasing degrees of active state support.[53] Nevertheless, the notion of 'state-sponsored terrorism' is more complex than can be described by a simple list of rogue states.

State support and resources can range across four overlapping categories, each with increasing support and control over the terrorist campaign:

- Sponsorship or direction. The state actively controls and directs terrorist activities as an instrument of policy.
- Support. The terrorists are not controlled by the state, yet the state encourages terrorist activities, and provides active support such as training, equipment, funding, and transportation.
- Toleration. The state makes no effort to arrest or suppress terrorists, and may passively grant them moral legitimacy, although it does not actively support them.
- Inaction. The state, because of political factors, legal restrictions or inherent weakness, cannot or will not prevent terrorist activity within its borders.[54]

Thus, one might describe four types of states, according to their level of support to transnational terrorists:

- *Sponsor*: the state provides substantial material support, e.g. command and control, training, weapons and documents.
- *Harborer*: the state actively maintains a primarily permissive relationship,

providing varying active and passive support in safe haven, tacit support for smuggling or recruiting, or the benefits of corruption with organized criminal elements that assist terrorist logistics, communications, etc.

- *Hideout*: the state maintains an indifferent or hostile relationship with the terrorist group, which enjoys a substantial presence on the state territory, but the state is unable to, or unwilling to risk the consequences of, disrupting or destroying the terrorist group.
- *Target*: the state maintains a consistently and manifestly hostile stance toward the group, which considers that state as a target.[55]

Thus, there is a continuum of sponsorship that states can afford a terrorist movement. As states are still the dominant actor in international law – and the only legal signatories of international agreements – states can impose accountability for varying levels of sponsorship of, or submission to, illegal NSAs. This can be done by instantiating tools – clauses, incentives, recourse to remedies, penalties, etc. – in international agreements that recognize and are responsive to a more complex continuum of potential sponsorship of illicit activity. Of course, as illustrated above, not all forms of sponsorship are voluntary, and some states (e.g. target states) can be powerless or constitutionally prohibited to cease their particular forms of support. International agreements should also provide incentives to minimize support to terror and strengthen governments to confront terrorism domestically.

In addition to new tools for international law, there might be a requirement for significant change in institutions of international law, in order to confront sponsorship of terrorism. New tools of international law must be flexible enough to seamlessly address terrorism and sponsorship at the individual person, corporate or state level. This means that new tools of international law should be crafted in mind of the institutions that would adjudicate conflicts, in both civil and criminal law. For example, adjudications of violations of clauses – critical for more nuanced forms of sponsorship, but also applicable for blatant violations – can be conducted via mechanisms already in place for many international agreements (e.g. adjudication by the International Centre for Settlement of Investment Disputes). Other international agreements can provide for dispute and resolution by the International Court of Justice, including submitting to the advisory jurisdiction in matters involving corporations or non-governmental organizations. However, these measures would also want to leverage the tools of international criminal justice. This calls for new mechanisms of international criminal justice. At present, the only relevant international forum in existence – the International Criminal Court – has no subject-matter jurisdiction over terrorism, nor jurisdiction over corporations or associations. The ICC is not adequate presently to extend the criminal justice process to individuals or non-state entities that might be sought for terrorist activities or sponsorship. This leaves a seam in the fabric of international institutions to fight terrorist sponsorship.

New tools of international law must be incorporated in instruments of international discourse that lie beyond traditional security-related agreements such as anti-hijacking conventions and security alliances. They must be ingrained throughout the principles, processes and structures that underlie every sector of international relations – diplomatic, economic, technological, even environmental. In a seamless international economic system, transnational organized crime corrupts seamlessly. More dangerous, the global war against terrorism is a war of globalization, and every international agreement and instrument that propagates globalization must include a declaration of alliance in this war, in addition to real tools that hold the agreement's mechanisms and measures to the accountable pursuit of globalization. Al Qaeda's agenda is not about Palestine or American troops in Iraq or even Osama bin Laden and Ayman Zawahri – it is about the credibility of a way of life that is an alternative to peace, democracy, globalization and free trade. Like globalization, this war affects every aspect of the international community. As such, every aspect of the international community must be enlisted to fight terrorism.

These prescriptions are idealistic, but not impossible, and can overcome the notorious 'political exception' issue, which has undermined international anti-terrorism conventions in the past. In this unique juncture of human civilization, globalization overcomes a historical obstacle in international cooperation against terrorism. Enforcing distinctions and definitions of 'terrorist' activity has been fraught with political ambiguities in the past, such as might undermine international agreements that proscribe such activities. During the 1970s and 1980s, many international agreements and initiatives were undermined by the cliché 'one man's terrorist is another man's freedom fighter'.

The international system has moved beyond these obstacles. First, these obstacles may have been relevant when the globe was divided by the polar ideologies of the Cold War, and industrialized societies of the world were divided between democracy and communism. However, this is no longer a compelling justification to ignore international antiterrorism responsibilities – as the anarchists of the early twentieth century were not offering a viable alternative to the interests of the industrializing members of the global community, neither is the early twenty-first-century movement represented by Al Qaeda offering a viable ideological alternative to the interests of the globalizing members of international society. Second, Al Qaeda does not purport to offer an alternative way to join the international community – this war of globalization is not about different ways to globalize, it is about *whether* to globalize. In this context, the process and substance of recognizing terrorist activity and support – and adjudicating complicity – is removed of many of the political ambiguities and opportunities for vacillation that marked antiterrorism during the 1970s and 1980s. There will always exist the specter that signatories can use terrorist allegations as political leverage, rather than genuine efforts to fight terrorism. However, complicity can be evaluated within many of the adjudicative or dispute resolution mechanisms inherent in existing international political or economic agreements.

CONCLUSION: CRAFTING TOOLS FOR INTERNATIONAL LAW

There are two challenges to international law: recognizing illegitimate NSAs as enterprises and enforcing accountability of sponsorship. International law is struggling with recognizing and dealing with legitimate NSAs as enterprises, and many lessons can be learned about how to focus on minimizing the influence of transnational networks, especially when no one seriously doubts the illegitimacy of those networks. However, solutions garnered from dealing with legal NSAs will not necessarily apply across the board, especially in the area of accountability. Solutions to holding legitimate NSAs accountable, such as inviting them to the table, do not apply to illegitimate NSAs when they want either to corrupt the table or blow it up altogether.

This illustrates the second challenge to international law with respect to illegitimate NSAs: enforcing accountability. By considering the role of state sponsorship of these networks, international law might develop more powerful tools in holding accountable those individuals, corporate entities and states who provide illegal networks with enabling support. Focusing on the role of the state is, of course, a much more manageable question of international law. There are important questions regarding NSAs as instruments of state power, and whether they are open to influence, as one influences their patron states (this is a converse to the influence of NSAs on state actions). Many international NGOs are more directly dependent on the 'state world' than they would admit.[56] This is certainly the case with terrorism: as stated above, if a terrorism campaign is to be successful as a significantly deadly organization (and thus a significant potential influence on the international order), it requires some sort of support by states, especially real estate for training.

Holding state sponsors accountable requires more sophisticated tools – economic, political and diplomatic – than rogue state lists and UN Security Council resolutions. There must be more responses to terrorism than extradition and military attack. Forms such as the World Trade Organization, International Monetary Fund and regional trade blocs – not traditional forms for security issues – provide a fertile ground for considering new instruments to hold states and even multinational organizations accountable for varying and complex levels of terrorist sponsorship. Economic agreements and trade pacts can be crafted with a similarly nuanced awareness of the complexities of terrorism sponsorship and need for accountability, and international agreements can be directly tied to concerns of sponsorship of terrorism. For example, bilateral trade agreements can include statements of anti-terrorism principles, and even provide recourse if a state provides specific kinds of succor to terrorist groups. International law that seeks to regulate transnational networks without considering the role of state patrons will simply offer criminal states new entrepreneurial opportunities to develop or provide forbidden goods and services to those on the wrong side of the international community.[57]

Finally, international law offers a tool in the struggle for credibility in the Globalization Age. International law is a canon of common values. Power and influence have changed and shifted, but power also includes the means of projecting it. Two things can affect the ability of an entity to project power and influence outcomes: its legitimacy in the eyes of its own constituents, and its credibility in the eyes of others. The legitimacy of Al Qaeda's social alternative is not as controversial to lawyers in Washington DC lounges as it to impoverished youths in Gaza slums. International law can challenge both the legitimacy of an extremist worldview and its credibility as an alternative to world order.

International law offers the advantage of persistence over agility in the struggle for credibility. The community of states and legitimate NSAs will always be disadvantaged compared to the agility of terrorist and criminal networks to manipulate the media and 'cue' populations to information. As discussed before, this agility is an advantage in a struggle for credibility, which can eventually establish illusions, if not realities, of legitimacy. However, a common, persistent baseline of values is also important to the struggle for credibility – an advantage international law gives to states. The ability of any human endeavor to sustain a collective effort depends as much on moral as material factors. International law is more than the rule schema for state behavior in the international system – it is, at its best, a persistent, normative expression of legitimacy in the international system: the values and priorities shared among the states, and their collective vision for the character of the international system. Both roles of international law are critical in fighting the war of globalization against Al Qaeda's brand of extremism.

This persistence must pervade the international legal framework to be effective at winning credibility. Every international initiative – regardless of how far removed from security concerns – should be directly linked to promoting values of democracy and free flow of trade and ideas, while undermining the legitimacy and credibility of despotism and the violent culture of values that transnational terrorist movements propagate. It will not be enough to generally espouse peace as a component of trade and tourism.

Economic agreements, foreign direct investments, collaborative scientific research, trade pacts, developmental grants, agricultural programs, educational initiatives – all must link goals and objectives to the credibility of democracy, accountability for sponsorship of terrorism and the de-legitimization of *specific* extremist agendas. Connecting the moral poverty of specific terrorist actions and agendas to global networks and their state sponsors is critical to minimizing their influence, promoting the legitimacy of globalization and credibility of its benefits, and offering a peaceful, prosperous and democratic alternative of world order to globalization's malcontents.

NOTES

1. Arguably for the first time, at least since President Jefferson waged war against the Barbary pirates in 1801.
2. See, e.g., Alvin Toffler's *Power Shift* (New York: Bantam, 1990), or Jessica Tuchman Matthews' article of the same name in *Foreign Affairs* (Jan./Feb. 1997).
3. See generally Bruce Hoffman, *Inside Terrorism* (London: Victor Gollancz, 1998).
4. Joseph S. Nye, Jr, *The Paradox of American Power* (Oxford: Oxford University Press, 2002), p.74.
5. Ibid., p.60.
6. Thomas Risse, 'Transnational Actors and World Politics', in Walter Carlsnaes et al. (eds), *Handbook of International Relations* (London: Sage Publications, 2002), pp.255–6.
7. Ibid.
8. Ibid., p.225.
9. Ibid.
10. Risse, p.260.
11. Ibid.
12. Nye, p.47.
13. Hedley Bull, *The Anarchical Society: A Study of Order in World Politics* (London: Macmillan, 1977), pp.264–74.
14. Ibid., p.264.
15. See, e.g., A.T. Kearney, 'Measuring Globalization: Economic Reversals, Forward Momentum.' *Foreign Policy*, Vol.54 (March/Aprril 2004), p.141.
16. Defense Science Board, *Final Report of the Defense Science Board Task Force on Globalization and Security* (Washington, DC: Defense Science Board, 1999), p.5.
17. Ibid., p.68.
18. See Hoffman, pp.68–86.
19. Brian Jenkins, 'International Terrorism: A New Mode of Conflict', in David Carlton and Carlo Schaerf (eds), *International Terrorism and World Security* (Los Angeles, CA: Crescent Publications, 1975), p.15.
20. Yonah Alexander, 'Terrorism in the Twenty-First Century: Threats and Response', *DePaul Business Law Journal* (2000). See also Hoffman, p.68 ('The advent of ... modern, international terrorism occurred on 22 July 1968.')
21. Hoffman, pp.67–8.
22. Ibid., p.68.
23. Ibid., p.204.
24. Ibid., p.91.
25. Ibid.
26. Jenkins, p.15.

27. David Rapoport has termed this a 'second wave' a modern terrorism. David Rapoport, 'Fear and Trembling: Terrorism in Three Religious Traditions', *American Political Science Review*, Vol.78, No.3 (1984), pp.658–77.
28. Alexander, p.69.
29. Hoffman, pp.87–90.
30. Rapoport, p.659, quoted in Hoffman, p.89.
31. Richard Falkenrath et al., *America's Achilles Heel* (Cambridge, MA: The MIT Press, 1998), p.35.
32. Hoffman, pp.121–7.
33. The Third World War being the Cold War, also a war of ideals.
34. R. James Woolsey, address at the Center for the Study of Popular Culture, 16November 2002.
35. Ibid.
36. John Arquilla and David Ronfeldt, 'Fighting the Network War', *Wired*, December 2001.
37. See Walter Laqueur, *The Age of Terrorism* (Boston, MA: Little, Brown & Co., 1987), pp.48–51.
38. Nye, pp.66–7.
39. Laqueur.
40. Nye, p.75.
41. Ibid, p.74.
42. Ibid, p.53.
43. Anne-Marie Slaughter et al., *The Challenge of Non-State Actors*, 98th American Society of International Law Proceedings, 1998, p.24.
44. Risse, p.274.
45. Slaughter, pp.22–3.
46. Risse, p.276.
47. Slaughter, pp.22–3.
48. Lori Damrosch et al., *International Law: Cases and Materials* (St Paul, MN: West Group, 2001), p.1314.
49. Slaughter, p.33.
50. United States Department of State, *Patterns of Global Terrorism 2003* (Washington, DC: US Government Printing Office, 2004), p.85.
51. Jack Goldstone, e-mail exchange with author, 2002.
52. Robert J. Beck and Anthony Clark Arend, '"Don't Tread on Us": International Law and Forcible State Responses to Terrorism', *Wisconsin Intersnational Law Journal*, Vol.12 (1994), pp.153, 164.
53. United States Department of State, *Patterns of Global Terrorism 2001* (Washington, DC: US Government Printing Office, 2002).
54. Gregory M. Travalio, 'Terrorism, International Law, and the Use of Military Force', *Wisconsin International Law Journal*, Vol.18 (2000), pp.145, 150.
55. This taxonomy is taken from 'States and Terror Groups: Progress in Research Design', an unclassified draft work in which the author was a primary participant. A copy of the draft findings of the work is on file with the author.
56. Risse, p.260.
57. See e.g. Moises Naim, 'The Five Wars of Globalization', *Foreign Policy*, January/February 2003, p.35.

Terrorism, Crime and Private Armies

JOHN P. SULLIVAN

The societal changes associated with the accessibility of information technology that stimulate networked organizational forms are changing the nature of conflict and crime. New, increasingly non-state, entities and organizational structures are adapting to these circumstances and altering the global political landscape. As the United States and its allies pursue a 'global war on terrorism' we are seeing the transition from nation-states to market-states unfold before our eyes. This essay reviews the actual – and potential – interaction between terrorism, crime and private armies in order to describe the change in the organization of global conflict. As the ability to wage war devolves from hierarchical organizations to internetworked transnational actors we are witnessing the evolution of new warmaking entities capable of challenging the primacy and ultimately the solvency of nation-states. This potential was recognized by eminent military historian Martin van Creveld in his prescient observation that 'in the future, war will not be waged by armies but by groups whom today we call terrorists, guerrillas, bandits and robbers, but who will undoubtedly hit upon more formal titles to describe themselves'.[1]

NEW WARMAKING ENTITIES AND THE NETWORKED FRONTIER

For example, we see Osama bin Laden's Al Qaeda continually morphing to retain relevance as a malignant and mutated version of the emerging market-state. As economic, political and technological forces combine to fashion a new state form, new warmaking entities emerge to occupy the niches filled by the forms of the past state-form. This dynamic is described by Philip Bobbitt in his treatise *The Shield of Achilles*.[2] In a recent interview Bobbitt observes that technologies, such as the nukes, computers and communications that dominated the Cold War, are reshaping the nation-state into the market-state. According to Bobbitt, rapid computation and communication are fueling the transition. He notes that today's terrorists, such as Osama bin Laden have exploited the Internet, satellites and cell phones to take terrorism and transform it into a market model. Like Mastercard, Osama bin Laden provides financing and infrastructure avoiding tight vertical control of operations.[3]

The rise of new warmaking entities, as always, accompanies this geopolitical–economic shift. As a result, groups such as Al Qaeda and its kin are much more than state-less gangs. These new networked terrorist or criminal adversaries possess standing armies, treasury and revenue sources (even if derived from criminal enterprises), bureaucratic functions, intelligence services, welfare apparatuses and the ability to make alliances (with state and non-state entities). They also promote a common vision by promulgating policy and laws, and most importantly, as we have already experienced, declare war. Other 'non-state' groups also deserve attention. As Brian M. Jenkins observes in his essay 'Redefining the Enemy', the blurred distinction between war and crime continues to result in a policy quandary where 'we underestimate the power of militarily inferior foes, tribal loyalties, difficult terrain, religious conviction, unceasing hostilities, gruesome images broadcast on television, and other unconventional measures of power'.[4]

Netwar, the now and future postmodern war waged by irregular adversaries including terrorists, drugs cartels, criminal gangs and ethno-nationalist extremists, is a new mode of irregular conflict that blends terrorism, crime and war. RAND analysts John Arquilla and David Rondfelt identified this trend where technological and organizational changes that benefit relatively small actors fuel asymmetric threats. They succinctly noted that networks can prevail over hierarchies in this emerging postmodern battle or operational space: 'Power is migrating to small, nonstate actors who can organize into sprawling networks more readily than can traditionally hierarchical nation-state actors.'[5] Jenkins likewise notes that the enemies we face have fundamentally changed. In addition to our traditional adversaries – hostile or potentially hostile states – we now face 'terrorists, weapons proliferators, organized crime affiliates and cyberoutlaws' intertwined within the context of religious, ethnic or tribal conflict, yielding a set of 'dynamic, unpredictable, diverse, fluid, networked and constantly evolving' challengers.[6]

TOWARD CRIMINAL FREE-STATES[7]

Terrorists, criminal actors and private armies of many stripes have altered the ecology of both crime and armed conflict. In many cases, the two are intertwined. Several factors reinforce these links. Global organized crime, which increasingly links local actors with their transnational counterparts, coupled with chronic warfare and insurgency (which yields economic benefits to some of its participants) can propel local or regional conflicts into genocidal humanitarian disasters. The resulting instability or 'conflict disaster' can result in what Jenkins calls 'chronic ungoverned badlands'.[8] These regions, which are essentially criminal free-states, provide refuge and safe haven to terrorists, warlords and criminal enterprises.

Transnational crime is a threat to political, economic, environmental and social systems worldwide. This threat goes beyond the substantial illegal drug trade and its attendant violence to include major fraud, corruption and manipulation of both political and financial systems. Transnational criminal organizations (TCOs) potentially undermine not only civil society but also political systems and state sovereignty by normalizing violence, legitimizing corruption, distorting market mechanisms through the disruption of equitable commercial transactions, and degrading the environment by sidelining environmental regulation and safeguards. When these criminal actors employ violence against state institutions, they become 'non-state soldiers'. Jenkins calls these non-state soldiers the 'combatants of organized crime'. He notes that failed government institutions, collapsed authority and cities of unemployed young men – the factors that also foster terrorism – provide opportunity for criminal enterprises. This new operational space is ripe for exploitation and is found in 'badlands and bad neighborhoods' around the world.[9]

Organized crime and terrorism are related in complex and diverse ways. Crime of many varieties is frequently used to fund terrorist activity. This may include smuggling, identity theft, sales of counterfeit goods (cigarettes, clothing, videos, etc.), illicit technology transfer, gems smuggling, piracy, high-tech crime and many varieties of fraud. Money laundering is at the core of global organized criminal enterprise. It is in this fiscal transaction or enterprise where terrorists, gangsters and other illicit actors are most likely to cooperate. These links sometimes mature into alliances of convenience. This convergence may come from several directions at once. For example, investigators examining the *Eme Once* (11 March) attack on the Madrid Metro observe that the *jihadis* that conducted the attack funded the plot with the proceeds of drug sales. A coalition of extremist and radicalized gangsters came together to conduct the operation. Adherents of Takfir wal Hijira, an Islamist sect active in the European and North African criminal underworld, sold drugs as a weapon of jihad. The largely Moroccan cell coalesced quickly, demonstrating the 'potentially explosive combination of Islamic extremism and organized criminal networks'.[10] Similar links between the Camorra and Islamic terrorist actors involving arms exchanges have also been observed. The links between political operatives and criminal specialists is believed to be nurtured in prisons which bring the two together in a common space. Areas with long-standing smuggling networks, such as the North African zone including Morocco, Tunisia, Mali, Mauritania and Niger are of current concern in Europe due to the large diaspora communities. French intelligence officials note that 'most of the [extremist] structures [they] have dismantled have been financed by crime',[11] including robbery, drugs and fraud.

Terrorists or insurgents may exploit organized crime; criminal gangs may act as middlemen in small arms, explosives or human trafficking; drugs may finance operations; and actors on both sides of the house may facilitate or conduct attacks for each other. In the worst cases, criminals may facilitate the movement of weapons of mass destruction among established or novel smuggling routes or criminals may become 'sovereign outlaws' commanding states or semi-autonomous enclaves.[12] This convergence of terrorism and insurgency further demonstrates the resilience of hybrid terrorist networks. Al Qaeda and its loose confederation of affiliates have successfully converted local struggles in the Philippines, Indonesia, Pakistan, Afghanistan, Saudi Arabia, Yemen, Algeria, Morocco and Iraq[13] into full-blown insurgencies, while adopting the Chechen struggle to stimulate the transition from local jihads into the seeds for a global insurgency.

A range of TCOs (e.g., Chinese Triads, Russian Mafiya, Colombian cartels, the Japanese Yakuza, Sicilian Mafia and others) have engaged in global activities challenging state institutions and stability. While most, like Colombia's Cali cartel, avoid politics to pursue profit, their mixture of competition and cooperation with each other, governments and commercial entities can foster instability. Corruption, co-option and political manipulation can emerge as primary tools of destabilization once criminal groups become embedded within a society. TCOs are especially suited to network forms of organization. They often cooperate to maximize profits and circumvent interdiction by police, law enforcement agencies (LEAs) and governments. The networks established by these groups display a remarkable capacity to transcend borders and flow around legal or geographic boundaries. These networks are based on risk reduction (joining with locals to exploit local conditions or access corrupt officials), market extension (new products or outlets), or product exchange (e.g., guns for drugs) and can expand the capabilities of individual criminal entities, often minimizing competition and conflict.

Increasingly transnational in character, these organized drug or crime networks are essentially borderless and difficult to combat because opposing

LEAs are generally constrained by sub-national and national boundaries. Extending their reach and influence by co-opting individuals and organizations through bribery, coercion and intimidation to sustain their activities, these groups are emerging as a serious impediment to democratic governance and free market economies. At sub-national levels, such corruption can also have profound effects. At a neighborhood level, political and operational corruption can diminish public safety, placing residents at risk to endemic violence and inter-gang conflict, essentially resulting in a 'failed community', a virtual analog of a 'failed state'. Consider the impact of gang warfare in Brazil. In early May 2003, a short sequence of violence in Rio de Janeiro illustrates the impact of gang destabilization: a bomb explodes outside a Copacabana hotel, a bus in Botafogo is torched, and endemic gang gun battles periodically halt traffic. No longer confined to the *favelas*, drug gangs engage police on motorways, attack government buildings and shopping malls. Civilians are threatened and targeted to dissuade police from acting. Fierce gun battles between police and gangs demonstrate the potential of the 'parallel power' in Rio and Sao Paulo. Rio's 'Red Command' has attacked Rio's city hall and inhibited shopping and taxi operations. In Sao Paulo, the 'First Capital Command' attempted to bomb the Bovespa, Latin America's largest stock exchange.[14]

With the rise of the market-state and market-state actors, long-standing assumptions about warfighting and policing are being challenged. This includes definitions of victory and defeat, threat entities, battles and conflict itself.[15] Virtual space may become more important. As Robert J. Bunker and I noted in a 1998 *Transnational Organized Crime* essay entitled 'Cartel Evolution: Potentials and Consequences', criminal enclaves or free-states could emerge.[16] Then as now, the fullest development of a criminal enclave exists in the South American jungle at the intersection of three nations. Ciudad del Este, Paraguay, is the center of this criminal near-free-state. Paraguay, Brazil and Argentina converge at this riverfront outpost. A jungle hub for the world's outlaws – a global village of outlaws – the triple border zone serves as a free enclave for significant criminal activity, including people who are dedicated to supporting and sustaining acts of terrorism. Groups active include gangsters from Rio and Sao Paulo, Lebanese terrorists, Colombian *narcotraficantes*, Nigerian gangsters, Japanese Yakuza, Tai Chen (Cantonese mafia) and other Asian crime syndicates. This polyglot enclave illustrates the potential of criminal netwarriors to exploit the globalization of organized crime. The blurring of borders – a symbol of the postmodern, information age – is clearly demonstrated in the Tri-Border enclave. Mafias exploit interconnected economies, corruption and jurisdictional obstacles, and contribute to TCO power and reach.

Similar dynamics have been described in Karachi, Pakistan, where drug lords and co-opted government functionaries reportedly fuel gang wars, insurgency and terrorism. The Memon family syndicate and Dawood Ibrahim syndicate have been linked with transnational terrorism attacks (for example, the 1993 Mumbai serial bomb blasts), finance operations for terrorists (through *hawala* and money laundering enterprises), a range of logistical support enterprises for Al Qaeda, Harkat-ul-Ansar, Jaish-I-Muhammad and other Al Qaeda-affiliated actors.[17]

Such networked 'enclaves' or virtual 'market-states' could play a dominant role within a network of transnational criminal or terrorist organizations, and potentially gain political influence within the network of market-state actors.

PRIVATIZED VIOLENCE: BEYOND NON-STATE ACTORS?

Privatized violence is likely to become a feature of the transition to the market-state and beyond. German political scientist Stefan Mair notes that declining state power is mirrored by a rise in 'privatized violence' where terrorists and organized crime collude with warlords, rebels, governments, private companies and NGOs.[18] His observations fit well with this essay's focus on terrorists, criminals and private armies. Mair describes four ideal types of privatized violent actors: terrorists, criminals, rebels and warlords. While each uses violence to achieve their objectives, their motives, strategies and powers can be differentiated. In general terms, they sometimes share attributes. For example in Mair's typology, criminals and warlords have economic imperatives while terrorists and rebels have political ones. Rebels and criminals typically target other organs of force (security services, police, military and competing groups or gangs), while terrorists and warlords generally target civilians. According to Mair, warlords and rebels (i.e., insurgents) seek to supplant the state's monopoly on force within a limited geographic territory, while terrorists and transnational organized crime operate on a global scale (albeit frequently with a limited territorial base) and their use of violence co-exists with state violence.[19] I would add pirates to Mair's warlord class, and also add a fifth potential privatized actor to Mair's list: private military companies (PMCs). Thus, I argue that there are five potential types of non-state soldier: terrorists, criminals, insurgents, warlords (including pirates) and private military companies (PMCs). All can operate as 'private armies'. In addition, all can interact and blend or share attributes at given points in time. This is especially true in the case of *jihadi* terrorists that seek to foment a 'global insurgency'.

Terrorists

As Mair noted, terrorists are distinguished by their use of violence against civilian non-combatants. Contemporary terrorists as noted above increasingly operate in a networked fashion, with relatively autonomous cells operating much like market-driven businesses. The resulting networks or multi-networks (networks of networks), like Al Qaeda and its affiliates, are centrally inspired but not necessarily centrally directed.

Criminals (Organized Crime)

Mair, like Jenkins, observes that transnational organized crime (TOC) and terrorists have been influenced by many of the same geopolitical, social and technological forces. He observes that transnational criminal organizations (TCOs) are increasingly dominated by network(s) of small cells, cooperating with each other along lines of functional specialization. Colombian cartels/gangs focused on cocaine, Afghans on heroin, Nigerians, Turkish, Kurdish, Albanian and Russian groups as middlemen in drugs and human trafficking, etc.[20] TCOs also act as middlemen or facilitators for terrorists, warlords and rebels in insurgencies. The resulting division of labor as previously mentioned reduces conflict among criminal enterprises and maximizes profit. TCOs, like terrorists seem to have recognized the adaptive benefits of networks much more quickly than the legitimate state competitors they seek to infiltrate, corrupt, co-opt or control.

Rebels (Insurgents)

Traditionally rebels (or insurgents) pursue political motives and exercise discrimination in their use of violence, seeking to exercise territorial control. In the recent past, many rebel movements were state sponsored, acting as proxies in the Cold War struggle to determine the definitive form of nation-state (communist or liberal democracy, the earlier fascist contender largely eliminated at the end of the Second World War). Some insurgents have turned to drug production or trafficking to fund their operations, while others have relied on diamond (or gem) trafficking, extortion, kidnapping or other crime, exacerbating nascent links with organized crime. Compounding their dependence on organized crime, some have embraced international terrorist attacks as a method, while others offer safe havens to criminal gangs and terrorist groups.

Warlords (and Pirates)

Mair notes that warlords seek to maximize profit from state disorder. Within their territorial domain, warlords seek to exercise a monopoly on crime and taxation. They use force in a locally limited territory, yet can operate across state boundaries when doing so enhances their profit (as seen in the case of Liberia's Charles Taylor, who attempted to reach into Sierra Leone, Guinea and Côte d'Ivoire). Warlords and pirates, like rebels, can dominate entire regions and offer refuge to terrorists and organized crime.

Pirates are a sea-borne analog to the land-based warlord. Pirates seek to dominate a spatially defined area – usually sea lanes, shipping lanes, straits and similar segments of littoral regions. Piracy is on the rise in many contested regions of the globe.[21] Profit, plunder (greed), war, revolutionary motives and lawlessness are fueling this maritime variation of the land-locked warlord. The unpoliced sea and littorals are increasingly exploited, with piracy attacks tripling in the past decade. According to the International Maritime Bureau (IMB), 2003 accounted for 445 attacks, with 121 of those in the waters near Indonesia. A number of strategic chokepoints, straits and channels that are easily interrupted are especially at risk. These include the Straits of Malacca, Bab el-Mandab and the Straits of Hormuz. The Straits of Malacca, bordered by Singapore, Indonesia and Malaysia, for example, lead the world in piracy attacks. About 30 per cent of all globally traded goods transit the straits, which link the Indian and Pacific Oceans. Rebel armies, criminal gangs and *jihadis* thrive in the surrounding areas. The potential for convergence between terrorists and pirates in the global *jihadi* insurgency is a rising concern to many intelligence and security agencies.

Private Military Companies (PMCs)

Private military companies or firms are increasingly important players in international security and conflict. PMCs are currently engaged in a variety of roles in conflicts worldwide. This is especially visible in Iraq where profit-making organizations account for one out of every ten American 'soldiers' involved in the conflict.[22] At the time of this essay, PMCs are involved in every level of US defense from intelligence to combat planning, from logistical support to armed security services and, by many accounts, direct combat. PMCs (discussed in detail below) alter the traditional (at least during the recent reign of the nation-state) government monopoly on violence and are likely to become major players in future conflicts. Some private security firms (i.e., PMCs), for example in Africa, have linked up with insurgents and warlords for fiscal remuneration. PMCs and private security firms provide services to both states and non-state actors, including businesses and non-governmental organizations (NGOs) engaged in humanitarian aid. The role of PMCs will likely influence the disposition of civil peace, global security and the rule of law during the market-state transition. In essence, the PMC is civil society's counterpart to criminal private armies such as Al Qaeda and its network of market-state forces.

WARLORDS AND PRIVATE ARMIES

Warlords are the embodiment of the rule of the criminal gang and criminal free-state. As recent experience confirms, warlords challenge and provide an obstacle to the stable structures of liberal democracy and the nation-state. Typically, warlordism is the province of failed or near-failed states, yet as the example of gang or mafia/cartel controlled areas of urban 'failed communities' readily demonstrates, proto- or virtual warlords can occupy similar niches even in more stable polities. Warlords depend upon armed force to exert their will. They are facilitated by the usurption of the rule of law, and often – if not always – rely upon criminal support (arms and drugs trafficking, extortion, the black market, etc.) to ensure their reach. As such, warlords exploit the vacuum of weak states and corrupt regimes. Sometimes they are firmly linked to clans or criminal organizations; at others, they negotiate their existence with such actors. It should be noted, however, that not all warlords are the same and not all exercise total control over their areas of operations or interest. Rival warlords can contest each other for control of a zone, and can differ considerably in their level of power, authority, reach and military prowess.

As actors exploiting vacuums of power and state control, warlords are frequently linked to the diverse varieties of political (and criminal) violence: ethnic riots, genocide, gang assaults, ethnic feuds and terrorism. For example, consider the Senas (armies) of India and Pakistan. These paramilitary groups are often dedicated to regional ethnic causes and involved in sectarian violence of all stripes throughout the subcontinent. The Indian Senas are largely caste-based private armies. Examples include the Rajput affiliated Ganga Sena, Kisan Morcha, and Kuer Sena, the Bhumhar affiliated Ranvir Sena and the Pathan/Rajput Sunlight Sena.[23] Senas, 'with their varying mixes of gangsterism, violence, and party contacts, entertain political aspirations in their areas. Some have formed State governments, and most are ethnically based proto-parties.'[24]

Recent experience has reaffirmed the threat of warlords and illustrated the link between warlords and other networked threats. In Afghanistan, for example, warlords are seeking to exploit the vacuum left in the wake of the fall of the Taliban, itself a variation of a warlord regime. Terrorist networks such as Osama bin Laden's Al Qaeda have supported or exploited relationships with warlords in Somalia and Afghanistan to anchor their global terrorist actions. Similarly, warlords have stymied the progress of the rule of law throughout Africa, Asia and South America at various times and are attempting to exploit the instability of contemporary Iraq. In post-war Iraq, private militias challenge conventional military and PMC forces. Deployed on ethnic and religious lines, these militias challenge both the emerging state and Coalition state-builders for the monopoly on force. These private armies include the 60,000 strong Kurdish 'pesh merga' and a number of Shiite forces, including the Badr Corps, Dawa Army, and the belligerent Mahdi Army led by radical Shiia cleric Moktada al-Sadr. Coalescing in the milieu of insurgents and criminal gangs, these rogue

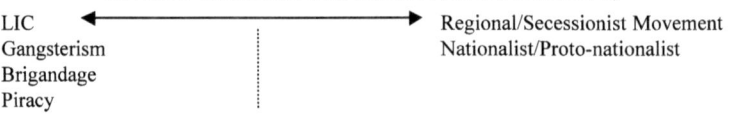

FIGURE 1

REVISED WARLORD CONTINUUM (OF INSTABILITY)

LIC   Regional/Secessionist Movement
Gangsterism   Nationalist/Proto-nationalist
Brigandage
Piracy

Transnational Warlordism/
Global Insurgency/Jihad/
Netwar (e.g., Osama bin Laden, Al Qaeda)
State Capture/Criminal Free-States
Virtual States

actors frequently stimulate recurrent riots, punctuated by terrorism, along the transition to warfare.

Not all warlords are the same, nor occupy the same niche in the continuum of instability.[25] Some occupy that niche of endemic low intensity conflict (LIC) dominated by gangsterism and brigandage. Others are aspiring nationalists or proto-nationalists driving regional/secessionst movements devoid of overt criminal motivations. A third variety, warlords who engage in netwar, also appears at the center of the continuum. This center position is the province of transnational warlordism, global *jihadi* insurgency, and potentially virtual states. That is the threat seen with bin Laden, Al Qaeda in Iraq, combined with the Taliban in Afghanistan, and elsewhere. Figure 1 depicts the warlord continuum.[26] In these instances, the networked warlords engage in state capture (or establishment of a criminal free-zone in failed regions) to solidify a node to export networked transnational conflict.

CORPORATE ARMIES: PRIVATE MILITARY FIRMS

The current conflict in post-war Iraq has brought the discussion of corporate mercenaries or more properly the private military sector into the realm of public debate. These private contractors are more the successors of the British East India Company (The John Company), its Dutch counterpart, European free companies, and others than of the mercenaries typified by 'Mad' Mike Hoare, Bob Denard or the Wild Geese of the conflicts in the late colonial era. Filling the voids that government forces cannot or will not provide, these modern day privateers, known as private military companies (PMCs) or private military firms (PMFs), are beginning to occupy a substantial niche in postmodern conflict.

> No longer confined to providing logistical support or specialty technical services, some security companies have formed their own 'Quick Reaction Forces', and their own intelligence units that produce daily intelligence briefs with grid maps of 'hot zones'. One company

(Blackwater) has its own helicopters, and several have even forged diplomatic alliances with local clans.[27]

Some even become engaged in direct combat operations; for example, Blackwater repulsed an April 2004 attack on US headquarters in Najaf, reinforcing its corporate commandos with its own helicopters and medevacing a wounded Marine.[28]

At this writing, several hundred PMCs operate in over 100 nations on six continents, generating over $100 billion in annual revenue.[29] They provide small teams of operators ranging from commandos to technicians, as well as large-scale logistical support and services. Peter W. Singer notes that PMCs (like other market-state actors) engage in specialization, with military provider firms offering services at the forefront of the battlespace (actual fighting), while military consultant firms provide advisory and training services, and military support firms provide rear-echelon support.[30] Some of these firms 'have committed severe abuses in the course of their operations and have been employed by dictatorships, rebel armies, terrorist groups and drug cartels'.[31] These firms are providing services in an atmosphere of international legal and regulatory ambiguity. While not covered by the general (and also ambiguous) proscriptions against individual mercenaries, international convention and law of PMCs is lacking. There is no comprehensive ban on mercenaries, and existing law does not cover the range of contemporary PMC activities.

This uncertain legal status has largely placed PMCs and their employees outside the rule of law. For example, in one notorious case several DynCorp employees were accused in several villainous acts including perverse, illegal and inhumane behavior and other immoral acts, including the self-videotaped rape of two young women by the firm's supervisor in Bosnia. No prosecutions were pursued due in part to an absence of applicable law.[32] More recently, 'the loose control of the 20,000-plus private enterprise soldiers in Iraq has been thrown into painful relief by the accusations that hired civilian interrogators and translators encouraged obscene tortures at Abu Ghraib prison and that one even allegedly raped an Iraqi boy in his cell'.[33] The law has not yet caught up with the shift in conflict and participants in market-state war. Indeed, in some ways, PMCs as quasi-state actors in the international community are representative of the shift to the market-state. In the worst case, this results in for-profit companies operating with little or no accountability to civilian or military authorities.[34] The market prevails rather than the rule of law or state identity, a reality confirmed by the migration of some US and UK special forces troops to PMCs for significantly higher rates of pay – for example, an SAS trooper earns £250 a week in Iraq, while private firms offer £5,000.[35]

Although they emerged in African conflicts over the past decade, contemporary PMCs have found their proving ground in Iraq, demonstrating the transition to the market-state. Security firms blend, sometimes uneasily, with their military and intelligence counterparts there. After an angry Fallouja mob ambushed two civilian security vehicles, killing four Blackwater contractors and then mutilating their remains in April 2004, recognition of the scope of PMC activity in Iraq started to publicly emerge. Shortly after the Fallouja ambush, Iraqi militias attacked a US government headquarters in Najaf and, once again, Blackwater operators were engaged, repulsing the attacking mobs.[36] As a result of these and other attacks directed against PMC security forces, many of whom are serving the US-led Coalition Provisional Authority (CPA), the PMCs there have started to coordinate operations and pursue mutual aid. This evolution is reflected in press reportage.

> Under assault by insurgents and unable to rely on U.S. and coalition troops for intelligence or help under duress, private security firms in Iraq have begun to band together in the past 48 hours, organizing what may effectively be the largest private army in the world, with its own rescue teams and pooled, sensitive intelligence.[37]

PMCs are demonstrating a potential to inter-operate and serve common needs, clearly a signal of a change in the relations and roles among military institutions – state, non-state, and market-state. These trends are a consequence of the erosion of the ability of states to contain and counter violence in developing and newly emerging states, where weak states contract to private armies to raise national armies to fulfill security roles they cannot address, potentially signaling a shift in state identity.[38]

CONCLUSION: STATE TRANSITION AND THE NEW MILITARY

> The pirate is not bound by the rules of war, but is the common enemy of everyone.

Cicero[39]

Epochal transitions are frequently violent. As new technology and social and economic orders emerge, they frequently do so fueled by innovation in military arts – that is, new methods of warmaking. The current war on terrorism is an example of this oft-repeated theme. Freebooting and piracy plagued the late Roman republic with shadowy organizations of brigands conducting diffuse operations on land and sea. As Cicero noted, non-state soldiers operate outside the prevailing political and legal constitutions of their society. Their type of conflict – what is today called asymmetric warfare or fourth generation warfare (4GW) – exploits the uncertainty of irregular combat. Now as then, petty tyrants, loot seeking warlords, and warring tribes and clans challenge the forces of order.

Powerful ideology again stimulates conflict. At the forefront of recognition currently is the radical Islam of *salifists* and *jihadis*, but demographic change and rapid conversion to newly dominant strains of Christianity may yet do the same. Poverty and conflict seem to go together with corruption, organized crime and terrorism as dark forces stimulating political upheaval and war. Slums of the urban future, dominated by megacities, may also play a role in sorting out the functions of various market-state actors on the new political horizon. As Mike Davis notes in a prelude to his forthcoming book on slums and what we once called the Third World,

> The new urban poor, indeed, are the ghosts at the table of world politics. Every debate about the war on terrorism, the future of the Middle East, the AIDS crisis in Africa, and the international narcotics trade is haunted by their presence and growing desperations. The helicopter gunships that hover over the megaslums of Gaza and Sadr City, the nightly gun battles in Bogotá and Karachi, the bulldozers in Nairobi, Delhi, and Manila – is this not already an incipient world war between rich and poor?[40]

While it is too early to project the outcome of this transition, the emerging market-state will favor those entities that adapt quickest to the new political, economic and military-security realities: the OPFOR (opposing force) which our adversaries are adapting, as we have seen in the discussion of networked gangsters, terrorists and global insurgents. At the strategic level, we need to recognize the force and depth of the transition and configure our institutions – civil, judicial, military, police and intelligence – in ways which can adapt and maintain core liberties, values and security. New force structures within and among states may be needed. The emergence of PMCs and other market entities such as commercial open source intelligence (OSINT) firms demonstrates a capability gap in our existing nation-state structures – otherwise new providers would not emerge. At strategic levels, we may need new forces, for example a national or international gendarmerie, to augment conventional force in constabulary operations, peacekeeping or peacebuilding and counterterrorism missions. Another alternative would be to formalize international regulation of PMCs and develop an appropriate body of international law to regulate the conduct of private military actors and their relations with both state force and other private actors. Tactically, we need what Brian Jenkins described as 'the capability for networked, multilateral threat analysis – comparable to "real-time intelligence on the battlefield" – to generate information that can be packaged and used quickly by a soldier in Afghanistan, a magistrate in France, a cop in Singapore, a Marine in Haiti'.[41] Such a multilateral capability can and must be built, as is described in my essay with Robert J. Bunker on 'Multilateral Counter-Insurgency Networks' elsewhere in this collection. But efforts to do so will most likely face stiff bureaucratic resistance until we recognize the depth and reach of the epochal shift we are navigating. Whatever shape the new market-states take, terrorists, criminals and private armies are already influencing the shape of their security and military services.

NOTES

 1. Martin van Creveld, *The Transformation of War* (New York, The Free Press, 1991), p.197.
 2. Bobbitt posits that the market-state is a new state form supplanting the nation-state. Within that analysis, he sees terrorist networks (with Al Qaeda being an early example) as a malevolent form of market-state. See Philip Bobbitt, *The Shield of Achilles: War, Peace, and the Course of History* (New York: Anchor Books, 2002).
 3. See also Paul O'Donnel, 'Technology Is Killing Democracy', interview with Philip Bobbitt in *Wired*, June 2004, p.44.
 4. Brian M. Jenkins, 'Redefining the Enemy: The World Has Changed, But Our Mindset Has Not', *Rand Review*, Spring 2004, available at 〈www.rand.org/publications/randreview/ issues/spring2004/enemy.html〉.
 5. John Arquilla and David Ronfeldt, 'A New Epoch – and Spectrum – of Conflict' in idem (eds), *In Athena's Camp: Preparing for Conflict in the Information Age* (Santa Monica, CA: RAND, 1997), p.5. For a more recent exploration of netwar and its darker consequences, see also John Arquilla and David Ronfledt (eds), *Networks and Netwars: The Future of Terror, Crime, and Militancy* (Santa Monica, CA: RAND, 2001).
 6. Jenkins.
 7. See Robert J. Bunker and John P.Sullivan, 'Cartel Evolution: Potentials and Consequences', *Transnational Organized Crime*, Vol.4, No.2 (Summer 1998), pp.55–74 for a comprehensive treatment of criminal convergence underlying this analysis.
 8. Jenkins.
 9. Ibid.
10. Sebastian Rotella, 'Jihad's Unlikely Alliance: Muslim Extremists Who Attacked Madrid Funded the Plot by Selling Drugs, Investigators Say', *Los Angeles Times*, 23 May 2004, p.A1.
11. Ibid., quoting a DST official.
12. Jenkins term 'sovereign outlaws', where criminals command states, complements Bunker and Sullivan's concept of criminal free-states.
13. Marc Sageman, 'Killing the Hydra: Only Attacks on its Ideas Can Defeat a Network Like Al Qaeda', *Los Angeles Times*, 6 June 2004, p.M1.
14. Anthony Faiola, 'Brazilian Gangs Take Turf Wars Out of Slums', *Washington Post*, 15 December 2002, p.A37.
15. Robert J. Bunker, 'Epochal Change: War Over Social and Political Organization', *Parameters*, Vol.27, No.2 (Summer 1997), pp.15–24.
16. Robert J. Bunker and John P. Sullivan, 'Cartel Evolution: Potentials and Consequences', *Transnational Organized Crime*, Vol.4, No.2 (Summer 1998), pp.55–74.
17. See John Wilson, *Karachi: A Terror Capital in the Making* (New Delhi: Rupa & Co., 2003), esp. ch.4: Criminal Syndicates and ch.5: Terror Connection.
18. Stefan Mair, 'The New World of Privatized Violence', *International Politik und Gesellschaft (International Politics and Society)*, (2/2003), available at 〈fesportal.fes.de/pls/portal30/docs/ FOLDER/IPG/IPG2-2003/ARTMAIR.HTM〉.
19. Ibid.
20. Ibid.
21. See Simon Montake, 'Pirates Ahead!', *Christian Science Monitor*, 18 March 2004, for a representative journalistic overview of the rising threat of piracy. Available at 〈www.csmonitor.com/2004/0318/p13s02-woap.html〉.

22. Nicolas von Hoffman, 'Contract Killers: How Privatizing the U.S. Military Subverts Public Oversight', *Harpers Magazine*, June 2004, pp.79–80.
23. See 'Private Caste Armies in Bihar' at the South Asia Terrorism Portal, ⟨http://www.satp.org⟩.
24. David L. Horowitz, *The Deadly Ethnic Riot* (Berkeley, CA: University of California Press, 2001), p.246.
25. This analysis of a continuum of warlords draws upon the observations found in Paul B. Rich, 'Warlordism, Complex Emergencies and the Search for a Doctrine of Humanitarian Intervention', in D.S. Gordon and F.H. Toase (eds), *Aspects of Peacekeeping* (London: Frank Cass, 2001), pp.253–273.
26. The table here is a refinement of that presented in Robert J. Bunker and John P.Sullivan, 'Cartel Evolution: Potentials and Consequences', *Transnational Organized Crime*, Vol.4, No.2 (Summer 1998), pp.55–74.
27. David Issenberg, 'Corporate Mercenaries: Part 1: Profit Comes with a Price', *Asia Times*, online, 19 May 2004, available at ⟨atimes.com/atimes/Middle_east/FE19Ak01.html⟩; David Barstow, 'Security Companies: Shadow Soldiers in Iraq', 19 April 2004, available at ⟨www.nytimes.com/2004/04/19/international/middleeast/19SECU.html⟩.
28. Ibid.
29. Peter W. Singer, 'Peacekeepers, Inc.', *Policy Review*, June 2003, available at ⟨http://www.brookings.org/views/articles/fellows/singer20030601.htm⟩.
30. Ibid.
31. Peter W. Singer, 'War, Profit, and the Vacuum of Law: Privatized Military Firms and International law', *Columbia Journal of International Law*, Vol.42 (2004), p.523.
32. Ibid, p.525.
33. David Leigh, 'Who Commands the Private Soldiers?', *The Guardian* ,17 May 2004, available at ⟨http://www.guardian.co.uk/print/0,3858,4925466-103550,00,html⟩.
34. Barry Yeoman, 'Soldiers of Good Fortune', *Mother Jones*, Vol.28, No.3 (May–June 2003), p.42.
35. David Rennie, 'Weary Special Forces Quit for Security Jobs', *The Telegraph* online, 31 March 2004, available at ⟨http://www.telegraph.co.uk/news/main.jhtml?xml = /news/2004/03/31/wspec31.xml⟩.
36. Dana Priest, 'Private Guards Repel Attack on U.S. Headquarters', *Washington Post*, 6 April 2004, p.A01.
37. Dana Priest and Mary Pat Flaherty, 'Under Fire, Security Firms Form An Alliance', *Washington Post*, 8 April 2004, p.A01.
38. An early observer of this potential is Rutgers scholar Henry Sanchez. See Henry Sanchez, 'Why Do States Hire Private Military Companies', (n.d.), available at ⟨http://newarkwww.rutgers.edu/global/sanchez.htm⟩.
39. Cicero, *On Duties*, 3.107.
40. Mike Davis, 'Planet of Slums', *Harpers Magazine*, June 2004, p.22.
41. Jenkins.

US Counterinsurgency vs Iranian-Sponsored Terrorism

SEAN K. ANDERSON

NETWORKS: NON-STATE ACTORS, STATE-SPONSORS AND GRAY AREAS

Netwar is a form of low-intensity conflict involving actions falling short of conventional warfare and often involving non-violent as well as violent confrontation in which like-minded protagonists consisting of small groups, joined together in a network organization, use related doctrines, strategies and information-age technologies to communicate, coordinate, and campaign in an inter-netted manner without one central command.[1] During the 1990s, as state-sponsorship of terrorist groups appeared to be declining, new non-state terrorist groups, such as Hamas and Al Qaeda, which appeared to be loose networks operating without direct state sponsorship,[2] became more prominent. However, even networks of non-state groups operate in an international environment in which both state sponsors, as well as sanctuaries provided by areas not under the effective control of any national government, play important and indispensable roles. If the center of gravity in terrorism has shifted primarily to the non-state actors and away from their state sponsors then, according to the analysis of Jerrold Post, military retaliation and counter-insurgency operations may prove less useful in deterring future terror.[3] On the contrary, if state sponsors or 'sanctuary zones' play an indispensable role then military retaliation and pro-active counterinsurgency policies should prove effective in neutralizing the potentials of terrorist networks. The experience of the United States in countering Iranian state-sponsored terrorism in the 1980s provides empirical evidence that pro-active counterinsurgency efforts are indeed effective.

The role of state sponsors and of sanctuary territories in promoting civil unrest and insurgency was first measured quantitatively by Ted Gurr in his casual model of civil strife. While attempting to determine the various sources of civil strife, Gurr found that 'social and structural facilitation', rather than relative deprivation or political repression, turned out to be the strongest explanatory variable.[4] Social and structural facilitation was measured in three ways: an index of 'inaccessibility', that is, territory of the nation deprived of transportation networks and government services; the existence and effectiveness of organized revolutionary or insurgent groups, specifically, communist groups; and the extent of external support for such insurgent groups.[5] In the post-Cold War context such insurgent groups need not be limited to communist groups, although the Columbian FARN and ELN groups and the Peruvian Sendero Luminoso group are post-Cold War communist insurgent groups. The existence of remote jungles, deserts or mountainous terrain lacking government services provides such insurgent groups with sanctuaries and bases of operations while the external support of state sponsors provides the insurgents with weapons, logistics, training, intelligence and communications resources that they could not easily provide on their own.

While Gurr sought to define the 'inaccessibility' index with respect to areas within a given country clearly this concept can be applied as readily to remote sanctuaries and staging areas in territories outside, but adjacent to, a given nation-state under attack by insurgents. In the international context the equivalent of these regions would be the 'gray areas' defined by Xavier Raufer, namely ungovernable areas in developing nations over which unstable, weak national governments have but nominal control but which afford criminal syndicates or terrorist and insurgent groups excellent bases of operations from which they can conduct far-reaching operations against other targeted nations.[6] While Gurr focused on the impact of external support for insurgents and lack of government control over inaccessible areas, Max G. Manwaring developed a quantitative model of counterinsurgency that incorporated not only the existence of insurgent groups and their external supporters but also the variables of 'unity of effort and discipline of government forces' and 'external support' for the targeted regime. Whereas the Gurr model was able to explain 65 per cent of the variation in the levels of civil strife in 114 nations over a five-year period, the Manwaring model, which incorporated specific counterinsurgency variables, was able to explain 91 per cent of the variation in levels of insurgency in 43 nations over a 45-year period.

The implications of these previous studies for understanding terrorist netwar include the following. First, terrorist networks will benefit from and, within limits, seek the passive or active support of state sponsors. Second, such networks, requiring areas of sanctuary and bases of operations, will find these within several 'gray areas' existing in less developed nations or in transitional regimes with weak central governments. Third, external operations in support of regimes targeted by terrorists, or directed against regimes supporting terrorists, will weaken the terrorist network of support and so deter terrorism. Evidence for these propositions can be seen in the case of the most notorious netwar terrorist group, Al Qaeda. In spite of its alleged antipathy towards Shi'ite Muslims and the secular nationalism of the Ba'thist Party, the Al Qaeda group formed a working relationship with the Iranian Islamic Revolutionary Guards Corps as well as the Iranian-sponsored Shi'ite group, Hezbollah.[7] Similarly, on 16 September 2003 the US Secretary of Defense, Donald Rumsfeld, stated that there was evidence of earlier Iraqi aid to Al Qaeda in bomb construction and training in the use of chemical and biological weapons, which has been corroborated by other sources as well.[8] Al Qaeda's reliance on Sudan and Afghanistan as bases of operations has also been well documented by Gunaratna and others.[9] Following the 11 September ('9/11') attacks the withdrawal of Pakistani state support for the Taliban regime and Operation Enduring Freedom's subsequent destruction of that regime along with the Al Qaeda training infrastructure within Afghanistan have all arguably weakened Al Qaeda's ability to continue its operations, although the organization itself has not yet been destroyed completely. However the case of the Islamic Republic of Iran and its support of a network of various terrorist groups during the 1980s provides a more complete case and data from which to draw a more certain conclusion regarding the effectiveness of proactive counterinsurgency measures.

IRAN'S PROACTIVE SPONSORSHIP OF ANTI-US TERRORISM

The Islamic Republic of Iran was identified by the US Department of State as the most active state sponsor of terrorism in the period 1980–1998. US military interventions within Iran's self-defined sphere of interests and retaliatory actions in the period 1980–1990, during which the most serious acts of Iranian state-sponsored anti-US terrorism occurred, provide a test of the effectiveness of such responses in stymieing and suppressing such state-sponsored terrorism. Although state-sponsored terrorism is a form of coercion, backed up by the threat and use of violence, to achieve political ends, the political context of these terrorist tactics also involve the signaling of intentions and responses between the terrorist sponsor and those whom it targets which involve both official statements and armed actions.

The intentions and perceptions of the Iranian state towards US intervention were previously examined through statistical content analysis of official Iranian state-run media in order to determine whether Iranian-sponsored anti-US terrorism was due to proactive and deliberate Iranian state policy or else was 'reactive' in nature, either in responding to perceived external threats by the United States or else in response to factional politics within Iran, namely, as a way of ensuring internal unity by directing attention to an external enemy. The conclusion of this study was that there was little statistical support for the 'reactive model', whereas there was significant support for the conclusion that Iranian state sponsorship was deliberate, proactive, and a means to Iran's ends of projecting its own power within the Persian Gulf and wider Middle East theater.[10]

While the methodology of the previous study will not be described in full detail here certain aspects of it bear on the current study, namely, the definition of the dependent variable of Iranian state-sponsored anti-US terrorism. The dependent variable consists of cases of anti-US terrorism in the period 1980–1990 for which there is strong evidence of Iranian sponsorship, whether by state or sub-state actors, that has been materially corroborated by multiple and diverse witnesses. Two major sets of chronologies of international terrorism were separately developed, one by Edward F. Mickolus, spanning 1980–1987, and the other being the RAND Chronology of International Terrorism, spanning 1980–1988. Supplemented with other public reports, such as those contained in the *New York Times*, *Iran Times International*, the US Department of State's annual report(s) *Patterns of Global Terrorism*, and the annual chronologies published by RAND provided multiple and diverse sources for identifying cases in the period 1988–1992 not jointly covered by the Mickolus and RAND chronologies. All cases for which dual confirmation in the Mickolus and RAND databases was lacking (or lacking comparable diverse and multiple witnesses) were eliminated from consideration as instances of the dependent variable. The class of terrorist attacks was further narrowed by eliminating all instances of mere threats from the class of incidents and also eliminating most cases involving attacks on US or Allied troops in war-like situations. Following this step-wise elimination of dubious or inconclusive cases, only those cases for which dual confirmation of Iranian sponsorship existed were included in the list of all cases ($N = 24$) of the dependent variable, which are reproduced in Table 1.

The independent variables of this earlier study included quantitative measures of the following sorts of statements identified through content analysis of a systematic sampling of the main Iranian government newspaper organ *Ittila'at* over the period of study. Threat perceptions are those threats which are seen as directed by non-Iranians or by enemies of Islam against Iran, Iran's revolution or regime, Islam, or against Muslims in general. Threat

TABLE 1
TERRORIST ACTS AGAINST US TARGETS COMMITTED UNDER PRESUMED IRANIAN SPONSORSHIP,
21 MARCH 1980–21 MARCH 1990

Incident No.	References	Tactic	Nationality of target	Date	Place	Notes
1	80072203, 19800723	Assassination	Iranian	22/07/80	USA	RAND cited evidence of Iranian sponsorship in FBI and NSA electronic surveillance of cash transactions between American assassins of anti-Khomeini emigre, Ali Akbar Tabataba'i; and Iranian agents within the United States
2	80073102, 19800731	Assassination (attempt)	Iranian	31/07/80	USA	Attempted assassination of Tabataba'i associate Shah-Reis, followed death threats by same group lined by signal intelligence with backers of attackers in No.1 above
3	82071901, 19820719	Kidnapping	American	19/07/82	Lebanon	
4	83041801, 19830418	Car bomb	American	18/04/83	Lebanon	
5	83102301-02, 19831023 A1 B04 F241, 19831023 A1 B04 F059	Car bomb	American, French	23/10/83	Lebanon	
6	83121203-10, 19831212	Car bomb	American, French	12/12/83	Kuwait	
7	84011801, 19840118, A1 B06 F001	Assassination	American	18/01/84	Lebanon	
8	84031601, 19840316, A1 B01 F001	Kidnapping, murder	American	16/03/84	Lebanon	
9	84050801, 19840510 A1 B01 F000	Kidnapping	American	06/05/84	Lebanon	
10	84092001, 19840920 A1 B04 F023	Car-Bomb	American	20/09/84	Lebanon	

TABLE 1 – *CONTINUED*

Incident No.	References	Tactic	Nationality of target	Date	Place	Notes
11	84120402, 19841204 A1 B03 F007	Hijacking, murder	American	04/12/84	UAE, Iran	
12	85010802, 19850108 A1 B01 F000	Kidnapping	American	08/01/85	Lebanon	
13	85031601, 19850316 A1 B01 F000	Kidnapping	American	16/03/85	Lebanon	
14	85052801, 19850528 A1 B01 F000	Kidnapping	American	28/05/8	Lebanon	
15	85060902	Kidnapping	American	09/06/85	Lebanon	
16	85061404, 19850607 A1 B03 F001	Hijacking, kidnapping, murder	American	14/06/85	Greece	
17	86090903, 19860909 A1 B01 F000 I000	Kidnapping	American	09/09/86	Lebanon	
18	86091203, 19860912 A1 B01 F000 I000	Kidnapping	American	12/09/86	Lebanon	
19	86102102, 19861021 A1 B01 F000 I000	Kidnapping	American	21/10/86	Lebanon	
20	87012402, 19870124 A1 B01 F000 I000	Kidnapping	American	24/01/87	Lebanon	
21	87041001, 19870409 A1 B07 F000 I000	Conspiracy	American, Israeli	10/04/87	Turkey	
22	87061702, 1987061? A1 B01 F00 I000	Kidnapping	American	17/06/87	Lebanon	
23	LA Times, NY Times	Kidnapping	American	17/02/88	Lebanon	
24	LA Times, NY Times	Murder	American	31/07/89	Lebanon	

Notes: References are from Mickolus and RAND.

projections are those warnings or threats by Iran directed against governments, groups or persons outside of Iran viewed as enemies of Iran or of Islam but here specifically threats against the United States. Factional strife statements are those statements that either indicate perceptions of intramural threats coming from persons or groups within Iran or else which are warnings directed at such groups or persons.

Statistical regression analysis would reveal whether any significant association existed between any of these variables and the dependent variable of anti-US terrorism. In fact there was no association between the 'threat perception' variable and anti-US terrorism, whereas there were multiple strong and leading indications found with the 'threat projection' variable and also a weak association with the 'factional strife' variable. One definite conclusion to be derived from the foregoing statistical analyses is that anti-US terrorist actions do not increase as spontaneous reactions of 'the Arab street' to perceived threats from either the United States or the West in general. Terrorist actions do not arise automatically through the community-wide mobilizing force of the Islamic resurgence, itself supposedly the inevitable outcome of historical and cultural 'root causes' and grievances. Instead a more simple explanation consistent with the statistical analyses would be that the anti-US terrorist actions have resulted from the deliberate calculations and decisions of certain identifiable officials and institutions associated with the Islamic Republic of Iran.

The real contending explanations are, then, two proactive models: a factional politics model and the state sponsorship model. The statistical analyses conducted in the earlier study concluded that threat projections played a predominant positive and significant role. While the analysis seemed to indicate that factional indicators were also significant, they were much less significant than the threat projection variable. Such factional strife seems to motivate subsequent efforts at regime consolidation through intensified anti-US mobilization and propaganda, including 'armed propaganda' in the form of terrorist actions.

THE IMPACT OF US MILITARY INTERVENTIONS

This earlier study examined only the impact of threats and warnings originating from the Iranian government but did not examine in tandem the effects of US military responses to Iranian threats and actual state-sponsored terrorist actions. This current study introduces US military interventions in response to Iranian state-sponsored terrorism to determine the effects of such intervention: do US military interventions against state sponsors help to reduce levels of terrorism? Or do they merely feed a supposed 'cycle of violence' leading to more and deadlier anti-US terrorism?

Measures of US Military Interventions

The Federation of American Scientists' Military Analysis Network maintains an on-line database of US military operations based on 39 other published works or electronic databases and has documented at least 187 major US military operations since the end of the Cold War.[11] The 'self-perceived sphere of Iranian interests' was defined by Ayatollah Khomeini's pronouncement ordering the 'exportation of the revolution' on 21 March 1980, in which he designated the entire Muslim world as the scope of the Islamic revolution. However, Khomeini has shown special concern for those nations that form the 'core' of the Islamic states, such as Egypt, Iran, Iraq, Jordan, Lebanon, Libya, Palestine, Saudi Arabia, Syria and the emirates of the Arabian Peninsula such as Kuwait, the United Arab Emirates, Qatar and Oman, as well as the island state of Bahrain. Iranian authorities developed a tactical alliance with Ba'thist Syria against Iraq and also sought to develop a presence among the Shi'a of Lebanon. Khomeini believed there was a particular obligation to 'liberate' Palestine from the Israelis and the holy cities of Mecca and Medina from Saudi control. Iran sought to develop close ties with Libya and Syria as fellow states that rejected any accommodation with the State of Israel. As Egypt was the key Arab state, without which the other Arab and Muslim states could not vanquish Israel, the Islamic Republic also targeted the Egyptian regime for its separate peace with Israel in the Camp David Accords. The mere presence of US military troops, naval vessels or aircraft in any of these regions is considered provocative and US attacks on allied states, such as Libya, or material support given to effective enemies, such as Egypt or Kuwait, are considered even more provocative, as would be any attacks on Iranian forces or those of its client groups, such as Hezbollah in Lebanon.

US military intervention can consist either of the mere presence of US forces in one of these sensitive regions, without accompanying military actions, or else could include military actions as well. For purposes of analysis it is useful to separate observations of actual hostile actions from those indicating the mere presence of US troops or forces without action. Therefore two variables were created to separately record these two qualitatively different measures of US military intervention. In Table 2 there are 16 major operations listed involving extensive US deployments of troops and ships within this region as well as several incidents involving actual US use of military force. The provocation of mere presence is coded at the rate of '1' for each monthly period in which US forces are deployed or deployments during which there was no active combat. Each incident involving armed combat is coded at the rate of one per target struck per period. Thus the entry corresponding to observation no.71 is '1' for the month of US deployment in the Gulf of Sidra while that of observation no.73 is '5' for five targets struck

TABLE 2

ACTS OF US MILITARY INTERVENTIONS IN REGION OF PRESUMED IRANIAN INTERESTS
21 MARCH 1980–21 MARCH 1990

Incident	Obs. No.	Date	Military Operation	Location	Quantification	Notes
1	2	24/4/80	Operation Eagle Claw	Iran/Desert One	2 = 1 P	US military rescue mission enters eastern Iran but is unable to perform mission due to catastrophe at 'Desert One' base of operations.
2	17	18/8/81	Gulf of Sidra	Libya	17 = 2A	In the course of freedom of navigation exercises in the Gulf of Sidra the US Sixth Fleet F-14 Tomcats shot down two Libyan Su-22 fighter-bombers.
3	19–20	6/10/81-1/11/81	Operation Bright Star	Egypt	19 = 1 P; 20 = 1 P	Operation Bright Star involved joint US-Egyptian military exercises involving the 552nd AWACs and 963rd Airborne Air Control Squadron as well as infantry units of the Rapid Deployment Joint Task Force.
4	30–48	25/8/82-26/2/84	US and Multinational Force	Lebanon	30 = 1 P, 31* = 1 A, 32 = 1 A, 33 = 30, 34 = 1 P, 35 = 1 P, 36 = 1 P, 37 = 1 P, 38 = 1 P, 39 = 1 P, 40 = 1 P, 41 = 1 P, 42 = 1 P, 43* = 2A, 44 = 1 P, 45* = 1A, 46 = 1 P, 47 = 1 P, 48 = 1 P	US forces were deployed in Lebanon following the Israeli invasion of June 1983 in an effort to create stability within Lebanon.

TABLE 2 – *CONTINUED*

Incident	Obs. No.	Date	Military Operation	Location	Quantification	Notes
5	31	22/9/82	US and Multinational Force	Lebanon	31 = 1A	Two US Marine Units deployed in Lebanon and engaged in actions to relieve Lebanese Armed Forces leading to conflicts with Shi'ite militias.
6	43	27/9/83	US and Multinational Force	Lebanon	43 = 2A	1st Battalion, 8th Marines Headquarters established at Beirut International Airport housing Battalion Landing Team with two aircraft carriers stationed offshore in Lebanese waters for air and artillery support. Marines and artillery deployed against allies of Lebanese Shi'ite militias.
7	45	4/12/83	US and Multinational Force	Lebanon	45 = 1A	In response to Syrian anti-aircraft artillery attacks on two F-14s flying over Lebanon on 3 December 1983 on the following day aircraft from the USS *Kennedy* and USS *Independence* attacked Syrian positions but both were shot down, killing one pilot and resulting in another being taken captive.
8	52	15/7/84	Operation Intense Look	Red Sea, Gulf of Suez	52 = 1P	USS *Shreveport* deployed to Red Sea through Suez Canal and Helicopter Mine Countermeasures Squadron Fourteen (HM-14) located and neutralized mines believed to be of Libyan origin. US military operations close to holy cities in Western Arabia always regarded as provocative by Iranian government.

TABLE 2 – *CONTINUED*

Incident	Obs. No.	Date	Military Operation	Location	Quantification	Notes
9	67	7/10/85	Achille Lauro	Egypt, Sicily	67 = 1A	EgyptAir 737 airliner carrying Palestine Liberation Front hijackers of *Achille Lauro* cruise ship forced by two F-14A Tomcats and an E-2C Hawkeye from the USS *Saratoga* to land in Sicily, at the Sigonella NATO base where the terrorists were taken into Italian custody.
10	71–73	26/1/86–29/4/86	Operation Attain Document	Libya	71 = 1 P, 72 = 2 A, 73* = 5 A	Following Libyan-sponsored terrorist attacks on the Rome and Vienna airports in December 1985 US Navy conducted freedom of navigation exercises in the Gulf of Sidra. On 24–25 March after two SA-5 missiles were fired at US aircraft from a Libyan SAM site the US Navy engaged and sank two Libyan patrol boats.
11	73	17/4/86–19/4/86	Operation El Dorado Canyon	Libya	73 = 5 A	In retaliation for Libyan-sponsored bombing of discotheque in West Berlin US aircraft bombed five targets within Libya.
12	88–100	24/7/87–16/7/89	Operation Earnest Will	Persian Gulf	84 = 1 P, 85 = 1 P, 86 = 1 P, 87 = 1 P, 88 = 1 P, 89 = 1 P, 90* = 1 A, 91* = 2 A, 92 = 1 P, 93 = 1 P, 94 = 1 P, 95 = 1 P, 96 = 1 P, 97* = 3A, 98 = 1 P, 99 = 1 P, 100* = 8 A	Following several Iranian attacks on oil tankers leaving Arab ports in the Persian Gulf the United States reflagged Kuwaiti oil tankers and engaged in daily confrontations with the Iranian naval and Islamic Revolutionary Guards Corps speedboats.

TABLE 2 – *CONTINUED*

Incident	Obs. No.	Date	Military Operation	Location	Quantification	Notes
13	90	26/9/87	Operation Earnest Will	Persian Gulf	90 = 1 A	US Navy forces sank the Iran *Ajr* mine-laying vessel and took ten Iranian survivors prisoner.
14	91	19/10/87	Operation Earnest Will	Persian Gulf	91 = 2 A	US Navy SEAL teams attacked and demolished two oil platforms in the Rostam offshore oil field that were being used as bases for attacking shipping.
15	97	17/4/98-19/4/1988	Operation Praying Mantis	Persian Gulf	97 = 3 A	US Navy attacked Iranian frigate *Sahalan* and destroyed two oil platforms in the Sirri and Sassan offshore oil fields that were being used as attack bases.
16	100	3/7/88	Operation Earnest Will	Persian Gulf	100 = 8 A	US naval forces engage Iranian navy in battle sinking two Iranian frigates and damaging five others.

Notes: "Obs. No." refer to months in time series from No.1 (March 1980) to No.120 (Feb. 1990). Therefore "3 19–20" means that in incident No.3 the observations were made in the nineteenth and twentieth months of the time-series. 'Date' denotes the day on which an operation took place or the dates of the period of the military exercise. In the Quantification column "1 = P" means that during first month of observations there was a US military presence while "17 = 2A" means that during the seventeenth month of observations there were two US military offensive actions. When an observation of a US attack is asterisked in the Quantification column this indicates it will receive elaboration as an incident separately from other overall military exercise or action during which it occurred.

within Libya during that one month period. Like the threat perception, threat projection and factional strife variables these quantified measures of US military intervention consist of three-month averages and its lagged variables.

RESULTS OF STATISTICAL ANALYSIS

As the independent variables of *Ittila'at* data and US military interventions are in the form of percentages, and hence are parametric measures, they can be statistically analyzed using regression analysis which can provide measures of the strength of association, coefficients of correlation, and some measures of how the independent variables contribute together to explaining the variation in the dependent variable. The dependent variable is measured as discrete terrorist events while the measures of US military presence and US military attacks are also discreet events. If, however, one uses three-month moving averages of both the dependent and independent variables, the measures of the dependent variable and discreet military variables are also transformed to percentage measures which can be analyzed using an ordinary least-squares regression model.

A stepwise multiple regression algorithm was used with the three-month moving average of anti-US terrorist events as the dependent variable with lagged values from month $(t - 1)$ to month $(t - 12)$ for the three-month moving average of each independent and lagged variable. The regression algorithm retained only those independent and lagged variables that are significant at the 1.0 per cent level of confidence and the final regression model is presented in Table 3.

The final regression model contains none of the lagged values of the threat perception variable. This suggests that anti-US terrorist attacks have not been

TABLE 3
REGRESSION OF IRANIAN-STATE SPONSORED ANTI-US
TERRORIST ATTACKS ON CONTENT VARIABLES DERIVED FROM
ITTILA'AT DATA AND US ARMED INTERVENTION VARIABLES

Variable		B	Standard	T-Value	Error
(Constant)		− 0.091	0.050		− 1.837
Threat projection	t − 5**	1.241	0.263		4.711
Factional strife	t − 10**	1.299	0.273		4.755
Threat projection	t − 9**	1.512	0.280		5.409
US presence	t − 2**	− 0.244	0.056		4.351
US presence	t − 9**	0.227	0.057		4.008
US attacks	t − 6**	− 0.123	0.033		− 3.527

R-squared = 0.505; F Value = 16.692**
Adjusted R-squared = 0.475; Signif F = 0.0000
*P < 0.05 and **P < 0.01

reactive in nature, that is, defensive actions by Muslim fundamentalists against perceived threats from the United States or the West. The most significant variable appears to be the nine-month lag of the threat projection variable: for every 100 per cent increase in the measure of threat projection one should expect about a 151 per cent increase in anti-US terrorist incidents ten months later. This is consistent with the state sponsorship model in which the Iranian state acts as a single actor in making its threat projections and subsequently carrying them out. There is another threat projection variable at a lag of five months preceding terrorist actions. The existence of more than one significant lagged value of the threat projection variable is also consistent with a communications model of terrorism in which the state sponsor may repeat its threats before actually carrying them out in order to underscore with its target audience the consequences of its non-compliance with those threats.

There is one lagged value of the factional strife variable, at ten months, that is also positively correlated with following incidents of anti-US terrorism. This positive correlation is consistent with the factional strife theory which views Iranian sponsorship of anti-US terrorism as being a spill-over effect of factional struggle within Iran and quite possibly the work of sub-state groups within the Iranian state rather than the Iranian state itself operating as a unitary actor. As this is the earliest leading indicator this would support an explanation of Iranian-state sponsorship of terrorism as being motivated as a regime-consolidating and unifying tactic in response to internal domestic challenges to the regime rather than in response to perceived external aggression.

The sequence and significance of the factional strife and threat projection variables can be explained by efforts by the Iranian state to divert its supporters from divisive intramural controversies by directing their energies and attentions proactively against external enemies. This is an example of what Schmid and Graaf called 'deflecting public attention from a disliked issue by bombing it from the frontpages',[12] as well as an example of morale-boosting and solidarity-building through concentration upon an external enemy.

In the previously-mentioned study these two threat projection and single factional strife variables together accounted for about 26 per cent of the variation in the levels of Iranian-sponsored anti-US terrorism.[13] However when the two US military intervention variables of US military presence and US military attacks are included among the independent variables the predictive power of the model increases to account for about 47.5 per cent of the variation in levels of terrorism, a gain of over 82 per cent. Two lagged US military presence variables, one at a two-month lag and the other at a nine-month lag, have small coefficients, nearly equal but opposite in sign, that are significant at the one per cent confidence interval. They may be interpreted as follows: whenever US military forces enter a region of strategic concern to Iran then in the following two month period there will be an average drop in anti-US terrorism of about 24 per cent. However, if this US military presence continues without actual hostilities or military engagements the average anti-US terrorism rebounds after nine months by about 22 per cent, returning it to almost the same pre-US presence level but still slightly lower. However, US military interventions involving actual attacks lead to a 12 per cent decline in anti-US terrorism which tends to persist. These findings disprove the claim that US intervention breeds more anti-US terrorism. In fact US military intervention appears instead to weaken Iranian state-sponsored terrorism rather than to generate more terrorism in some purported 'cycle of violence'. Nonetheless, the larger size of the coefficients of the threat projection and factional strife variables indicates that the internal decision making and political dynamics of the Iranian regime have been more important determinants in causing anti-US terrorism than either free-floating perceptions of an intangible 'external threat', which apparently plays no role, or even the reality of US actions invading the perceived sphere of interests of the regime, which in fact slightly deter the regime from anti-US adventurism.

CONCLUSIONS

The foregoing statistical analysis demonstrates that anti-US terrorist actions resulted from the deliberate calculations and decisions of certain identifiable individuals or groups associated with the Islamic Republic of Iran. Iran carried out its terrorism through a panoply of various non-state groups, such as the Lebanese Hezbollah and Islamic Jihad groups, similar groups in Saudi Arabia and other Gulf sheikhdoms, and also overseas contingents of the Islamic Revolutionary Guards Corps. These groups have exploited the various sanctuaries provided by other state sponsors, such as Sudan and Syria, as well as in the 'gray areas' of the Bekaa Valley, Sudan and the waters of the Persian Gulf and Arabian Sea. The factional indicator was significant and may herald subsequent efforts at regime consolidation in part through intensified anti-US mobilization and propaganda, including 'armed propaganda' in the form of terrorist actions. However the main policy implication of this finding for administrators of US foreign policy is that factionalism within Iran neither pre-occupied nor distracted this regime from carrying out its external terrorist agenda. None of this motivation appears to depend on autonomous public opinion of some purported 'Arab street' or 'Muslim street'. If the factional politics model accounted for most of the anti-US terrorism the United States would face the dilemma of seeking to punish the radicals within Tehran at the cost of undermining the position of alleged 'moderates' within the Tehran government. However, as Jerrold Post indicated in his study of terrorist group structure and locus of authority, when state-sponsored terrorism is the outcome of strategic choice then retaliatory policies that reduce the marginal utility of terrorism to the sponsoring state are both effective and morally justified.[14] In fact, this appears to have been the case with the Iranian regime which in the decade of the 1990s shifted from terrorist attacks on US targets to a more narrow state terror directed towards expatiate dissidents viewed as enemies of the state, such as the People's Mujahideen group or the Kurdish national-separatists.

The current study concludes that the Iranian state sponsored anti-US terrorist actions committed in the period 1980–1990 proactively as a rational actor autonomously pursuing its geopolitical agenda and not merely as reactions to perceived or real aggressions against it by the United States. The decline in state-sponsorship of terrorism by the Syrian and Libyan regimes, the failure of Iraqi attempts to foster anti-US terrorism and the change in Iranian state terrorism from targeting foreigners to targeting largely Iranian expatriates viewed as enemies of the regime must all be attributed, at least in part, to the success of US military and diplomatic policies aimed at isolating and punishing the state sponsors of terrorism. Although US military and diplomatic personnel have put themselves into greater risk of being targeted due to the active interventions of the United States in various parts of the world, such instances of anti-US terrorism as do occur are not proportional to the potential impact of US military retaliation against the perpetrators of such attacks, whether by state sponsors or non-state groups. When confronted by firm and consistent counter-terrorist policies by the United States and other targeted liberal democracies, the state sponsors have given way in the last decade to abstaining from sponsorship of anti-Western terrorism. However a more comprehensive program to counter such terrorism should not only punish state sponsors with military reprisals but also attack more proactively the non-state groups sponsored by such regimes, and reduce the availability of sanctuaries in the 'grey areas' through diplomatic and economic policies to restore governability and stability to such areas.

NOTES

1. John Arquilla and David Ronfeldt, *The Advent of Netwar* (Santa Monica, CA: RAND, 1996).
2. Steve Emerson, 'A Terrorist Network in America?', *New York Times*, 7 April, 1993.
3. Jerrold M. Post, 'Rewarding Fire with Fire: Effects of Retaliation on Terrorist Group Dynamics', *Terrorism*, Vol.10 (1987), pp.23–36.
4. Ted Gurr, 'A Causal Model of Civil Strife: A Comparative Analysis Using New Indices', *American Political Science Review*, Vol.62 (December 1968), pp.1122–3.
5. Ibid., pp.1115–17.
6. Xavier Raufer, 'Gray Areas: A New Security Threat', *Political Warfare: Intelligence, Activities, Measures and Intelligence Report*, Vol.20 (Spring 1992), p.1
7. Rohan Gunaratna, *Inside Al Qaeda: Global Network of Terror* (New York:Columbia University Press, 2002), pp.146–9.

8. Several sources document the Iraqi Ba'thist–Al Qaeda connection: Laurie Mylroie, 'Iraq and the Clinton Presidency', *Journal of Counterterrorism and Homeland Security*, Vol.8, No.2 (2002), pp.10–15; Laurie Mylroie, 'Going after Iraq', *Journal of Counterterrorism Homeland Security*, Vol.8, No.4 (2002), pp.10–13; Mansoor Ijaz, 'Saddam and the Terrorists: A Marriage (Now Ended)', *National Review*, Vol.55, No.12 (30 June 2003), pp.17–18; Con Coughlin, 'Mohammad Atta's Iraqi Conection', *London Telegraph*, 15 December 2003, available at ⟨http://www.frontapgemag.com/Articles/Printable.asp?ID = 11313⟩.

9. Gunaratna, pp.30–45; US Congress, Senate Committee on Foreign Relations (2001), *The Global Reach of Al-Qaeda*, 107th Congress, 1st session, US Senate (Washington, DC: US GPO Y 4.F 76/2:S.HRG. 107–390), p 5 et seq.

10. Sean K. Anderson, 'Warnings versus Alarms: Terrorist Threat Analysis Applied to the Iranian State-Run Media', *Studies in Conflict and Terrorism*, Vol.21 (Fall 1998), pp.277–303.

11. Federation of American Scientists Military Analysis Network, ⟨http://www.fas.org/man/dod-101/ops⟩, maintained by John Pike.

12. Alex P. Schmid and Janny de Graaf, *Violence As Communication: Insurgent Terrorism and the Western News Media* (London and Beverly Hills, CA: Sage Publications, 1982), pp.53–4.

13. Anderson, Fig.1

14. Jerrold M. Post, 'It's Us Against Them: The Group Dynamics of Political Terrorism', *Terrorism*, Vol.10, No.1 (1987), p.34.

PIRA Lessons Learned: A Model of Terrorist Leadership Succession

ANDREW GARFIELD

Much has been written about Al Qaeda and its leader Osama bin Laden since 11 September 2001 ('9/11'), although most books and papers have under-standably focused on the period before that fateful day. Much less has and can be written about Al Qaeda post 9/11 because it has been driven 'underground' as a result of the global war against terrorism. What we do know is that those remaining members of the Al Qaeda leadership not already arrested or killed are on the run or in hiding. It seems certain that bin Laden himself is still alive and probably holed up in Pakistan close to the Afghan border. Other leaders have dispersed globally and are probably hiding within and moving covertly between sympathetic Islamic communities right across the Middle East, Europe, the Far East and Africa. Whilst it is certain that the global war against terrorism led by the United States has severely impacted Al Qaeda's operational capabilities and freedom of maneuver, it has not prevented this group from reorganizing, as well as recruiting and training limited numbers of new operatives. The group itself, or its affiliates and those inspired by it, have also continued to conduct deadly operations in numerous countries, although so far not on the scale of 9/11.

In the face of the most concerted and coordinated international effort ever implemented to defeat terrorism, how has this group managed to survive? How has it reorganized and who is now leading it? Just as important, who are the likely future leaders who will eventually replace the last remaining 'founding fathers' like Osama bin Laden? These are serious questions that even the combined might of the US intelligence community is struggling to answer. This is understandable, given the nature of this now highly secretive, ethnically diverse and globally dispersed network. In the absence of, at the very least, adequate open source data, how can we answer these vital questions and predict the next evolution of this deadly menace? One possible solution is to study the emergence and evolution of leadership within another terrorist organization. Such analysis will not tell us whom the new and emerging leaders of al Qaeda actually are but it might help us to frame the right questions to ask our intelligence collectors. To that end, this essay will re-examine the leadership succession of the Provisional Irish Republican Army (PIRA) for possible indicators that might be useful in our battle with Al Qaeda.

INTO THE ABYSS

The catalyst for the re-emergence of terrorism in Northern Ireland was the neither the unifying nationalist ideology of the minority Catholic population nor the twin pillars of republican resistance: 'abstention' from the UK-controlled political process and the 'armed struggle' against the British 'Crown'. In fact, what rekindled terrorism in that long-troubled province was the response of the majority Protestant community and the British authorities to the large-scale civil rights movement that emerged in the late 1960s to protest against the real and perceived oppression, discrimination and injustice felt by the Catholic community in Northern Ireland.

Most Protestants felt significantly threatened by Catholic demands for equal representation, equality and security and responded to the protests and marches with aggressive and often violent action. The authorities effectively condoned attacks by large vigilante gangs of hard-line Protestant 'loyalists' by not stopping them. By the summer of 1969, violent attacks on Catholics were commonplace and reports began to surface of Catholics being intimidated into leaving their homes. This inevitably led to rioting and chaos.

Against this background of civil rights protest and often-violent confrontation between nationalists on one side and the police and loyalist gangs on the other, the Irish Republican Army (IRA) was able to do very little to defend the Catholic community. Indeed, as Catholic communities burned in August 1969, some even suggested that the IRA actually stood for

'I Ran Away'. To add insult to injury, it was the British Army and not the IRA that deployed to protect the nationalist community as law and order broke down.

This situation came about because, by the late 1960s, the IRA had become dominated by leaders, based in Eire, who espoused a Marxist–Leninist political approach rather than 'abstention' and the 'armed struggle'. These leaders had come to prominence following the defeat of the IRA in the 'border war' that ended in 1962. As a result of this military defeat, the twin pillars of republicanism were rejected and a predominately political campaign was embraced. The military wing became largely dormant, little training was undertaken and arms caches were not maintained and replenished. As a result, in the fall of 1969, the IRA was not in a position to rally its remaining 'volunteers' even to defend Catholic communities then under 'attack'.

There were, however, a number of senior IRA figures in Northern Ireland who had always opposed this political approach and they continued to advocate 'abstention' and the 'armed struggle'. These leaders were incensed at the IRA's failure to defend Catholics in the ghettos of Belfast and Derry, claiming that the southern-based leadership was out of touch with reality on the ground. They also realized that the social conditions were right to rekindle the republican flame. They therefore moved quickly to displace the old leadership, forming a new 'Provisional' IRA. What remained of the old IRA called itself the Official IRA and continued in existence for many years, also carrying out a more limited terrorist campaign. It was the 'Provisionals', however, who went on to dominate the war in Ireland.

INDIVIDUAL MOTIVATIONS – WHY DO THEY BECOME TERRORISTS?

All too often our understanding of the mindset of terrorist leaders is unduly influenced by the actions of the group and our own feelings of anger, revulsion and an understandable desire for justice/retribution. In reality the reasons why a person might resort to terrorism and become a terrorist leader are multifaceted and complex. In the case of the early leaders of the PIRA this was certainly the case. It is also important to remember that the vast majority of Catholics who joined the PIRA did so for what seemed to them and their community to be the most honorable of reasons. These individuals and their extended families did not view themselves as 'murdering cowards' but as 'patriots', 'soldiers' and 'freedom fighters'. Given this abiding belief in the legitimacy of their cause and of their actions, it is necessary for us to develop an in-depth understanding of their motivations.

Ideology
The IRA entered the current conflict with a hard core of supporters and operatives whose main motivation was no different than their

ancestors – the withdrawal of the Crown and the creation of a United Ireland. Whilst the southern-based leadership may have embraced a political approach in 1962, many in the North held the firm belief that the republican cause would only succeed through 'abstention' and a return to the 'armed struggle'. This type of absolutist cause had particular appeal to the many young people in the nationalist community who had little hope in their lives.

Tradition

The Republican tradition was literally handed down from father to son and daughter and even today, some 30 years later, family/tribal allegiance to the cause continues to fill the ranks of the PIRA. Gerry Adams is typical – his father, grandfather and several uncles were leading republicans and he married into a family with a similar tradition and pedigree.

Desperation

Many of those who joined the PIRA from 1969 onwards were not from republican families. The discrimination experienced by most Catholics in the 1960s had created a large Catholic underclass of angry, bored and somewhat impoverished young men and women who were easily persuaded that a campaign of civil disobedience was the only way to improve their lot. A common theme from interviews conducted with this generation was the sense of hopelessness, despair and betrayal (by the system) they all felt. The attitude of many was not that dissimilar to that felt by many Palestinians today and worryingly by second generation Muslims living in European countries – 'when one has nothing, one has nothing to lose'. When seen from this perspective it is a short walk from civil disobedience to groups like the PIRA and Al Qaeda.

Anger

The authorities' draconian and violent crackdown on the civil rights movement, combined with its failure to control the loyalist mobs, further radicalized many nationalists. The early aggressive response of the British Army and the policy of internment further alienated this nationalist community and provided the PIRA with a large pool of willing recruits who were motivated by feelings of anger and a desire for revenge.

Self-Defence

Another theme from interviews was the feeling that it was one's duty to join the PIRA to defend one's community from the threats it faced. This is a powerful emotion that was ruthlessly exploited. Many of those who joined the PIRA in the early days appear to have been motivated far more by this essentially honorable desire than by any broader republican aspirations or advocacy of an 'armed struggle'. The majority of those motivated by this desire eventually left the movement but a significant minority were efficiently indoctrinated and joined the ranks of the PIRA.

Religious Extremism

Religion did not define the PIRA and did not motivate the majority of Catholics to join the group but it did provided a bedrock of devotion and tradition that benefited the PIRA, enabling it to use the power of the parish priest to maintain control of the community in which it operated. These 'radical' clerics also provided divine justification and absolution for terrorist acts. The religious dimension was also used to exaggerate the pre-existing division that existed between the two traditions in order to further enflame ethnic hatred and rivalry.

Youthful Exuberance

A further dimension should not be underestimated as a factor for joining a terrorist movement – the idealism, recklessness and exuberance of the young. Many under the age of 25 were also caught up in the excitement and romanticism of the 'armed struggle' and were easy prey for terrorist recruiters. This was particularly true in the poor working-class areas of Belfast and Derry, where mass unemployment and boredom had already created a disillusioned young underclass who actively sought external dangerous stimuli, for example 'joy riding'. Again, we are seeing a similar situation develop amongst young second-generation Muslim immigrants in most European countries.

Group Dependence

Worth noting as a factor that motivates individuals to remain in the group, if not join it, is group dependence and reinforcement. Once a volunteer has joined he or she becomes almost totally isolated from normal society, grievances and prejudices are reinforced and psychological interdependencies are created. A collective mindset also emerges that reinforces the shared ideology. The group becomes the only source of information, the only source of confirmation and in the face of external danger, the only source of security. A sense of 'regimental spirit' is also created, so that 'not letting anyone one down' becomes a powerful driver. This was demonstrated during the PIRA hunger strikes, when 'staying the course' and not 'letting down those who had already died' became as important as the actual reasons for the strikes. In such circumstances, defection from the group is a destructive act for oneself and one's friends and cannot be contemplated. Terrorist leaders of course encourage this group dependency.

Poverty – Not a Factor

Poverty, as we would understand the term, was not a significant factor that encouraged many to join the PIRA. Whilst many Catholic youths were unemployed they still benefited from the United Kingdom's relatively generous welfare state and the support of family members who had employment. That said, relative to the Protestant majority and the rest of the United Kingdom, most Catholics had less wealth, felt disadvantaged and believed that they were being denied equal status. Their own faith and traditions, political intransigence and opposition to the state also contributed to this sense of discrimination, humiliation and inferiority. It is important to bear this in mind, because many Muslims, who do enjoy relative wealth in the West, appear to feel similarly disadvantaged, discriminated against and denied basic freedoms. They too tend to exclude themselves because of their faith, traditions and ethnic background. If Al Qaeda and other Islamic extremists can tap into this discontent as successfully as the PIRA did, we could see as much as 10 per cent of any Muslim immigrant community become active supporters of the terrorists.

TERRORIST LEADERSHIP

Three-Generation Theory

Based on an analysis of the PIRA, it is assessed that there have been at least two and possibly three distinct generations of leadership in that group. It is important to note, however, that although these three generations have emerged sequentially, they may well all be in positions of power at the same time. These generations are designated as; early or founding leaders; follow-on and continuity leaders; and embryonic leaders (See Table 1).

Early leaders are those individuals who formed/established PIRA and led this group during the first period of its existence (1969–75). Follow-on and continuity leaders are those individuals who replaced the 'early leaders' after the group had been operating for some time. They were usually much younger, even more committed/devout and more capable, they also shared many of the same motivations and traits as the early leaders. Initial follow-on leaders joined the group when it was formed and where often personally recruited by the early leaders. There is, however, a distinct transition between these two generations, as the 'follow-on' leaders fundamentally redefined and reorganized the movement, taking it in a new strategic direction.

Third generation 'embryonic' leaders are defined as individuals who do not fit the profile of most or all previous leaders. They have not yet taken up senior leadership roles but are in a position to do so. They are young and highly motivated and could modify or expand the 'cause,' change the goals and

TABLE 1
PIRA LEADERSHIP GENERATIONS

	Early founding leaders (1st generation)	Follow-on and continuity leaders (2nd generation)	Embryonic leaders (3rd generation?)
Time period	1969–1975	1978 to present	Present
Examples	MacStiofain; McKee; O'Bradaigh; O'Conail	Adams; McGinnis; Sands (+ clients for CL)	Not identified
Leadership role	Formed/established PIRA	Redefined/reorganized movement in new strategic direction	Junior middle ranking
	Developed military strategy	Developed dual track (military & political) strategy	Implement political strategy
	Provide strategic direction and tactical control	Provide strategic direction but devolved tactical control	
Description	Working class	Working class & middle class	Working class & middle class
	Veteran terrorists	Joined group when formed	Attracted to Shin Féin over PIRA
	Street smart rather than educated	More capable via universal education	Well educated (up to and including graduate level)
	30s & 40s	Early 20s	20s & Early 30s
	Command respect but not charismatic	Cult of personality formed	'Political' constituency organizers

objectives of the movement, reorganize and restructure, or adopt a new strategic direction if they eventually take control.

The Early Leaders

Not unlike Al Qaeda, with its links to the Afghanistan war, the early leaders of the new Provisional IRA were already experienced terrorists, most of whom had been blooded in the failed border campaign which ended in 1962. These 'hard-men' from Northern Ireland had watched in frustration and anger as the southern-based leadership adopted a Marxist–Leninist political approach that rejected the principals of 'abstention' and the 'armed struggle'. The events of 1969 further inflamed their passions and the failure of the IRA to adequately defend the nationalist community stiffened their determination to break from the current leadership and re-launch the fight, at least in the North. In this respect, their reputation and in most cases long family tradition, were vital factors ensuring the success of their succession. They had credibility as both leaders and fighters and had earned the respect of most IRA men in Northern

Ireland. Individuals such as MacStiofain, O'Bradaigh, O'Conail and McKee dominated the newly created Provisional Army Council, with MacStiofain (an Englishman who had joined the republican movement in the 1950s) becoming its first chief of staff.

This new leadership was mature, in their 30s and 40s and they came from broadly similar working class backgrounds. Whilst few could be described as well educated, most were intelligent and all were 'street-smart'. To varying degrees, they understood the dynamics of the socio-economic and political activism of the time and correctly recognized that it afforded them an opportunity to re-ignite the 'armed struggle'. MacStiofain in particular was able to think strategically and he drew up a plan which attempted to shape more than simply a day by day war: first, to promote the PIRA as defenders of the people; second, to retaliate against those responsible for the violence and discrimination in order to provoke a disproportionate reaction; and last, to escalate the 'armed struggle' in order to 'eject the Brits'.

Whilst none of these leaders could be described as particularly charismatic, thanks to their established reputation as seasoned veterans and in some cases by dint of their personal efforts to defend nationalists against the Loyalist mobs, these leaders did command respect. It also helped that they were perceived as men of integrity, given that they had remained ideologically committed to the 'armed struggle' and abstention when many others had not. Their reputation as ruthless killers also ensured that they were feared. They were able to exploit this respect and fear to develop a 'cult of personality' that allowed them to persuade most volunteers to switch to the Provisionals. They were also able to motivate many young Catholics to join the PIRA in 1969 and 1970. It is doubtful if these leaders could have carried the support of the bulk of the old IRA without an established reputation and the resulting 'cult of personality'. In this respect, leaders like MacStiofain stand comparison with the first leaders of Al Qaeda.

Follow-on Leaders

Inspired to join the PIRA with those early leaders were a large number of much younger men, some of who would eventually become successful commanders and leaders in their own right, including one Gerry Adams. This cadre included individuals with an established republican background who were radicalized by their experiences in 1968/69. It did not take much to persuade these individuals to join the PIRA given that they had been indoctrinated from a very early age. Many were of good intellect and all had at least a high school education. Few went on to university, mainly because they choose instead to join the PIRA. It is important to remember that outside of the United States there is not the same drive to seek a higher education after school. Terrorist leaders may not have an undergraduate degree but they often are highly intelligent and extremely able.

At the same time, an even larger group joined the PIRA inspired not by any republican ideology but by a desire to defend their community; by anger resulting from the overreaction of authorities; and for a few by a thirst for revenge. The resolve of many of this intake quickly melted away but a substantial hard core were persuaded to become full-time volunteers. From this cadre emerged leaders such as Martin McGinnis and Bobby Sands. Both intakes were far more sophisticated in their understanding of the dynamics of the crises and the opportunities it presented than were the 'early leaders' of the PIRA. This was due in no small part to the impact of universal education.

These follow-on leaders very quickly had the opportunity to demonstrate their prowess and bravery as 'fighters' and/or their cunning and guile as strategists as the campaign of violence escalated. By 1972, the number of terrorist operations could be numbered in the thousands. Martin McGinnis, for example, rose from street punk to commander of the Derry Brigade in less than five years and had become chief of staff of the PIRA by 1978. In the process, he demonstrated his willingness to take significant risks, his capabilities as a commander and his ruthlessness as a terrorist. He therefore earned the respect of his men 'in the trenches' and had the credibility as a 'fighter' that Gerry Adams never quite achieved. As a result, he built up a 'cult following' that has never waned, even after he joined Shin Féin and appeared to embrace the peace process. Indeed it could be argued that it was his acceptance of the peace process that won over many skeptical volunteers and junior commanders.

Gerry Adams's own rise to the leadership of the PIRA was similarly spectacular. However, his emergence was due more to his abilities to manipulate the organization and as a strategist rather than as a 'fighter'. Although there is some circumstantial evidence that he personally took part in operations there was also a considerable amount of exaggeration of his 'war record'. This lack of 'street cred' might have prevented Adam's from leading the PIRA were it not for the fact that his chief ally has long been Martin McGinnis. Adams could never have persuaded the PIRA to adopt the 'long war' strategy and the 'bullet and ballot box' approach without the support of seasoned and respected field commanders like McGinnis.

These much younger men, mostly in their early 20s, were far more dedicated than the early leaders and were prepared to fight on when these older leaders sought to develop a political dimension to the struggle. This is somewhat ironic given that Gerry Adams himself eventually developed his own dual-track approach. Despite their relative youth, they had strength and clarity of purpose but also flexibility of mind and the ability to think laterally. All believed that 'the end justifies the means' and each had a considerable degree of moral flexibility. Very few ever showed genuine remorse for their victims, only for the damage some atrocities did to their cause. The only limiting factor that these individuals placed on the level of violence used was the damage excessive casualties might do to the cause.

The chief success of this 'follow-on leadership' was their ability to accommodate both the 'military' men, who were predominantly driven by the 'cause', to a lesser extent revenge and a belief in the 'military' route, with strategic thinkers who viewed violence as an arrow in the quiver but were also able to look beyond it and to bend its use in order to facilitate the transition to other strategies. In Belfast in the early 1970s the thinker Adams partnered with 'military men' like Ivor Bell to form the ideal combination needed to take control of that brigade. This approach was echoed at each level of Adams' leadership and reached its fulfillment in his relationship with Martin McGinnis.

The rise of these 'follow-on leaders' was rapid, facilitated in no small part by the success of the UK government's counter-terrorist effort, which eliminated a considerable number of the 'early leaders'. It is somewhat ironic that far more dangerous leaders emerged as a direct result of the success of the UK's counter-terrorism strategy. It is clear, therefore, that a strategy that focuses on senior leadership and does not also include their many able followers runs the risk of missing emergent leaders.

Subsequent changes in leadership were necessitated in part because of attrition but more usually either as a result of manipulation of the mechanics of the organization or because of violent splits. The successful 'follow-on leaders' like Adams were usually able to keep one step ahead of the authorities either by remaining in hiding or by avoiding any action that could directly link them to a terrorist offence. Like mafia leaders many were/are well known to the authorities but they were/are exceptionally difficult to arrest and convict. These leaders were also able to correctly read or engineer opinion within the movement and 'on the streets' in order to time and direct their leadership moves. As part of this manipulation they saw utility in provoking police and Protestant over-reaction in order to establish cause and legitimacy, and to further radicalize the people.

These leaders were almost all utterly dedicated to the ideology of the republican cause and have never wavered from it. They may have embraced a dual track approach but there seems little doubt that their long-term objective remains a United Ireland by any means. Despite advancing age, it is likely that these leaders would quickly revert to the 'armed struggle' if they fail to achieve their goals via democratic means. How long they are prepared to give the peace process is the $64,000 question.

As time passed, a new sub-category of second-generation leaders began to emerge who for the purposes of this essay are designated as 'continuity leaders'. Continuity leaders share essentially the same ideology, background, motivations and traits as the remaining follow-on leaders and may well have been groomed by them for leadership roles. They are likely to be supporters of the remaining follow-on leaders and owe their status and allegiance to their mentors. For that reason they are unlikely to radically change the structure or strategic direction of the organization. They are generally happy to maintain the status quo and are willing to continue to steer the movement in broadly the same direction as the remaining, usually more senior, follow-on leaders like Gerry Adams and Martin McGinness. For these reasons it is assessed that follow-on leaders and continuity leaders are both second generation.

Based on this experience, and in the context of Al Qaeda, it is possible to conclude that the emergent leadership of that network will be drawn from those young hard-core followers personally recruited by Osama bin Laden and other senior leaders during the 1990s. At the present time, many of these potential leaders are probably commanding cells abroad or remain close to one of the senior leadership. The great concern is that, if they follow the PIRA pattern, they will be even more dedicated, ruthless and capable than the current leadership and much more secretive and therefore even more difficult to find. By dint of their dedication, commitment and 'combat record', they too will be able to exploit a 'cult of personality' to motivate the organization and inspire its members to risk or give their lives for the cause.

Third-Generation Leaders

Since the Good Friday agreement in 1997 the PIRA has suspended its combat operations, although it continues to recruit, train and equip its forces. It seems certain that the PIRA will be using this ceasefire to collect intelligence, to enhance its capabilities and to develop new tactics. Its leadership is almost certainly developing a new military strategy to be employed if and when the peace process fails. That leadership has now been in charge of the PIRA, largely unchanged, for over 20 years. Since 1997, few if any have been arrested and none have been killed. Indeed, many jailed leaders have been released as part of the peace process, some of whom are bound to have resumed their 'duties' despite the terms of the peace agreement.

That is not to say that a third generation has not emerged in the wider republican movement. Rather than swelling the ranks of the PIRA, however, these junior and middle ranking leaders have been attracted to Shin Féin instead, probably because this is the most publicly active division at present. Many are middle class and well educated (up to and including graduate level). They appear to be equally committed to the republican cause and are both highly intelligent and cunning. Having advanced within the political wing of the IRA, they have proved themselves highly adept at fund raising, campaigning and the organization of a 'political' constituency. If the peace process breaks down it is conceivable that at least a minority of this possible third generation will become terrorists themselves. Indeed, some would agree that their membership of Shin Féin already puts them in that category. If they do become terrorists they may well prove to the most dangerous and capable leaders yet.

Within the limitations of the law, it is therefore vital that this third generation is monitored and profiled in case the peace process does break down.

Leadership Motivations, Traits and Ambitions

As with all members of a terrorist/irregular group, the motivations of the PIRA leadership are multi-various. These motivations differ little between early and follow-on leaders. The most common single motivating factors are either the 'the cause' or a perceived need to 'defend ones community'. More usually, however, leaders are motivated by a combination of these and other factors. These can include hatred of the authorities, another community or a different religious tradition, and revenge for real or perceived wrongs including the death or arrest of family and group members by the authorities.

Like leaders in most other areas of human endeavor, many terrorist leaders are driven by a strong desire for power and the status accorded to those in positions of authority. For a few, the lack of any alternative way of life drove them into the organization but was not a significant factor in their leadership aspirations. The buzz and intellectual challenge of terrorist violence was, however, and a substantial minority developed a fondness for violence. Only a tiny minority of terrorist leaders have been principally motivating by money, as this is not a 'business' in which the 'management' gets rich, unless of course the group evolves into a criminal gang, which some have.

Leadership Style

There is no common style of leadership in the PIRA. The most successful leaders combine a number of styles to best effect. Leaders do, however, fall into distinct categories. 'Early leaders' usually inspired respect through the strength of their personality, by their commitment to the 'cause', and because of their success as tactical commanders. They were the ideological focus of the group, its public face and its military commanders. This of course exposes them to capture or worse.

'Follow-on leaders' usually fell into two different categories. First, there were those who had demonstrated their suitability for command by participating in and eventually leading successful operations. As word of their exploits spread, they gained the respect and support of the 'volunteers'. With these sound operational credentials they were able to rule through reputation, success, fear and strength of character. Martin McGinnis would definitely fall into this category. Then there were those who have charismatic personalities and the strategic vision necessary to inspire members and build a powerful constituency within the group, despite having little or no operational experience. They had the intellect to plan and lead a multi-faceted campaign and the political skills needed to manipulate the organization in order to engineer their own rise to prominence. They were also accomplished 'spin doctors', able to publicly promote themselves and the movement, goad the authorities and manipulate the media.

All of these leaders used a combination of carrot and stick, patronage and punishment in order to control the group. Supporters were raised to key posts to ensure that a leader's plans were implemented and as a reward for loyalty. However, failure, indiscretion or insubordination was usually punished ruthlessly. All these leaders were/are well aware that fear is a proven and powerful tool in irregular forces both to dissuade challenge and maintain order. There is plenty of circumstantial evidence, for example, that the leadership of the PIRA have used violence, including severe beatings, 'knee-capping' and execution, to maintain 'good order and discipline'. Of particular note is the ability of certain leaders to keep both supporters and rivals constantly off balance through intentional inconsistency in their leadership style. Maintaining an element of doubt and fear in the minds of even loyal supporters is a particular effective way of keeping them 'honest'.

Successful terrorist leaders have also shown their ability to modify their leadership style depending on external circumstances and the prevalent mood of the organization. The leadership of the PIRA has on occasions shown an apparent willingness to listen to supporters and the wider movement but then switched to a dictatorial style in order to drive through a new policy or a change in strategy. When necessary, they have also shown the ability to switch between a centralized command and control structure to maintain tight 'rule', for example during ceasefires, and then devolve significant command responsibility to subordinates in order to preserve the security of the organization during conflict.

Another aspect of leadership style common to the PIRA and most terrorist groups is a tendency to rely on a very small group of trusted advisers. These advisors are allowed to act for the leader at some levels of the organization, communicating ideas and canvassing responses. Indeed sometimes these advisors float new concepts as their own, in case they receive a negative response from the membership. Gerry Adams has been particularly adept at selecting advisors he can trust and who can provide him with useful advice. These have been drawn from both the military wing and from Shin Féin. The danger, of course, in a system based on the 'cult of personality', is that these advisors will tell the leader what he wants to hear rather than what he needs to hear. They were also able to exert undue influence on the leader. This of course can be an advantage for security forces if exploited intelligently.

CONCLUSION

The PIRA is a hugely successful terrorist organization that has come close to defeat several times since 1969 but each time has adapted in order to overcome the challenges presented by the United Kingdom's best efforts to combat this particular terrorist menace. The author would therefore suggest that, despite the obvious differences in culture and ideology, there is much that can still be learnt from this group with regard to how Al Qaeda might evolve and who might emerge as its new leaders.

11 September 2001 has shown all too vividly that, in the global war against this adversary, we have to look for every edge we can find. Reviewing the emergence and evolution of other terrorist groups might just give us that edge. At the very least it can provide pointers. We must undertake such analysis because we cannot afford to leave any stone unturned.

Challenging the Hegemon: Al Qaeda's Elevation of Asymmetric Insurgent Warfare Onto the Global Arena

KIMBRA L. FISHEL

INTRODUCTION: AL QAEDA AS A GLOBAL REVOLUTIONARY POWER

On 11 September 2001 ('9/11'), America woke up. The war that had been declared against the United States in 1996[1] by Osama bin Laden's Al Qaeda network finally struck in that country's mainland. The attack on the United States not only destroyed the Twin Towers in New York City, struck the top of the US military hierarchy, the Pentagon, and caused the crash of a commercial jetliner in Pennsylvania before it could reach its designated target, it also ushered in a realization that, whether it desired it or not, the US was involved in a global war of epic proportions. Al Qaeda had succeeded in doing what no other terrorist organization had previously accomplished. It succeeded in elevating asymmetric, insurgent warfare onto the global arena.

Much has been written about asymmetric insurgent warfare at the local and regional levels. One of the most prominent contemporary theories utilized by practitioners as well as scholars is the 'Sword model', or Manwaring paradigm.[2] This model is derived from a succession of security studies that initially stemmed from a 1984 call by then Vice Chief of Staff of the Army, General Maxwell Thurman, to examine the correlates of success in counterinsurgency. The Manwaring paradigm identifies and analyses those variables that affect the outcome of insurgent warfare, drug operations and peace operations. It has been established through both quantitative and qualitative analysis and identifies seven dimensions that are critical to success. These studies all focus on threats within the existing international system and have not yet been applied to entities that challenging the international system itself.

Similarly, under the rubric of grand theory, realist international relations scholars have discussed extensively the imperial or revolutionary state power that seeks to overthrow the existing international system. Classical realist Hans Morgenthau[3] wrote of imperial state powers operating outside the international structure with the goal of overthrowing the existing system to place something else in its stead. Nazi Germany, under Adolf Hitler, is a case in point. Robert Gilpin,[4] relying heavily on economic theories, discusses power distributions among states and how uneven growths in technological, military or economic power over time may convince an unhappy power that the benefits of attempting to change the existing international structure may outweigh the risks. Such crisis situations destabilize the international system. They can result in a specific type of warfare, hegemonic warfare, engaged in to overthrow the existing system. This is a fundamentally different type of warfare than that which is engaged in within the existing international structure. Grand-scale theories on international change such as those by Morgenthau and Gilpin apply to states, and asymmetric entities are not expanded upon.

Neither regional insurgency theories nor grand-scale theories are adequate for explaining Al Qaeda's actions. Al Qaeda has elevated the tools and techniques of the regional revolutionary onto the global level, something only states had previously been able to accomplish successfully. Al Qaeda has transformed an asymmetric, non-state actor into a power that it perceived as capable of challenging the existing international system, dominated by what it calls 'the West' and headed by the United States. Why Al Qaeda perceived such a goal was possible and how it evolved into a global insurgent power, in effect, declaring 'hegemonic war', are questions that this essay seeks to answer. Insights to those answers may be found in utilizing the Manwaring paradigm and the concepts of international revolutionary state powers, and modifying and applying these theories to the objectives of Al Qaeda, the development of Al Qaeda's strategy and its ability to adapt that strategy to US response.

THE MANWARING PARADIGM

According to the Manwaring paradigm, the successful prosecution of seven dimensions is critical to success in insurgent warfare: legitimacy, unity of effort, military actions of intervening power, support actions of intervening

TABLE 1
DIMENSIONS OF THE SWORD MODEL

Original Sword dimension	Dimension as applied to Al Qaeda
Legitimacy	Legitimacy
Unity of effort	Unity of effort
Military actions of intervening power	Al Qaeda strategy against counter-terrorist actions
Support actions of intervening powers	Al Qaeda strategies against support actions
External support to insurgents	External support to Al Qaeda
Actions versus subversion	Al Qaeda's actions versus subversion
Host country military operations	Al Qaeda strategy to weaken host military actions

power, host country military actions, actions against subversion including intelligence/psychological operations/population and resource control, external support to insurgents. Because these dimensions are applied to conflict within a state and external powers seeking to aid states in counterinsurgent, counter-drug or peace operations, it is necessary to rename the dimensions so that they better apply to challenges to the international system itself, when there is in effect no 'external power' to come to the aid or rescue of the weaker power.[5] Table 1 shows the original dimensions and the corresponding 'new' name for each dimension as applied to Al Qaeda. These dimensions, when applied to Al Qaeda strategy, illustrate how Al Qaeda has elevated insurgency onto the global level.

Al Qaeda's strategy, like all strategy, consists of three main components: objectives or goals (ends), the tactics or operations brought about to acquire those goals (ways), and the ability to obtain the resources necessary to support its operations and achieve its stated goals (means). The manner in which ends, ways and means are integrated with the seven dimensions of insurgent warfare is illustrated in Table 2.

Al Qaeda's global revolutionary nature is inherent in its goal, that of overthrowing the existing world structure, destroying the United States and instituting in its place Al Qaeda's version of the next Islamic caliphate. For Al Qaeda, the existing system is illegitimate because it deviates from their version of what the world should be. One need look no further than the pre 9/11 Taliban's rule in Afghanistan to find Al Qaeda's model of the ideal state. The way in which Al Qaeda seeks to bring about the downfall of the West is through warfare, relying primarily on the tactic of terrorism, although conventional battles are fought as well. In addition, Al Qaeda continually seeks to push conflict from the low intensity and conventional realms into the high intensity realm through the acquisition of weapons of mass destruction (WMD). The resources needed to support these goals and operations include money, which requires an international financial network, support of other

TABLE 2

MODIFIED MANWARING DIMENSIONS AND AL QAEDA STRATEGY

Al Qaeda strategy dimensions	Ends	Ways	Means
Al Qaeda strategy against counter-terrorist actions and military actions	Creation of Islamic front with nuclear capability	Direct attacks on US military such as USS Cole and Al Khobar barracks	Planners, operators, equipment, explosives, arms, finances, misc.
Al Qaeda strategy against support actions of intervening power	Establish roots of problems of Muslim world lie with US	Al Qaeda bombings of US embassies in Africa	Same as above
Legitimacy	Identify fatwa's and Koran – de jure; est. of Islamic caliphate in Saudi Arabia – de facto; destruction of US and the West – de Facto legitimacy	International legitimacy is rejected: Use of mass casualties to gain legitimacy among supporters and establish a new global legitimacy	Planners, couriers, recording equipment, computers and same as above
External support to Al Qaeda	Expand global support network	Global operational infrastructure with satellite organizations	Leaders, planners, recruiters, communicators, coordinators, followers, other organizations
Al Qaeda actions versus subversion	Obtain effective intelligence; establish world view	Observations/involvement in conflicts around the globe; indoctrination of recruits	Intel planners, intel operators, intel analysts, propagandists, educators, finances, equipment
Al Qaeda strategy to weaken military actions of host country	Subvert host country military	Collect intelligence on military; infiltrate supporters into host country military	intel planners and operators, sympathizers in high places, highly placed recruits
Unity of effort	Creation of 'true Islamic' states in Middle East	Vertical leadership structure; horizontal network of compartmentalized cells; ability to shift from vertical to horizontal	Leaders, planners, network, communications, finances

governments friendly to Al Qaeda and factions within states willing to give Al Qaeda aid, sanctuary and personnel.

Al Qaeda's Strategy: Ends

Al Qaeda has been anything but reticent in its stated goals or its desire to kill Americans. The United States recognized this threat as well, although it did so more in legalistic terms rather than appraising and responding to an enemy that had declared war. For example, the United States indicted Osama bin Laden, and in 1999 the United States compiled a list of statements by bin Laden and associated organizations that included the following:[6]

1. Osama bin Laden's 1996 declaration of jihad from Afghanistan, 'Message from Usama bin Laden to his Muslim brothers in the Whole World and Especially in the Arabian Peninsula: Declaration of Jihad Against the Americans Occupying the Land of the Two Holy Mosques; Expel the Heretics from the Arabian Peninsula.'
2. The February 1998 fatwa Against American citizens in which bin Laden and Ayman al Zawahiri endorsed a fatwa, 'International Islamic Front for Jihad on the Jews and Crusaders', that stated Muslims should kill all Americans anywhere in the world.
3. The May 1998 fatwa issued by the 'Ulema Union of Afghanistan' in which bin Laden endorsed a declaration of jihad against the United States and its followers and termed the US Army the 'enemies of Islam'.
4. Osama bin Laden's 1998 statement entitled the 'Nuclear Bomb of Islam', in which he states it is the duty of Muslims to prepare as much force as possible to terrorize the enemies of God.

In Al Qaeda's communiqués and declarations, it invariably attempts to rely upon de jure legitimacy in an attempt to acquire universal de facto legitimacy among Muslims. De jure legitimacy, or legitimacy grounded in law, for Al Qaeda is found in the many fatwas released according to shariah law and its attempt to invoke the Koran to support its position. This attempt at de jure legitimacy is only one part of an attempt to gain de facto legitimacy, perceived legitimacy among Muslims for their cause, for their war against the United States and the West, and comes directly from the strategic ends of global revolution.

However, Osama bin Laden is not endorsing the killing of Americans merely for the sake of killing Americans. Al Qaeda has both short-term and long-term goals with evolving strategies. Prior to the attacks on 9/11, Al Qaeda's immediate goal was the US withdrawal of forces from Saudi Arabia and the establishment there of an Islamic caliphate.[7] Al Qaeda is attacking the legitimacy of the Saudi government while at the same time attempting to acquire de facto legitimacy for its actions based upon a type of theological global nationalism among Muslims. In an interview with Al Qaeda expert Peter Bergen, bin Laden stated that in his view the main problem of the Islamic world was the injustices visited upon Muslims by the United States. Therefore, he would foment a revolution in Saudi Arabia, and there a new regime would be established to rule in accordance with the seventh-century precepts of the Prophet Muhammad.[8] Here, Al Qaeda attempts to delegitimize the country in which it is operating, Saudi Arabia, and focuses the blame for perceived injustices by Muslims upon the outside or intervening power, the United States.

Al Qaeda's medium-term goal was what bin Laden referred to as the ouster of 'apostate rulers' in the Middle East, including those in the Arabian peninsula. In their place, true Islamic states would be created. More and more Islamic states would be created so that Al Qaeda's long term goal could be realized – the creation of an Islamic front of states with nuclear capability to wage war on the United States.[9] This goal incorporates the creation of the external support network required for global insurgent actions, seeks to attack and counter the military operations of the intervening power, the United States, through the acquisition of nuclear capability, and finally attempts to create a unity of effort among what Al Qaeda considers 'true' Islamic states. Table 2 illustrates where these specific actions, showing Al Qaeda's strategic ends, fall within the Manwaring dimensions.

In Al Qaeda's strategic goals can be found the following: a virulent hatred of the existing international system that it sees as dominated by the United States and its allies, and oppressing Muslims throughout the world; a desire to overthrow the existing system through a series of stages; and an organization based upon a particular ideology of Islamist fundamentalism.

Although Al Qaeda would never use this language, by implicitly adapting the Sword model and attacking the modified Manwaring dimensions of legitimacy, unity of effort, external support to Al Qaeda, actions against counter-terrorism and military actions of the intervening power and attacking support actions of the intervening power, Al Qaeda has become representative of the traditional global revolutionary or imperial power discussed by Morgenthau or Gilpin. Nazi Germany, the classic imperial power as defined by Morgenthau, shared similarities with these strategic goals, including relying on a type of fanatical ideology to propel it. Although Adolf Hitler was a not a religious leader, he nonetheless invoked fanaticism as the essential element of the Nazi movement. Mobilization of the masses could only be achieved by a total lack of humane consideration and a relentless pursuit of objectives. According to Hitler, 'the greatness of each great movement is rooted in a religious fanaticism totally convinced of its own rightness, intolerant against everything else'.[10] The difference now is that the challenger is not a state that has risen to power to challenge the existing global structure, by rather an asymmetric, non-state entity.

Al Qaeda Strategy: Ways

Al Qaeda has chosen the tactic of terrorism with the underlying concept of jihad as its primary vehicle for achieving it strategic goals. Al Qaeda has organized in such a way that allows it, as an asymmetric power, to elevate its terrorist operations and tactics onto the global arena. The Manwaring dimensions given in Table 2 are again useful in illustrating those actions that Al Qaeda has taken to globalize is strategic ways, thus showing that Al Qaeda's operational infrastructure and organization are unprecedented – at the level of the international system.

At the time of 9-11, Al Qaeda's core base was set in Afghanistan with satellite terrorist organizations spanning the globe. In addition, Al Qaeda relies upon a conglomerate of Islamist political parties and other affiliated terrorist organizations to support its operations.[11] This has truly globalized Manwaring's concept of external support to an insurgent power to far-reaching, global support for a challenging asymmetric organization. It goes far beyond the state support of insurgent organizations prevalent during the Cold War. Al Qaeda's high command consists of a vertical leadership structure that provides 'strategic direction and tactical support to its horizontal network of compartmentalized cells and associate organizations'.[12] In this way, Al Qaeda created strong unity of effort within the terrorist network but, perhaps more importantly, Al Qaeda's structure allowed for fairly rapid shifting of operational control.

The US invasion of Afghanistan dealt a major blow to Al Qaeda's core base, but Al Qaeda has shifted its strategy to rely more on horizontal compartmentalized cells rather than strictly vertical chains of command, thus preserving a working degree of unity of effort. Thus, Al Qaeda has achieved a strategic adaptation of ways to achieve ends, particularly through unity of effort and external support. It is the degree to which Al Qaeda has proved adaptive to counter operations that has allowed it to maintain its global revolutionary status over two years since its attacks on the United States.

One way of conceptualizing Al Qaeda's operational framework has been described as concentric circles.[13] The inner circle consists of the Al Qaeda organization itself, composed of several hundred members who have sworn allegiance to Osama bin Laden. The second ring consists of several thousand 'holy warriors' who trained in the terrorist camps of Afghanistan. The third ring consists of thousands of Islamist militants who trained in Afghanistan over the past ten years, many of whom were to fight with the Taliban against the Northern Alliance. Finally, the outer ring consists of those Muslims around the world who subscribe to Osama bin Laden's particular view of the West as the enemy of Islam.[14] Its very way of organization is one of the factors that enabled Al Qaeda to become the global revolutionary power that its strategic goals require – it gives Al Qaeda a global presence while at the same time allowing it to shift control over operations from the vertical to the horizontal as necessity dictates.

Al Qaeda's structure and global reach allow it to carry out such diverse terrorist operations as the 1993 bombing of the World Trade Center, the 1995 bombing of the Al Khobar barracks in Saudi Arabia, the 1998 bombing of US embassies in Nairobi and Dar es Salaam, the October 2000 attack on the USS Cole, and the 2001 attack on the US mainland. Despite clear attacks on US interests that were, in fact, acts of war, only a direct attack on the US mainland was sufficient to place the US on a war footing.

Al Qaeda's direct attacks against US interests fall under the dimension of Al QAEDA strategy against the support actions of the United States as well as its strategy against US military actions. While Al Qaeda carried out its offensive terrorist operations, its 'ways' of achieving objectives also fall under the Al Qaeda actions versus subversion dimension. This includes intelligence, psychological operations and population and resource control.

Al Qaeda was heavily involved in and/or observant of conflicts around the globe including Somalia, Chechnya, Iraq and the former Yugoslavia, particularly Bosnia. Al Qaeda's involvement and observation of conflict around the globe and the way the United States handled those conflicts is a primary factor in Al Qaeda's perception of its ability to successfully challenge the power of the United States and its massive attack on 9/11. Al Qaeda operatives observed and reported on US tactics in these areas and regularly pointed to what it perceived to be the US defeat in Somalia and Lebanon and even Iraq (due to the fact that Hussein was left in power after the First Gulf War when the Americans left Iraq.) It was therefore possible to wage a successful war against this hegemonic power that lacked staying power. Al Qaeda's world view and propaganda as well as its perceived capabilities were indoctrinated in recruits through the madrassas, or religious schools, primarily in Pakistan. Thus religious schools became a vehicle for both psychological operations as well as a means of population and resource control. Recruits were indoctrinated with Al Qaeda's goals and mission and equipped with a belief in victory while at the same time trained or organized to become fighters, supporters and financiers of Al Qaeda's global network.

In addition to terrorist operations, guerrilla involvements and other subversive activities, Al Qaeda's quest for weapons of mass destruction plays an integral role in achieving its strategic objectives and is rather interestingly linked to a new form of legitimacy. For Al Qaeda, in the end, only organizations and states with nuclear weapons are seen as capable of destroying the United States and its followers. This is why the weapons of mass destruction—terrorism—rogue state nexus is important. With the rise in weapon states and the dispersion of nuclear material as well as scientific and technological capabilities following the collapse of the Soviet Union, Al Qaeda has the potential ability to acquire nuclear devices to go along with its will to use them. It is this concerted quest for ultimate destructive power and will combined with capability that distinguishes Al Qaeda from other terrorist organizations, in addition to its scope and organizational structure. Despite its utilization of the tactic of terror, Al Qaeda believes that the final way of destroying the existing structure will be through the use of WMD, most notably nuclear weapons.

Political terrorism is the deliberate attack on civilians to achieve a political goal or purpose. Traditional, terrorist organizations have killed handfuls of people in their attacks. Those attacks from typical terrorist organizations that have taken the most lives have killed hundreds. The 1993 Bombay bombings killing 235 people, the 1998 bombing of Pan Am flight 103 over Lockerbie Scotland killing 278 people, and the 1979 arson attack in Abadan, Iran killing 477 people are cases in point.[15] Terrorists seek to create fear and havoc while at the same time making a demonstration of their abilities to gain attention to their cause. They are indiscriminate in their killings in that theoretically anyone could be targeted. However, there is a certain level of restraint traditionally exercised so that organizations do not lose the support they have from their followers and also so that they can entice the state into overreacting to the point of alienating their own populations. All this occurs just short of the state taking strong enough actions to actually destroy the terrorists.[16] This is one theory that has been advanced as to why terrorists thus far have not 'gone nuclear'. Besides the difficulty in acquiring and using such weapons, inflicting mass casualties actually works against the objectives of most non-state actors.[17] According to terrorism expert Brian Jenkins, 'terrorists want a lot of people watching, not a lot of people dead'.[18] Once the threat level is deemed high enough by the state, all states, including liberal democracies, will respond accordingly.

Whether or not the theory that inflicting mass casualties is counter-productive is actually correct, Al Qaeda differs from other terrorist organizations in that it has demonstrated a willingness and the ability to inflict mass casualties on a large scale. 9/11 demonstrated this as the result of a conventional terrorist attack.[19] The attempted attack on the World Trade Center in 1993 also demonstrated such willingness, although the operation itself was unsuccessful in that outcome. There is no doubt that, as British Prime Minister Tony Blair stated, had they been able to kill hundred of thousands rather than thousands they would have done so. Such willingness and ability may be a requirement for an asymmetric power to become a global revolutionary power. Concerns of maintaining 'international legitimacy' by not inflicting mass casualties are not relevant for this type of power. Since Al Qaeda is operating outside the existing international structure, which it sees as illegitimate and seeks its destruction, it is attempting to create a new legitimacy, with a base of supporters that *seeks* that type of mass destruction. The more Al Qaeda can inflict damage and casualties, the more its base of supporters will legitimize its actions. Both Muslims and non Muslims who reject Al Qaeda's actions are irrelevant as both must be destroyed – the first because, according to Al Qaeda, they are not true Islamists but rather Muslims who have been Westernized, and the other because they are infidels who bring misery upon the Muslim world. As Tony Blair was correct in his comments, President George W. Bush was equally right in stating just a few days after the attacks on the United States: 'these were more than acts of terrorism. These were acts of war.' And those acts of war were engaged in by an asymmetric power that took Manwaring's dimensions for success in insurgency and revolutionized them onto the global arena itself through strategic means including the use of mass casualty terrorist attacks to help form a new legitimacy. This use of legitimacy turns the original idea of legitimacy inside out and is something new in asymmetric global warfare.

Al Qaeda's Strategy: Means

In order to support its global revolutionary goals and maintain its operations, Al Qaeda must be able to obtain the necessary resources. Table 2 illustrates how Al Qaeda's means for achieving its strategic operations and goals correspond to the modified seven dimensions of the Manwaring paradigm.

Al Qaeda has established a vast financial network across the globe. One commonality of terrorist organizations, especially when confronting democratic states, is that they seek to exploit the weaknesses or vulnerabilities of open societies. The openness and liberal policies of democratic states are focal points. One way Al Qaeda finances its operations is through apparently innocuous means such as mosques and religious charities. When these types of organizations are closely monitored by governments, it inevitably brings ridicule upon government agencies by certain segments of an open society. Surely those agencies are violating the privacy and rights of charitable and religious organizations, probably due to their particular faith. Al Qaeda is well aware of this aspect of liberal societies and incorporates it into its strategic doctrine and training manuals.

Charitable and non governmental organizations may be mere fronts for terrorist organizations, meaning the people involved in the organizations know who they are contributing donations to and that the money contributed goes straight to Al Qaeda or its affiliates. In addition, legitimate organizations have been infiltrated by Al Qaeda personnel who misdirect the money to fund terrorist activities. Still, some organizations have dual roles, one supporting a legitimate charitable cause and one supporting Al Qaeda, a method also used by both Hamas and Hezbollah.[20] Besides charities, Al Qaeda also has business investments; Osama bin Laden's vast global financial network developed to fund the Afghan mujahideen, as well as criminal activities, fund their operations.[21]

In addition to finances, Al Qaeda requires personnel. Contrary to the 'poverty causes terrorism' theory, the main core of Al Qaeda personnel are educated and at least moderately well off. They appeal to a certain segment of Muslim society that defines itself as Islamic terrorists. The importance of this type of identification must be stressed in the context of how the Manwaring dimensions are elevated to the global insurgent realm. As Islamic expert and scholar Bernard Lewis points out, the majority of Muslims are not fundamentalists and the majority of fundamentalists are not terrorists. Although Muslims may complain that the media speak of terrorist movements as 'Islamic' and ask why the media do not identify other terrorist organizations, such as the Basque terrorists or the IRA as 'Christian', there is a simple answer. Those organizations do not identify themselves as such, whereas 'most present day terrorists are Muslims and proudly identify themselves as such'.[22] Indeed, the proud self-identification plays into the de facto legitimacy that Al Qaeda seeks to acquire in setting up a new international structure based upon a new legitimacy. Without this type of self-proclaimed identification, it may not be possible to mobilize supporters on a global level, using a fanatic religious basis in an attempt to reform the world. It is the self-identified Islamist terrorists that have put in place the organizational structures to span the globe and become the asymmetric, global revolutionary threat that exists today.

AL QAEDA AS GLOBAL REVOLUTIONARY

The modified Manwaring paradigm dimensions illustrate how Al Qaeda attempted to take the dimensions that determine outcome in insurgent warfare and elevate them from operations existing within a given international system into a strategic framework for challenging the existing international structure. However, to understand what that may mean requires the addition of concepts from grand scale theories as they apply to revolutionary powers. The fact that in the past those powers have been states is no longer relevant as the Manwaring dimensions have shown how an asymmetric power can attain the same type of position.

From Gilpin comes the idea that perceived benefits in attempting to change the existing international system outweigh the perceived costs on the part of the revolutionary power. Through its exploitation of the modified Manwaring dimensions, Al Qaeda had succeeded in building up a global support base and extending its reach to such an extent that it had the operational capability of striking out at the United States in numerous places in various parts of the world. Its indoctrination of supporters with Al Qaeda propaganda and its view of Islam combined with its interpretation of US defeats in previous conflicts changed the dynamic in which Al Qaeda saw its challenge to the United States and the existing international structure. Technological innovations including communications and mobility combined with linkage networks established by Al Qaeda indicated that shifts in position and power could occur. The use of terror as a mass casualty tactic on the US homeland and the use of insurgent warfare combined with terrorist actions through the world in areas such as Afghanistan, Iraq and the Middle East, the Philippines, Asia and the former Soviet Union all fed into the Al Qaeda perception that it could successfully challenge a global superpower for control over the structure of the international system.

Whether or not these tactics and operations alone could actually destroy the United States is not important because Al Qaeda's final strategic way of achieving its ends relies not on conventional means but on the acquisition of weapons of mass destruction and the creation of Islamic states with nuclear capability. Terrorism, insurgency and conventional warfare are all means to weaken the United States, shake its resolve and enable Al Qaeda to strengthen its hold over its areas of operation. Thus, nuclear weapons and WMD become the big technological jump whose hope of acquisition enables Al Qaeda to further readjust its perception of its ability to defeat the United States. Thus the concept of hegemonic war, as originally discussed by Gilpin, brought on by perceived changes in technological, economic or military power, does apply.

Whereas the Manwaring dimensions have previously applied to conflicts within the existing international system, and operations have often been engaged in to maintain that system, concepts gleaned from Hans Morgenthau apply particularly to Al Qaeda. What Morgenthau calls imperial powers operate outside the existing international system. Their purpose is to overthrow that structure. Therefore the normal rules and procedures, which apply within that structure, may not be useful in combating such a power. Organizations and states that seek to exist within the current international structure may find it particularly difficult to recognize revolutionary or imperial powers for what they are. While entities existing within the system seek means within the system to combat the challenging power, the challenger turns the system against itself while utilizing means defined as illegitimate by the system to accomplish its goal. Al Qaeda's use of mass casualty terrorism as a source for its own legitimacy is a case in point.

Because Al Qaeda is a non-state, terrorist organization rather than a peer competitor state, the problem of understanding Al Qaeda as a global revolutionary power is exacerbated. This may explain why the United States in the 1990s treated Al Qaeda mainly as a law enforcement problem rather than as an enemy in war. Understanding the nature of the threat is an important first step in defeating an enemy who in effect has declared hegemonic war upon an existing international system and maintains a determination to destroy the United States and its allies. By understanding those factors which best lead to success in insurgent warfare and how those factors have been adapted and changed through elevation of insurgent warfare onto the global arena by an asymmetric power, the United States and its allies can be better prepared to fight and defeat an enemy who remains both resourceful and determined.

NOTES

1. For an online transcript of this fatwa, 'Declaration of War Against the Americans Occupying the Land of the Two Holy Places,' see ⟨http://www.Pbs.org/newshour/terrorism/international/fatwa_1996.html⟩. This fatwa was originally published in a London based newspaper, *Al Quds Al Arabi*, in August 1996.
2. See Max G. Manwaring and John T. Fishel, 'Insurgency and Counter-Insurgency: Toward a New Analytical Approach', *Small Wars & Insurgencies*, Vol.3, No.3 (Winter 1992) pp.272–310.
3. See Hans J. Morgenthau, *Politics Among Nations: The Struggle for Power and Peace*, revised by Kenneth W. Thompson (New York: McGraw Hill-Publishing Company, 1985).
4. Robert Gilpin, *War & Change in World Politics* (Cambridge: Cambridge University Press, 1993).
5. The dimensions of the Manwaring paradigm or Sword model were created by factor analysis. Variables in the analysis ended up in seven clusters or factors. Those factors were then called dimensions and given specific names. In John T. Fishel's work, *The Savage Wars of Peace*, those dimensions were applied to peace operations and were renamed accordingly to better fit the circumstances of peace operations, but the variables making up each dimension remained the same. I have done the same here, changing the names of some of the dimensions to better fit the circumstances, but the variables making up the dimensions remain unchanged.
6. There is a wealth of information regarding statements made by Al Qaeda available to the public. See ⟨http://usinfo.state.gov/topical/pol/terror/99129502.htm⟩ for government documents relating to statements by Al Qaeda and its war against the United States. This site from the US Department of State International information Programs refers to FBI websites documenting evidence against bin Laden and illustrates US knowledge of the Al Qaeda threat even in 1999.
7. Rohan Gunaratna, *Inside Al Qaeda Global Network of Terror* (London: Hurst & Co., 2002), p.89.
8. Peter L. Bergen, *Holy War, Inc., Insider the Secret World of Osama bin Laden* (New York: The Free Press, 2001).
9. Gunaratna, p.89.
10. See Walter Lacquer, *No End To War Terrorism in the Twenty-First century* (New York: Continuum International Publishing Group, 2003).
11. Gunaratna, p.54.
12. Ibid.
13. See Peter Bergen, 'The Dense Web of Al Qaeda', *The Washington Post*, 25 December 2003, p.A29. Bergen describes Al Qaeda and its supporters as a structure of concentric rings in which different parts or different rings may take place in different operations.
14. Bergen.

15. Richard A. Falkenrath, Robert D. Newman and Bradley A. Thayer, *America's Achilles Heel Nuclear, Biological, and Chemical Terrorism and Covert Attack* (Cambridge, MA: MIT Press, 2001), p.47.
16. For a full discussion of terrorist tactics and strategies see Kimbra L. Thompson Krueger, 'The Destabilization of Republican Regimes: The Effects of Terrorism On Democratic Societies', *Low Intensity Conflict and Law Enforcement*, Vol.5, No.2 (Autumn 1996), pp.253–77.
17. Falkenrath.
18. Brian M. Jenkins, *Will Terrorists Go Nuclear?*, RAND Report P-5521 (Santa Monica, CA: RAND: 1975), p.4. Also quoted in Falkenrath.
19. Although what are known as apocalyptic groups have always been willing to die for their chosen cause, and take everyone with them, they have not as yet acquired the means to do so.
20. See William F. Wechsler, 'Strangling the Hydra: Targeting Al Qaeda's Finances', in James F. Hoge, Jr and Gideon Rose (eds), *How Did This Happen: Terrorism and the New War* (New York: Council on Foreign Relations, 2001).
21. Ibid.
22. See Bernard Lewis, *The Crisis of Islam, Unholy War and Unholy Terror* (New York: Modern Library, 2003), p.137.

Applying Order-of-Battle to Al Qaeda Operations

LISA J. CAMPBELL

WHY WE SHOULD APPLY ORDER-OF-BATTLE TO AL QAEDA

Terrorism has come to be defined as war and Al Qaeda is in the forefront of terrorist groups who are enemies of the United States. Even North Korea, one of our bigger state enemies, does not currently cause the United States to fear an attack in the heartland or on its ports, as Al Qaeda does. As a result, in some respects Al Qaeda has the attributes of a superpower — not in the weight of its destructive firepower, but in its capacity to potentially collapse a large nation with the use of disruptive targeting. With a conventional state *opposing force (OPFOR)*, we systematically analyze their capabilities and intent, and then build advanced weaponry, technological advances, psychological warfare, political influence and other tactics accordingly. To treat Al Qaeda as a nation-state would be a mistake. However, examining their capabilities and intent, via their order-of-battle (OB), is necessary if we are to put ourselves in a position to make predictions and assess our own OB and counter-methodology accordingly.

A comparison of the OB of Al Qaeda vs that of a traditional nation-state will bring several things to light. Specifically, a one-on-one comparison will reveal a complete mismatch of capabilities. Not in the lopsided way of the United States vs Iraq, but in a way that our conventional OB will not be functional against that of Al Qaeda. Furthermore Al Qaeda's OB is fluid. That is, it is often borrowed, rented or stolen (e.g., a rental truck packed with explosives), which makes the bulk of their weapons temporary and disposable, economically feasible and most importantly, exempt from targeting (Table 1). These *just-in-time* weapons are a phenomenon that allows Al Qaeda to maintain an essentially constant element of surprise. Finally, we will need to reconsider our own conventional forces to keep pace with the emerging threat from Al Qaeda and its affiliates, while maintaining enough conventional OB to counter residual state enemies.

THE NINE ORDER-OF-BATTLE CRITERIA

The nine OB criteria are elements tracked over time and evaluated by intelligence analysts to become sufficiently acquainted with the enemy to know their intent and assess their probable courses of action. Intelligence analysts track OB criteria because they are looking for things that provide indications and warnings of future operations.[1] When observed, subtle and not-so-subtle changes in OB criteria provide warnings to analysts that the enemy is in action. The nine OB criteria are as follows:

· Composition
· Disposition
· Strength figures
· Tactics
· Training
· Logistics
· Combat effectiveness and efficiency
· Electronic technical data
· Miscellaneous data

An expanded definition of these criteria is set forth below.

A basic definition of OB is the identification, strength, command structure and disposition of the personnel, units and equipment of any military force.[2] To some, the definition also includes how an enemy mixes and matches his

TABLE 1

AL QAEDA EQUIPMENT ORDER OF BATTLE (OB)

OB category	Nomenclature	Role	Developmental stage
Air Force	Remote controlled aircraft	Air-to-ground	R&D
	Commercial jet	Air-to-ground/logistics	Used in combat
	Light aircraft	Logistics, training, combat	Used in combat
	Ultralight aircraft	Unknown	R&D
	Crop duster	Unknown	R&D
Missile	Surface-to-air (SAM)	Anti-aircraft (offensive)	Used in combat
Naval	Small craft	Anti-ship/suicide attack	Used in combat
	Cargo ships	Logistics, arms transport	In inventory
	Scuba diving gear	Anti-ship, surveillance	R&D
	Ferry boat	Surveillance, weapons platform	R&D
Ground	RPG	Anti-aircraft/surface-to-surface	Used in combat
	Anti-aircraft guns	Surface-to-air	Used in combat
	Commercial vehicles	Logistics, anti-infrastructure, anti-personnel	Used in combat
	Fuel truck	Bomb	Used in combat
	Horses	Logistics	Inventory (by region)
	Small arms	Conventional, hijackings, assassinations	Used in combat
Ordnance	Grenades	Anti-personnel/vehicle/building	Used in combat
	Rockets (various)	Ground attack	Used in combat
	Mines	Anti-personnel/vehicle	Used in combat
	Shoe bomb	Anti-Infrastructure (aircraft)	Attempted use
	Nitrocellulose bomb	Anti-Infrastructure (aircraft)	R&D
	IEDs	Anti-personnel/vehicle/infrastructure	Used in combat
	Camera IED	Assassination	Used in combat
	Explosives (various)	Anti-personnel/vehicle/Infrastructure	Used in combat
	Detonating devices: remote triggers/timers/sensors	Detonation	Used in combat
Misc	Night vision devices	Night operations	Inventory (possible)
	computers, communications equipment	Secure&open comm., cyber attack, psyops	R&D/used in combat

forces.[3] OB plays into the intelligence cycle (collection, production, processing, dissemination, planning), and in near-term planning and analysis is considered along with weather and terrain.

The best way to observe the criteria is to set up combat files and track changes, done by producing lists and sub-lists — a combat file. Producing and maintaining combat files on Al Qaeda will be highly complex and will need to incorporate more intelligence collection methods, such as OSINT, CYBERINT and increased HUMINT.[4] When no changes are occurring, things are *normal*,[5] which, in principle applies to any enemy — nation-state (hierarchical) or networked non-state. Setting up initial combat files to examine Al Qaeda, however, will call for modification of the OB criteria to accommodate their creative use of the *five*-dimensional battlespace[6] (including cyberspace) and their disrespect for traditional rules of engagement (ROEs). Furthermore, intelligence analysts will need to network in order to obtain OB information on Al Qaeda. John P. Sullivan writes: 'To be effective, this intelligence must embrace network attributes and effectively fuse with networked operational forces.'[7]

The nine OB criteria will become more important over time, especially if Al Qaeda is not destroyed. Even if Al Qaeda is dissolved, their now-evolving type of warfare, often described as fourth-generation warfare (4GW), which includes terrorism, will likely not. Instead, other similar or worse non-state enemies will utilize 4GW. History has shown that wars against terrorist groups usually are long.[8] During times where no terrorist acts are occurring, whether because of successful offensive operations or because Al Qaeda (and/or its affiliates) are inactive, more attention will need to be paid to even subtle changes in OB. Observation of OB criteria during such a terrorist lull can be compared to that of seismic activity of the New Madrid Fault. At some point there will be an earthquake. Predicting when and where the epicenter will be is attempted by tracking changes in seismic activity. Similarly, when Al Qaeda is on the run, OB changes may be artificial. In the 1980s and 1990s the OB of Al Qaeda was detected to a degree but not influenced. During that timeframe they were allowed to evolve naturally — no one was aggressively chasing them.

HOW THE OB OF AL QAEDA IS DIFFERENT FROM THAT OF A NATION-STATE

Al Qaeda is an international network comprised of independent cells, as opposed to a conventional state hierarchy. They have no real equipment or weaponry that can be appreciably targeted — and what they do have is chameleon-like in nature. Al Qaeda is entrenched in guerrilla warfare in several countries and their weapons often take on the character of the country in which they operate. In Chechnya, for example, Al Qaeda might use only AK-47s, whereas in Yemen they may use several types of firearms from multiple producers. The observation of the activities of Al Qaeda becomes exponentially more complicated as we exit the arena in which they are labeled guerrilla fighters and enter countries such as the United States, where they are more likely to be labeled as terrorists. For instance, a donkey transporting weapons in the middle of downtown Los Angeles would stand out; whereas, an SUV would blend in with the environment. Conversely, in the mountain passes between Afghanistan and Pakistan, a donkey would look like day-to-day traffic, while an SUV would likely get noticed. Unlike Al Qaeda's unusual ability to blend its OB in with its environment, most OB elements of a conventional military will almost always be visible, stand out in its environment. In or out of garrison, conventional militaries, with the exception of special operations components, will for the most part have known and standard equipment. Of any military entity, Al Qaeda has the most OB variety, which allows it to adapt and conceal itself in multiple worldwide environments.

In addition to its unconventional methods and worldwide dispersal of assets, Al Qaeda has established its own coalition, similar to NATO or the former Eastern Bloc, only loosely arranged and written into the worldwide cyber-infrastructure. For nation-states, equipment, doctrine and even tactics are often obtained from one or more supplying countries with the means to produce them. Still, their OB criteria are analyzed independent of one another. Increasingly, Al Qaeda merges operations with other terrorist groups. Therefore the OBs of Al Qaeda and its affiliates will have to be looked at as if they were one. In guerilla warfare environments, observing combined operations is possible. But in the more networked terrorist environments, observing combined operations is more difficult because they are concealed. Furthermore, failed states will also offer their OB to terrorist and criminal alliances, if these alliances have not already appropriated them clandestinely or by proliferation. An Al Qaeda affiliate may have a signature weapon type that will identify it only in the aftermath of an attack. In the future, non-state groups may blend and coordinate so much that their OBs increasingly may have to be determined by location as well as by group.

APPLYING ORDER-OF-BATTLE CRITERIA TO AL QAEDA

The subsections below will apply the nine OB criteria to Al Qaeda, compare it with that of a nation-state, and show modifications for better application to the emerging threat.

Composition

Composition includes unit identifications and organizational line and block charts. When observing a conventional force, equipment and personnel are numbered. Diagrams of echelon of command are drawn for each branch of service and parent unit. Identification of units, what comprises them and how they are organized will answer many questions about a conventional enemy. Developing a historical picture of the unit composition of Al Qaeda will enable intelligence analysts to understand it. Constant monitoring of this picture will allow for detection of changes in structure. Identifying only one unit or cell of Al Qaeda at a time may have to suffice because of their ability to conceal themselves. But any single revelation of a unit or cell may lead to projections of others like them.

Echelons are hierarchical structures, that is, units by level of importance or responsibility. Intelligence analysts draw units as line-and-block charts. Line-and-block analysis for conventional forces is hierarchical and comprised of combinations of firepower as its primary base. For Al Qaeda, echelons may be applicable only to their top leadership, which may be diminishing as leaders get captured and interrogations reveal the locations of others. But Al Qaeda may have a type of middle management, or underground bureaucracy,[9] that provides logistical support for terrorist operations to occur. Regardless of echelon, line-and-block charts for Al Qaeda will look different than those of a conventional force. However it may be best to combine line-and-block charts on Al Qaeda with link analysis. The reason for the inclusion of link analysis is that Al Qaeda is comprised of specialty-focused people and, unlike conventional enemies, does not have a tangible military. A cursory look at types of units for Al Qaeda is outlined in Table 2. Overall the challenge of line-and-block analysis for Al Qaeda will be due to the ongoing offensive and capture of Al Qaeda leaders, changing organizational structure as a result of the global war on terror (GWOT), linking up with affiliated terrorist and criminal groups, and the global scope (at least 60 countries)[10] and use of cyberspace Al Qaeda has at its fingertips into which it can disappear.

TABLE 2
AL QAEDA PERSONNEL ORDER OF BATTLE (OB)

Size	Strength	Remarks
Main force	Tens of thousands	Multi-national, personnel vary by specialty vs branch of service, across 60 + countries
Leadership	Unknown	Spiritual leaders, top planners
Suicide squads	Tens to hundreds	By region
Cells	3–5 per cell	World-wide (60 + countries)
Asymmetric units	Varies	Special operations
Individuals	Est. hundreds	Worldwide; suicide bombers, loners, criminals
Sleeper agents	Unknown	Worldwide; may be cell-sized or individual
Support network	Tens of thousands	Worldwide; provide money, assistance, weapons, safe-houses, logistics, recruitment, etc.

To detect changes as indicators line-and-block charts will need to be developed for emerging new leaders and alliances, as well as for lower cell structure interface.

Disposition

Geographical location, tactical deployment and movements make up the disposition of a conventional force. The disposition of most nation state militaries is routinely observed with the use of reconnaissance assets such as spy planes and satellites. For the most part, when significant enemy movements take place we become aware of them and are alerted in time. There are two types of deployment for conventional forces: peacetime and wartime. With Al Qaeda, there is no *peacetime* disposition — all is war, the exact geographical locations of which are becoming very difficult to determine. Instead of the identification of airfields, ports, military bases and cities (conventional), the disposition of Al Qaeda involves identifying caves, enclaves, mosques, apartments and even internet cafes. The tactical deployment of a conventional enemy is observed by looking at an array on a battlefield or aircraft on strip alert. Observation of tactical deployment and movement of Al Qaeda depends heavily on communications intercepts and informants.

The physical relocation of a unit or of several units signifies the conventional enemy's next course of action or a new capability. Units may move to an attack position or to reinforce or replace another unit. For obvious reasons enemy movements need to be constantly monitored. Movement within Al Qaeda may take on different meanings, especially since their units are much smaller than those of a conventional military and are concealed. Examples of movements within Al Qaeda might be the short- or long-stay residency of its members in neighborhoods of varying type (e.g., wealthy, poor, Arab-dominated, Hispanic) or evidence of a meeting held between an Al Qaeda leader and that of an affiliate. The relocation of relatives of Al Qaeda leadership just prior to an attack may be considered a movement — and an indicator. In the guerilla warfare battlespace, Al Qaeda members may cross a country border or move into an urban enclave to assist their brothers in jihad. Movement of this type may be an indication of a near-term asymmetric attack. Finally, movement for Al Qaeda may take shape in such less obvious but no less significant ways as the relocation of a new website on the Internet.

Strength Figures

Strength figures are statements that number personnel, weapons and equipment, and portray types of units. Strength figures will be the most difficult to track for Al Qaeda; however, comparisons with studies of conventional forces may highlight the advantages Al Qaeda has over a state

OPFOR. Conventional forces are heavily dependent on logistics and support, with actual fighters being a low percentage of the overall unit makeup. Al Qaeda, on the other hand, is made up of many warriors and comparatively few logistics needs, which makes it a cost-effective operation as well as a more mobile and efficient one. With warriors spread out all over the globe, and with lack of traditional uniforms, stealth figures into the equation as well. The logistics and support of conventional forces are part of the unit and mobilize with it, which is both costly (requires heavy transportation) and observable to the public. Support for Al Qaeda, on the other hand, appears to be voluntary and its logistics elements are often pre-positioned, like an underground railroad. An example of ground OB for a conventional force is shown below for a 1996 estimate of the Russian Federation:

> As of 1996 the Ground Forces of the Russian Federation were estimated to number approximately 670,000 officers and enlisted personnel. Of that number, about 170,000 were contract volunteer enlistees and warrant officers, and about 210,000 were conscripts. Presumably, the remaining 290,000 were commissioned officers, suggesting that some 43 percent of ground forces personnel were officers. These figures strongly suggest that most of the notional 'divisions' of the Russian Army consisted of a base, equipment, and officers, but no more than a handful of soldiers to actually operate equipment.[11]

The excerpt above shows how cumbersome conventional ground forces of a nation state can be and what a small percentage of their personnel may actually be operators. During the 1994–1996 war in Chechnya many successes of the Chechens over the Russian military highlight how non-state actors can overcome a state actor in measurable strides using asymmetric tactics at low cost. During the two-year timeframe the Chechen tactic was 'small, tightly knit units who enjoy[ed] great autonomy in decision-making'[12]. They were (and still are today) often family members or otherwise related, and used surprise attacks. The Russian forces, by contrast, were 'mainly young conscripts who depend on commands from higher officers, leaving them highly vulnerable in the heat of battle'.[13] The Chechens held steady for 21 months of fighting causing the Russians to retreat and resort to attempts at peace talks.

Unlike most conventional forces, Al Qaeda makes significant use of sleeper agents. Like North Korea, the use of sleeper agents makes it difficult to determine real strength figures for Al Qaeda. And the problem is compounded because of the worldwide dispersal of Al Qaeda and its propensity for stealth and deception. Its number of agents and support personnel may have to be estimated based on past attacks. It has been estimated from the 11 September attacks ('9/11'), for example, that a number of support personnel worldwide were involved in the planning and logistics of the event along with the 19 identified hijackers. Instead of straightforward OB calculations, the number of personnel involved in future or anticipated attacks may have to be systematically calculated. The number of sleeper agents for Al Qaeda can also be calculated by pre-incident indicators (e.g., eyewitnesses) and other volunteered information from worldwide humint sources.

A breakdown of strength figures for conventional OPFORs looks like this:

- Number of casualties, loss of aircraft, etc.
- Numeric Changes (e.g., number of replacements)
- Effective strength (formula: initial strength (tables of organization and equipment, TO and E) minus losses, plus replacements)
- Types of units and their correlation to each other
- Replacement system
- Eligible manpower
- Reserves
- Mobilization potential
- Mobilization system

It is nearly impossible to calculate the above strength figures for Al Qaeda and this largely remains a gray area. In areas like Afghanistan, Yemen and countries where the leadership is committed to the GWOT, it is possible to determine the number of captured Al Qaeda members because claims of these captures are frequently in the news. Replacement figures for Al Qaeda, however, are less likely to be determined accurately or in a timely manner. The blending of groups will make accurate counts even more difficult, especially in areas such as Afghanistan or Iraq, where there are also former regime loyalists, rival tribes and parties, criminal elements, foreign fighters and terrorists.

Al Qaeda uses the addition of warriors of various ethnic backgrounds, as well as women and teenagers. The ratio of new types of warriors to regular or traditional-looking conscripts of Al Qaeda is worth observing. Changes or additions to personnel types may provide an indicator, yet the evidence may not surface until after attacks occur or are thwarted. The weapons used by Al Qaeda fighters should also be tracked and analyzed, including experimentation with conventional, non-conventional, homemade, improvised and chemical, biological, radiological, nuclear (CBRN) weaponry (Table 3). Solicitation of expertise by Al Qaeda is worthy of tracking as well. Weapons that are crude or improvised and have the potential to be used asymmetrically by Al Qaeda should be categorized as *real* weapons in its inventory. Also, if conventional weapons are used for another purpose, they should be re-categorized and re-analyzed. For example, if an air-to-air missile

TABLE 3
AL QAEDA WEAPONS OF MASS DESTRUCTION (WMD)

Type	Stage	Remarks
Chemical	R&D	Cyanide, pesticides, insecticides, hybrids (cyanide/sulphur), poisons
Biological	R&D	Ricin, possibly anthrax
Nuclear	R&D	Enriched uranium purchase, recruitment of specialists
Radiological	R&D	Enriched uranium purchase, Jose Padilla arrest, information from documents confiscated in Afghanistan

(acquired from a failed state) were modified and consistently used by Al Qaeda in a ground attack role, then it should fall under the *Ground OB* category and not the *Air OB* category. Planning for and countering the threat from Al Qaeda will be facilitated if weapons are analyzed according to actual use, and not textbook use. The *Blackhawk Down* scenario in Somalia is an example of how a conventional ground weapon was used differently, or asymmetrically. Somali warriors used rocket-propelled grenades (RPGs) not only against an air target for which it had not been designed — a helicopter — but they used several of them in a swarming type of tactic to ensure success in shooting it down.

Tactics

Tactics criteria are broken down into conventional, unconventional, and/or nuclear.

> During the eight-week period between 6 October 2002 to 28 November 2002, al-Qaeda and its affiliates executed no fewer than six significant attacks. The strikes spanned six countries and included civilian, military and commercial targets.[14]

The paragraph above shows a deviation in tactics from what was previously normal for Al Qaeda. That is, prior to 9/11 they executed large, spectacular attacks approximately every two years (Khobar Towers, US embassies in Africa, and the USS Cole). Tactics for Al Qaeda will differ from those of conventional forces, mostly because of their unique OB, their networked operation and their fundamental ideology. Tactics of any military are tracked for both offensive and defensive operations, by echelon and branch of service. Observing changes in tactics for Al Qaeda will enhance development of indicators by intelligence analysts, which could lead to assessments of the type and scope of attack that will occur next. A starting point is observing the components of the Al Qaeda attack cycle and the length of time involved in planning an attack. A longer planning period could indicate a more sizeable attack.

The following is a list of additional tactics by which Al Qaeda can be tracked:

- Teams or cells (e.g., how many used in an attack)
- Planning cycles
- Use of smuggling or drug routes
- Secondary attacks
- Weapons (e.g., movement and use)
- Day or night planning or operations
- Logistics (e.g., use of ships, passports and student visas)
- Personnel (e.g., use of personnel with varied backgrounds)
- Amphibious operations
- Airborne tactics
- Ground operations (e.g., ambush tactics, kidnappings and assault)
- Use of terrain (e.g., urban operations)
- Operations security (OPSEC)
- Tactical doctrine (e.g., the use of weapons of mass destruction)
- Rhetoric (e.g., intent of Al Qaeda leadership which is sometimes stated)
- Use of the Internet (e.g., psychological operations (PSYOPS), misinformation, recruitment, exchanges and global reach)
- Use of time (e.g., understanding cultural differences in time can affect the timing of preemptive- or counter-operations)
- Deception (e.g., intentional or stealth tactics): whether intentionally or not, Al Qaeda has created a *phantom* OB by which they appear more formidable than they actually are.

Training

Obtaining information on training for conventional state OPFORs is straightforward; such information is often available in publications or on the Internet. Al Qaeda has adopted many of our Marine and Special Operations unit tactics simply by acquiring the manuals. Finding Al Qaeda manuals and CD ROMs following the war in Afghanistan has presented intelligence analysts with insight into the training Al Qaeda conducts, which has given insight into such data as their numbers of personnel available to conduct attacks. By various calculations, the numbers of Al Qaeda personnel trained in Afghanistan over the last decade has become the current basis for how many fighters are in the system. Eventually this will have to be updated. The following is a list of known training elements that can be used to track Al Qaeda:

- Individual training (e.g., the location and nature of flight lessons)
- Unit training (e.g., evidence from terrorist training camps and terrorist manuals distributed to fighters via CD ROM)

- Size and scope of training
- Advanced training
- Training in CBRN
- Special operations unit training
- Training areas, cycles and schedules
- Political indoctrination
- Languages
- Cross-intelligence (e.g., adopting training from other groups who have used a particular tactic successfully)
- Terrorist vs guerrilla fighter training
- Specialized training: e.g., suicide bombers
- OPSEC

Logistics

Logistics is the study of how the unit is supplied. The principle behind logistics is the same for a nation-state as it is with Al Qaeda, with the exception that Al Qaeda will be more heavily weighted on the illegal side. Criminal influence, including the drug trade, will both complicate and facilitate tracking logistics. Use of existing drug- or people-smuggling routes, for example, may facilitate tracking logistics, if they are known by counter-drug or counter-smuggling agencies. New smuggling routes established via new criminal associations and hidden from our intelligence agencies will be difficult to detect (e.g., use of an improperly flagged boat with false documents and hidden compartments).

All channels and types of supply used by Al Qaeda should be tracked. Al Qaeda has the tendency to use equipment that is not their own, such as a US commercial 747 or a rental truck, which may be used for transportation of illegal arms or as a weapons delivery platform. When Iraq (under Saddam Hussein) used illegal means to acquire weapons it was difficult to assess what they actually possessed. A similar deception occurs with Al Qaeda, which can result in intelligence analysts attributing a capability to Al Qaeda that they do not actually have. The fear alone of a capability of Al Qaeda can result in misappropriation of military and civilian assets to counter them. Thus the accurate assessment of logistics for Al Qaeda is essential. Although the same logistics tracking guidelines that are used for conventional OPFORs are also used with Al Qaeda, it is necessary to track Al Qaeda on many other levels, of which the following are examples:

- Procurement sources (e.g., Chechen guerrillas, equipment of former regimes such as Afghanistan, gray or black market sources, the Axis of Evil countries, failed states, US allies, or other terrorist groups).

- Storage areas (e.g., caves, rental storage spaces, houses or underground burial).
- Equipment that is to be used one time, as with a suicide attack, may require no storage. Bomb components, however, may require storage space and time for assembly.
- Supply distribution system (e.g., use of smuggling routes, commercial transportation, land, sea, rail and air transportation as well as tracking distance and speed).
- Terminals, airports and ports. Travel is still an important part of Al Qaeda's operations because of its global nature. As with corporate business meetings, the Internet eliminates some travel needs, but not all.
- Evacuation, or escape routes (e.g., for non-suicide or martyrdom attacks, Al Qaeda may have an escape plan).
- Salvage capabilities (e.g., use of unexploded ordinance to build crude but effective incendiary explosive devices — IEDs).
- Support from outside groups. 'Internal self-managing teams plan and execute operations, while external linkages with a complex association of contributing groups provide a constellation of support activities.'[15] Support groups and individuals will play a greater role in OB than with a conventional force, and will distort numbers. Support groups may be considered an auxiliary element to the basic military structure of Al Qaeda and thus tracked as part of its OB.

Combat Effectiveness and Efficiency

Combat effectiveness and efficiency are enemy strengths and weaknesses, length of time committed to combat, experience, political reliability, geographical arena, national characteristics, and morale and esprit. By weighing the sub-criteria below against a conventional force, advantages of Al Qaeda become apparent.

Examples of Al Qaeda's Strengths include:

- Stealth
- Deception
- Dispersal
- Time
- Networking
- Global reach
- Propaganda spread
- Lack of tangible assets (target avoidance)
- Asymmetric weapons and tactics
- Disregard for ROEs: attacking the civilian infrastructure gives Al Qaeda more targeting opportunities than its enemies who abide by them

Examples of Al Qaeda's Weaknesses include:

- Communications intercepted
- Visibility during pre-operational planning and/or travel
- Many state enemies due to US crackdown on those states, former Al Qaeda supporters
- Diminishing areas to hold training camps
- Informants

A primary strategy for Al Qaeda — the length of time they commit to combat — is one of their strengths. Al Qaeda seems to be unaffected by time. Volunteer Al Qaeda fighters are apparently permanent, not bound by 2–4 year enlistments like recruits of conventional forces. The ability of Al Qaeda to make political objectives last a long period of time may also be an indication of strength. However, state entities may also have this strength. In a conflict, the side that is most future-looking, evidenced by the number of generations their influence will span, indicates a long-term commitment, and therefore, may also be a strength. In spite of the fact that Al Qaeda often changes enemies (Russians in the 1980s, the United States in the 1990s to present, and concurrently, all Westerners and moderate Muslims), they appear to have a long-term commitment to their conflicts — their jihad. Followed over time the sub-criteria below should provide more clues to understanding the effectiveness of Al Qaeda:

- Political Reliability — like some extremists in Yemen who have been converted to a more moderate stance, some Al Qaeda agents operating in the United States or Europe have the potential to become Westernized and less interested in being a terrorist. However, there will still be the extremists who live by the notion that waging war is the reason for their existence.[16]
- Geographical areas (e.g., indications of new areas being used, especially for training and/or weapons and personnel movement and harboring)
- National characteristics (e.g., universal appeal of the Al Qaeda ideology overcomes local and regional differences)
- Morale and esprit (potentially determined from communications intercepts and Internet website propaganda and chatter)

Electronic Technical Data

Communications and non-communications equipment may have the following characteristics:

- Cell phones/satellite phones
- Internet communication

- Radios
- Encryption, decryption and steganography
- Tape recordings or videos, especially from Osama bin Laden or other top leader
- Non-communications equipment (e.g., standard and non-standard detonating devices)

Miscellaneous Data

Miscellaneous data for a state OPFOR are personalities, unit history, code names and numbers, enemy identification (uniforms, insignia, etc.), administrative procedures (rates of pay, promotions, discipline, mail service, R&R, assignments and transfers, conscription and enlistment, etc.). Not all standard military data for conventional OPFORs will apply to Al Qaeda. How Al Qaeda fighters are paid is not well known, but there is certainly less administrative work than with a conventional force. Deployment orders, awards or promotions, if they exist at all for Al Qaeda, do not have the extensive administrative requirements that a conventional military does. Much of the requirement for administrative work is absent for Al Qaeda. For a conventional force administrative work uses a large portion of its personnel and commitments. Because of fewer personnel needed for administrative work, Al Qaeda is able to have more fighters. In the miscellaneous criteria listed above, there are variations used by Al Qaeda that may be tracked as indicators. Military uniforms for Al Qaeda, although far from standard, will exist, albeit in a non-traditional and often invisible form. The *uniform* of the 9/11 terrorists was that of a standard, well-groomed businessman. Stolen uniforms may also apply as another type of temporary or *just-in-time* OB, e.g., to gain access to a secure area or to look innocuous in the process of conducting an attack.

ADDITIONAL MODIFICATIONS TO AL QAEDA OB CRITERIA

The clandestine nature of Al Qaeda lends itself to the need to track anomalies as OB. Anomalies typically become known by incoming reports of observations, often not by a humint-trained soldier, but by common citizens, police or security officers. These may be reports of suspicious activity or an increase in activity surrounding a particular high-value infrastructure or node. The following anomalies[17] should be added, and may fall under one or more of the nine criteria above:

- Border security anomalies (disposition)
- Immigration anomalies (strength figures)
- Transportation anomalies (logistics)

- Infrastructure anomalies (tactics)
- Energy anomalies (tactics)
- Animal Disease anomalies (tactics)
- Nuclear facility anomalies (tactics)
- Medical anomalies (tactics)
- Internet anomalies (disposition)

Finally, some of the more complex concepts that define the emerging battlespace, such as bond-relationship targeting, mass disruption, netwar and cyberwarfare[18] and their constituents will increasingly become necessary OB criteria.

CONCLUSIONS AND RECOMMENDATIONS

When analyzing Al Qaeda, the nine OB criteria and associated data will be extensive. According to intelligence analyst Lt Colonel Ken Luikart, this responsibility should ultimately reside with our top intelligence agencies, preferably one apolitical cell. At all lower agency levels, ranging from local operations in Iraq to homeland security operations in a metropolitan area, the same criteria will need to be tracked and analyzed, then channeled to both higher and lateral agencies. With that, intelligence analysts should be able to make better assessments as to what Al Qaeda intends to do and what they might be targeting. Consequently, the United States and other targeted countries should be able to better align money and assets to counter only real threats from Al Qaeda, instead of all of the speculated threats. Tracking OB and making assessments will be ongoing due to the nature of terrorism and the long-term nature of the war on the same. While the use of a systematic approach in tracking the OB of a state OPFOR ultimately leads to development of a superior combat force and deterrence, tracking Al Qaeda may only serve to buy more time between attacks and/or make attacks less catastrophic. Conventional nation states should also see that conventional weaponry, tactics and strategies will need to be altered to counter Al Qaeda and other emerging non-state entities who pose a similar threat.

ACKNOWLEDGEMENTS

Special thanks for the contributions of Lt Col. Kenneth Luikart and Sara Haeckel

NOTES

1. Kenneth A. Luikart, 'Transforming Homeland Security – Intelligence Indications and Warning', *Air and Space Power Journal* (Summer 2003), pp.76–7.

2. HQ, Department of the Army, FM 30-5, *Combat Intelligence* (October 1973), p.7–1.
3. Correspondence with Lt Col. Ken Luikart, August 2003.
4. John P. Sullivan, 'Networked Force Structure and C4I', in Robert J. Bunker (ed.), *Non-State Threats and Future Wars* (London: Frank Cass, 2003), p.150.
5. Correspondence with Lt Col. Ken Luikart, August 2003.
6. Robert J. Bunker, *Five Dimensional (Cyber) Warfighting: Can the Army After Next be Defeated Through Complex Concepts and Technologies?* (Carlisle Barracks, PA: Strategic Studies Institute, US Army War College, 1998), pp.4–5.
7. Sullivan, p.150.
8. Brian Michael Jenkins, *Countering Al Qaeda*, MR-1620-RC (Santa Monica, CA: RAND, 2002), p.18
9. Ibid, p.5.
10. Richard H. Shultz and Andreas Vogt, 'It's War! Fighting Post-11 September Global Terrorism through a doctrine of Preemption', *Terrorism and Political Violence*, Vol.15, No.1 (Spring 2003), p.8.
11. Russian Army Order of Battle, 1996, ⟨http://www.globalsecurity.org⟩.
12. Bill Gasperini, 'Russia Goes All Out In War on Chechnya: Victory at Any Price?', *The Christian Science Monitor*, 9 January 1995.
13. Ibid.
14. Ben Venske, *Al Qaeda Wave Attack Assessment*, v1.0, 17/18, May 2003, p.5, ⟨http://www.intelcenter.org⟩.
15. Shultz and Vogt, p.10.
16. Jenkins, p.8.
17. Correspondence with Lt Col. Ken Luikart, August 2003.
18. Robert J. Bunker, 'Battlespace Dynamics, Information Warfare to Netwar, and Bond-Relationship Targeting', in Robert J. Bunker (ed.), *Non-State Threats and Future Wars* (London: Frank Cass, 2003), pp.97–107.

Operational Combat Analysis of the Al Qaeda Network

ROBERT J. BUNKER and MATT BEGERT

This essay is divided into sections focusing on network organizational structures, an overview of Al Qaeda, a discussion of the analytical approach used to conduct an operational combat analysis of the Al Qaeda network, the actual analysis of the Al Qaeda network, and the future potentials of this research. The work draws upon netwar and related concepts, fourth epoch war theory, and lessons learned from various counter-insurgency and counter-terrorism network operations and exercises. The insights gained should be considered informative rather than authoritative, given the experimental nature of networks and our own limited knowledge of their form, functions and capabilities.

The authors' intent is to further research into the military capabilities and, ultimately, vulnerabilities of network organizational structures. Networks represent the underlying foundation of postmodern military and police force structures. They will interact with modern (legacy) forces, based on hierarchical communication paths, both from the standpoint of supporting them (e.g. Terrorism Early Warning Groups) and opposing them (e.g. Al Qaeda and other non-state opposing forces [OPFORs]).

We are not required to understand the network organizational form perfectly – just better than the opponents of the nation-state form. In a 'war over future social and political organization', we will need many new capabilities to defeat our foes. Networks have been identified as one of the keys that will unlock those capabilities for our military and police forces.

NETWORK ORGANIZATIONAL STRUCTURES[1]

Organizational structures used by modern military and police forces are inherently hierarchical in nature. They resemble a pyramid with the key decision makers clustered toward the apex and command (rank) strata branching down much like a tree root system from general level officers (chiefs) all the way down to privates (deputies and beat officers). Information passes down from command level to command level at a relatively slow and ponderous pace. As part of the feedback loop, information is then passed slowly up the various command levels. This is an iterated process and well suited to mechanistic economic and military needs. Military personnel diagram these structures based on unit function and designation using 'line and blocked' charts. Law enforcement administrators engage in similar diagramming and typically allocate their personnel resources to specific geographic zones of a state, county or city operational area.

Over the last decades of the twentieth century, contemporary network organizational structures have gradually emerged as a challenge to hierarchical ones. They represent another aspect of the modern to postmodern epochal shift underway. A number of works have been written about networks with regard to society, business, and conflict and war. Some of the better known writers on this topic include Howard Rheingold, Kevin Kelly and John Arquilla and David Ronfeldt.[2] These new structures are characterized by:

- Cells/nodes
- Information channels
- Ease of connectivity
- Flat information integration

Free floating cells and nodes replaced rigid hierarchical tiers in this type of organizational structure. They are linked together via mutually beneficial information channels which form a web-like pattern between the various cells and nodes of the entity in question. These channels benefit from ease of connectivity which allows them to be established and terminated as required with little or no effort. Because the majority (if not all) of the cells and nodes can link to each other directly, middle layers are done away with, resulting in flat information integration. This effect creates a far flatter organizational structure than that found in pyramid-like hierarchies. These characteristics are important because they provide direct utility for conflict and war.

AL QAEDA OVERVIEW

In conflict and war, networks made their potential unequivocally known on 11 September 2001 ('9/11') with Al Qaeda's strategic suicide bombings against the United States. Al Qaeda is not an organization as defined by a hierarchical (bureaucratic) process and a formal chain of command or control common to the understanding of Western government. Al Qaeda represents a basis of Sunni extremist thought or a view of how the world should operate. Adherents to this common operating picture claim Al Qaeda as the basis for independent, networked action. Still, Al Qaeda possessed a leadership hub based on an emir, chief counsel, Consultation Council and Islamic Study, Military and Finance Committees as of February 2001.[3]

Al Qaeda, as a network structure, has gone through a four stage evolutionary process in its war against the US:[4]

Pre-War Years

Al Qaeda benefited from the years of funding to the Mujahadeen in the 1980s by the US, Saudi and other governments during the anti-Soviet jihad in Afghanistan. Osama bin Laden and others founded Al Qaeda in 1988 to expand the jihad. During this period, Al Qaeda began its global expansion. American troops deployed in Saudi Arabia for the First Gulf War brought Al Qaeda interests into direct conflict with the United States. Bin Laden moved from Afghanistan back to Saudi Arabia (forced into exile because of conflict with the Saudi government) then to Sudan (forced out by US pressure) and back to Afghanistan (invited in by the new Taliban government). Attacks against the United States during this period were sporadic. The World Trade Center car bombing of February 1993 and the Khobar Towers truck bombing in Dhahran, Saudi Arabia represent the most significant events. A number of failed operations (not taken beyond the planning stage) are evident as is Al Qaeda's training link to Somali tribesmen who killed 18 US troops in Mogadishu in October 1993.

Formal Declaration of War

In August 1996, Osama bin Laden issued a formal declaration of war against the US ('Declaration of War Against the Americans Occupying the Land of the Two Holy Mosques'). In preparation for this coming war, Al Qaeda had been editing the *Encyclopedia of Afghan Jihad*, a training manual for conducting guerrilla warfare and terrorism, since 1989. The manual was based on lessons learned from fighting the Soviets and doctrine culled from US and British field manuals. It was printed in 1996 (with CDs first appearing in 1999) and was to be used in the training camps that had been set up in Afghanistan to train tens of thousands of Al Qaeda recruits. The manual was also exported to radical Islamic forces in Chechnya, Bosnia, the Kashmir and Mindanao. During this period, Al Qaeda continued its global expansion and eventually formed network nodes in 60 countries. Attacks on the United States were highlighted by the embassy bombings in Kenya and Tanzania in August 1998 and the USS Cole attack in Yemen in October 2000. Interdicted attacks include those against the embassy in Kampala in 1998 and Los Angeles International Airport in December 1999. The US military response during this period was cruise missile strikes against terrorist training camps in Afghanistan and a pharmaceutical plant in Sudan thought to be linked to bin Laden. Osama bin Laden was also indicted for the embassy deaths of US citizens and UN sanctions against the Taliban for harboring him were imposed.

9/11 and US Counterattack

The 9/11 attack elevated Al Qaeda, in the eyes of the United States, from a terrorist group engaging in criminal activity (a police concern) to that of a direct military threat to the US homeland (a military concern) This showed that Al Qaeda had gained the nation-state capability to engage in warfare without being limited by geography (political boundaries) and legal constraints (as defined in international law). The US response in the autumn and winter of 2001 was to target Al Qaeda cells worldwide and invade Afghanistan in order to destroy the Taliban government, the terrorist training camps and the Al Qaeda headquarters in Tora Bora. Taliban and Al Qaeda fighters were also targeted along with attempts to kill or capture Osama bin Laden and as many senior Al Qaeda officials as possible. Al Qaeda activity became disrupted during this period as its membership went deeper underground and surviving Al Qaeda forces in Afghanistan fled into the rugged mountains of the neighboring Pakistan border region.

Adaptation and Counter-Strikes

Al Qaeda adapted to the loss of its Afghani sanctuaries and some of its star-hub C^2 structure by devolving more of its functions to the extremities of the network. Targeting switched from the larger and more impressive attacks to more frequent attacks on softer targets worldwide. While a planned Singapore attack was thwarted in December 2001, attacks began to once again take place in the autumn of the following year. During this period, the Bali nightclub bombing took place in October 2002 and in November 2002 surface-to-air-missiles (SAMs) were targeted against an Israeli passenger aircraft taking off from Mombassa, Kenya in coordination with the Paradise Hotel bombing. In the last two years, attacks have taken place in Saudi Arabia, Iraq and Spain with probable linkages to additional bombings in Chechnya, Uzbekistan and Pakistan. With the loss of the Afghani training camps, Al Qaeda has adapted by increasing its use of the Internet for propaganda, recruiting and training purposes in addition to its continued reliance on madrasahs (those not shut down), mosques and prisons. One trend of concern has been Al Qaeda's recent ability to engage in foreign policy with governments, such as Spain, to arrange cease-fire agreements in return for troop withdrawals from areas of operations such as Iraq. In its earlier days, Al Qaeda was bought off by some Middle Eastern governments in return for not creating network nodes within their countries. This backroom criminal extraction of 'extortion' or 'protection' money (depending on how you view it) is now evolving to the point that it is being legitimized by overt truce offerings that are being accepted by some governments.

ANALYTICAL APPROACH

The operational combat analysis will be derived from a basic weapons systems analysis approach. This traditional form of analysis is normally focused upon the tactical level and characterizes weapons systems, such as the tank, by their speed, offensive and defensive attributes. A triangle figure is usually drawn with each of the three sides representing one of these attributes. Typically tradeoffs exist with speed sacrificed for defense and vice versa because of the weight of protective armor. Scout tank and battle tank examples can be viewed in Figure 1.

Scout tanks trade offensive and defensive capability for extra speed. Battle tanks emphasize offensive and defensive attributes, in varying combinations, over speed. These tradeoffs allow for mission specialization and synergies to develop between different tank types. A more developed analysis may include cost, weight, and maintenance and logistical need requirements.

FIGURE 1

TANK WEAPONS SYSTEMS ANALYSIS (TACTICAL)

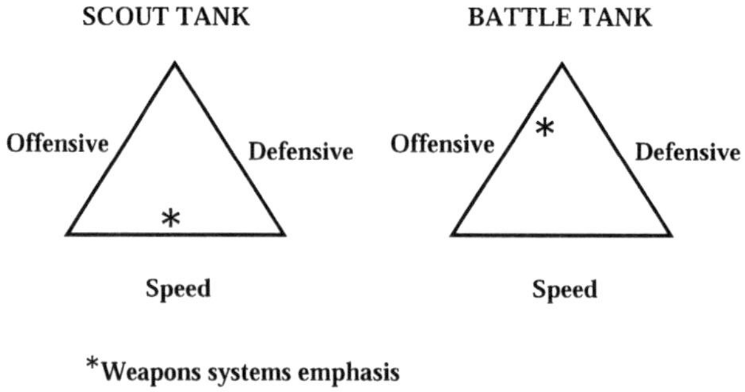

SCOUT TANK   BATTLE TANK

Offensive   Defensive   Offensive   Defensive

Speed   Speed

*Weapons systems emphasis

Abstracting this form of analysis to networks requires two issues to be addressed. First, the level of focus needs to be expanded from the tactical to the operational level of analysis. Second, traditional weapons systems are self-contained things with their own acquisition, targeting and offensive capabilities. Networks, by their very nature, are not self-contained and instead have combat functions distributed across their system of nodes. Because of the distributed nature of networks and analysis focused on the operational, rather than the tactical, level, tradeoffs between attributes do not exist as they do for stand-alone weapons systems. As a result, a network may or may not gain multiple capabilities without the expense of other capabilities. The defining modifier for network capabilities will likely be a function of its organizational form: chain, star, all-channel network or hybrid.[5] Access to such information about non-state OPFORs will be problematic because of our incomplete knowledge (nodes and linkages not identified, blurred associations, etc.) and the sensitivity of this information (much of it is beyond open source intelligence).

In addition to speed, offensive and defensive attributes a fourth attribute, derived from the concept of a combat multiplier, will be added to reflect the unique operational advantages possessed by network organizational structures. The combat multiplier attribute represents an operational plus that networks gain over hierarchies. It is an attempt to portray some of the benefits that networks possess because of their inherent non-linear dynamics based on such ideas as collective vision (leaderless C^2) and emergence (spontaneous intelligence).[6]

No visual representation of these four attributes for a network currently exists. For our purposes, Table 1 portrays how these attributes apply to Al Qaeda. It is surmised that young and less-developed non-state OPFORs will possess basic speed, offensive and defensive attributes but not the combat multiplier attribute possessed by a mature network, such as Al Qaeda, because of their small size and lack of outside network linkages.

OPERATIONAL COMBAT ANALYSIS OF AL QAEDA

Al Qaeda operational combat analysis is divided into the four attributes of speed, offensive, defensive and combat multiplier as previously mentioned. These attributes are further subdivided into specific capabilities. Each of these capabilities is described and then one or more Al Qaeda examples of utilizing that capability are provided:

Speed

The attribute of speed in this situation will be based upon commander or officer-in-charge (OIC) decision making, information processing and

TABLE 1
OPERATIONAL COMBAT ANALYSIS OF THE AL QAEDA NETWORK

Attribute	Al Qaeda example
Speed	
Increased information flow	Cross-linkages between nodes
	World-wide nodal sensor network
	Flatter organization/less middle-management between C^2 star-hub and nodes
	No legal or bureaucratic limits on information gathering capabilities
Reduction of information seams	*Encyclopedia of Afghan Jihad* (1996)
Filtering/fusion capability	Recognition of Spain's center of gravity (March 2004)
Parallel processing (multi-tasking)	Nodal target set identification (pre-September 2001)
	Nodal target set identification and attack authority (September 2001 on)
Offensive	
Swarming capability	Fallujah, Iraq (March 2004)
	Riyadh, Saudi Arabia (May 2003)
	Gardez, Afghanistan (February–March 2002)
Distributed sensor-to-shooter links	Mogadishu, Somalia (October 1993)
Bond-relationship targeting (BRT)	Yanbu, Saudi Arabia (May 2004)
	Madrid, Spain (March 2004)
	Baghdad, Iraq (September–November 2003)
Attack masking/virtual network	LJ Cells; Al Qaeda affiliate (2002–2004)
	Haganah denial-of-service attacks (October 2003)
Defensive	
Stealth-masking its members (forces)	Al Qaeda and Taliban Survival Kit Instructions (February 2004)
	Riyadh, Saudi Arabia (November 2003) 9/11 (September 2001)
	USS Cole incident, Yemen (October 2000)
Impervious to decapitation strikes	Network evolves towards independent operational nodes (2001)
Offers protection against precision fires	Gardez, Afghanistan (February–March 2002) 9/11 (September2001)
	USS Cole incident, Yemen (October 2000)
Provides redundant information channels	Al Qaeda C^2 star hub nodal links
	Al Neda website
Self-healing ability	Post-9/11 node and linkage replacement (2001 +)
Information security	Al Qaeda and Taliban Survival Kit Instructions (February 2004)
	Military Studies in the Jihad Against the Tyrants Manual (December 2001)
	9/11 Strike force structure (September 2001)
Combat multiplier	
Increasing returns as the network expands	Nodes in 60 countries bring their own expertise, lessons learned, regional contacts, and unique access to resources
Ease of growth	Derived from common Al Qaeda threads justifying deviations in accepted behavior patterns (*jihadis* with western lifestyles, criminal behavior, Pakistani suicide bombers)
Mission tailoring	Paradise Hotel/Israeli airliner in Mombassa, Kenya (November 2002)
Criminal–warfighting orientation	Use of crime as a form of warfare, fielding of criminal–soldiers, breaking of western rules of warfare
Collective vision	Restoration of the Islamic caliphate
	Destruction of the US and Israel
	Overthrow of apostate Islamic regimes
Adaptive behavior	Network morphing (1988, 2001)
	'Losing and learning doctrine' and 'Goal oriented and not rule oriented' protocols
Emergence	Unknown

reaction cycles rather than traditional forms of tactical or operational mobility. US Air Force Col. John Boyd's well-known observe–orient–decide–act (OODA) loop which allows opponents to get within each others' decision cycle best describes this attribute:[7]

Increased Information Flows. Networked structures possess increased information flows due to the vast number of information channels (cross-linkages) that exist between the various cells/nodes. This results in many more times the amount of information being shared by the organizational structure and provides an 'information multiplier' effect. Over time, the 'information multiplier' will grow even more pronounced over that of hierarchies with the advent of broadband communications that will provide a greater initial baseline of information being sent into an organization. Networks, unlike hierarchies, will be better suited to handle these increased information flows. Real-time information being received by those who can immediately capitalize upon it also takes place as organization structure allows processing speeds to increase.

Al Qaeda Example: Al Qaeda nodes represent a world-wide sensor network which collects information and feeds it back into the organization. Information transmitted back to the C^2 leadership star hub travels fewer (middle-management) levels than in a hierarchical organization because of its flatter design. Information increasingly transmitted between nodes via Internet chat rooms and websites ranges anywhere from open source information to information collected and/or purchased via criminal means. Al Qaeda criminal-soldiers, in many cases, have access to better, more accurate and timely information than governmental forces because no limits are placed on their information gathering capabilities by legal or bureaucratic systems.

Reduction of Information Seams. The term 'information fiefdoms' has been used to describe how groups within hierarchical organizations hoard information and do not share it with other groups. The term 'black hole' has also been used to describe governmental agencies that gladly accept information but do not engage in quid pro quo. These descriptions are indicative of information seams within an organization and between organizations. Networked organizations reduce the amount of information seams that exist by allowing a freer flow of information to take place. Information sharing is viewed as a sum–sum game (everyone wins) by networks rather than a zero–sum game (some win and some lose) as it is viewed by hierarchies. This overcomes the limitations of artificial institutional and geographic boundaries imposed by modern political systems.

Al Qaeda Example. The creation of the multi-volume 7,000 (possibly 8,000)-page *Encyclopedia of Afghan Jihad* over a five-year period and its subsequent publication in 1996 shows a willingness by the Al Qaeda network to eliminate the information seams between its current and future nodes concerning the learning of guerrilla warfare and terrorism. As one analyst stated, 'The *Encyclopedia* was attempting to diminish, if not eliminate, the master-pupil tutelage that forced terrorists and would-be terrorists to gather together in one spot for prolonged study. The volumes were a portable university for the common militant. Its ultimate aim was to democratize terrorism.'[8] In addition, the lessons are 'modular' and can be learned in any sequence or tailored for specific operational conditions in different countries.[9] This allows Al Qaeda to engage in far quicker criminal–soldier (*jihadi*) fielding than ever before utilized by traditional terrorists – akin to cellular division (replication) as opposed to modern industrial production methods.

Filtering/Fusion Capability. Once information seams have been limited or done away with, true information filtering and fusion capability takes place. This results in bits of information being brought together and merged in order to come up with new insights. For example, if a number of precursor chemicals for sarin gas were found within an operational area and an individual linked to a terrorist group (or a free agent with a chemistry degree) was also detained, these pieces of information are far more valuable fused together than kept compartmentalized by different groups working in that operational area. In other instances, lack of information is not the problem but too much information (noise), which must be filtered out, represents the problem. Network structures are beneficial in this regard because they allow for the sifting and filtering of information as it is distributed between the numerous nodes in the system. This allows for essential elements of information (EEI) identification to take place.

Al Qaeda Example. Filtering and fusion capability is represented by the Madrid train bombings of 11 March 2004. The identification of Spain's vulnerable political will (center of gravity) and the assessment to time the Madrid bombings coincident with a critical election demonstrates a situational assessment and an ability to execute an operation based on shared, filtered and fused information. Fusing the tentative Spanish political will, the opposing view of the political candidates on the issue of troop deployment to Iraq, and the network-distributed opinion that the strategy of the 'Jihadi Iraq' should include strikes against the enemy close to his home, demonstrates accurate information filtering and selection of an effective course of action.[10]

The results of this action were influential. The expected election outcome was reversed, Spain began withdrawing its troops in accordance with the newly elected official's campaign promise, and Spain entered into an agreement with the Al Qaeda network for 'protection' of its returning troops in compliance with bin Laden's 'stop shooting at Muslims' negotiation. In this one event, Al Qaeda has reduced the number of foreign troops in Iraq and attained the diplomatic and use-of-force status of a nation-state.

Parallel Processing (Multi-Tasking). When engaging in real-time problem solving, networked structures also possess another advantage over hierarchical structures. In this instance, rather than an apex decision maker working top-down on a problem, the problem gets tasked out and broken down among the network participants. The best example of this phenomena to date was the Ricin Alert Incident which took place in January 1998 in the United States. It was based on a rumor that drug traffickers were using a chemical warfare agent to booby-trap loads of methamphetamine. This rumor was proven to be false within six hours by an open-source network of law enforcement and public safety groups, linked together over the Internet and phone lines, who simultaneously worked on this problem while constantly updating each other regarding new elements of information which were collected. As a side note, those agencies and groups which were not connected into this network continued to broadcast this erroneous and disruptive rumor for days and, in some cases, months.

Al Qaeda Example. Al Qaeda nodes have always been responsible for target selection in their sphere of operations. Prior to 9/11, potential target groupings were presented by the nodal members to cut-off and senior Al Qaeda members who belonged to the Shura (Consultation Council). The senior members decided which specific targets to attack and provided network funding and expertise to the node or nodal members that would engage in the attack. During this period, nodal multi-tasking for potential target selection was thus taking place in dozens of locations throughout the world. Since 9/11, Al Qaeda nodes have increasingly been deciding on their own which targets to attack and conducting the attacks utilizing their own resources. This migration of network authority results in additional forms of nodal multi-tasking to now take place.

Offensive

The offensive attribute utilized by networked structures can either be destructive/seizure in nature (thing targeted) or disruptive in nature (non-thing targeted). It should be noted, however, that destructive/seizure attacks – based on destructive firepower – are generally associated with how hierarchical structures engage in conflict and war. Networks, on the other hand, tend to utilize disruptive firepower when engaging each other and hierarchies:

Swarming Capability. Swarming is a scheme of maneuver based on a convergent attack of five or more semi-autonomous (or autonomous) units on a targeted force in a specific physical place.[11] It allows that force to be hit from all directions which greatly increases its level of vulnerability as flank and rear attacks are normally more devastating than frontal attacks. After the attack, the various attacking units quickly scatter for defensive purposes. Swarming is dependent upon a robust flow of information, therefore, to use it, you must protect the information flow in order to maintain an advantage. Conversely, one should consider attacking/disrupting the information flow of an opposing force in order to counter-swarm.

Al Qaeda Example. The four civilian contractors killed in Fallujah, Iraq on 31 March 2004 were ambushed and then swarmed in a possible Al Qaeda-staged attack. While making a turn in their two vehicles the contractors were attacked by a group of men (faces covered by headscarves) who split into two groups. These groups threw hand grenades into the contractor's vehicles and sprayed them with small-arms fire. This was immediately followed by the crowds encircling the vehicles, stoning them and dragging the contractors' bodies through the streets.[12] A more pronounced example of Al-Qaeda swarming can be seen in the multiple wave attacks in Riyadh, Saudi Arabia which took place in May 2003. Compounds (Al-Hamra, Cordoval and Jedawal) containing 'American, British, Italian, French and other Western nationals as well as some Saudis' were simultaneously attacked by breeching (assault) teams which cleared the gates of guards and obstacles followed by suicide bomber units which entered the compounds and detonated.[13] Probably the best swarming example, according to John Arquilla, can be found in the Gardez, Afghanistan operation which took place in February and March 2002, a few months after the United States and coalition assault on Tora Bora. Thousands of Taliban and Al Qaeda fighters, deployed typically in twos and threes, were distributed all over the mountainous battlefield. These small assault teams 'pulsed' to attack US and allied forces in order to achieve numerical superiority. One of their swarming targets was US helicopters and their troop drop areas.

Distributed Sensor-to-Shooter Links. Networked structures are not required to utilize traditional manned weapons systems that are composed of self-contained sensor/targeting, maneuvering, crew protection/defense and weapons firing capability. Rather, sensors and other items can be physically decoupled from weapons. This allows the greater network to assign priorities to targets with fire brought against them more efficiently by whatever weapon is designated and/or free to engage the target. This allows for massed fire rather than massed forces. Modem militaries see this fire as being predominantly destructive because of their hierarchical bias. This approach is also more cost effective in crew protection/defense costs because no crew would need to be protected in some of the distributed parts of this system such as in air-dropped acoustic and unmanned aircraft (UAV) sensors.

Al Qaeda Example. Somalis working and fighting for Mohammed Farah Adid were provided training by Al Qaeda. These fighters operated a distributed shooter-to-sensor network against Task Force Ranger in 1993 in the operation described in the book *Black Hawk Down*. Somali watchers could observe preparations for helicopter operations without obstruction because of the terrain surrounding the Ranger base and because of the established routine of always keeping the hangar doors open. These Somali 'sensors' would note the preparations for launch and send signals to the shooters, who could then prepare for an attack on the helicopters, sometimes before the actual launch. The advanced warning gave the 'shooters' time to position and camouflage the selected firing positions. In this case, the advanced weapons were rocket-propelled grenade launchers. The firing positions were modified so that the gunners took a prone position, facing up, with the launch tube extended into a hole on the ground and with the gunner concealed in some manner. The shooter could then fire at the helicopter with little movement other than aiming adjustment and the backblast, partially shrouded in the hole, disguised the origin of the shot. This modification of firing position was also derived from this low-tech, but effective distributed sensor-to-shooter network.[14]

Bond-Relationship Targeting (BRT). This form of attack is defined as 'rather than gross physical destruction or injury, the desired end state is a tailored disruption within a thing, between it and other things or between it and its environment by degrading, severing, or altering the bonds and relationships which define its existence'. It allows the bonds and relationships between things to be targeted rather than the things themselves. Terrorism and information operations, two types of warfare that network structures excel at, rely far more upon disruption than actual destruction. Because of that fact and various forms of advanced weaponry now developing, BRT-type disruptive attacks will almost certainly remain the preferred offensive targeting approach utilized by network structures.

Al Qaeda Example. Beyond the 9–11 attack, clear-cut BRT examples can be seen taking place in a number of Al Qaeda theatres of operation. Operative Mustafa Abdul Kader Abed Al Ansari and his brothers attacked Americans at the Saudi petrochemical and refinery complex at Yanbu on 1 May 2004. This attack sought to further weaken US business links to the Saudi regime and drive out American businesses and their personnel from the country.[15] Al Qaeda's Madrid railway bombings of 11 March 2004 killed 192 and injured 1,400. They achieved their goal by forcing the Spanish government to withdrawal its military forces from Iraq. Earlier on 22 September 2003 the United Nations headquarters in Baghdad was leveled by a suicide bomber vehicle. This subsequently crippled UN activities in Iraq. This bombing and others attributed to Al Qaeda, like the multiple Iraqi police bombings of 27 October 2003 and the Italian Carabinieri bombing of 12 November 2003, are also meant to break apart coalition forces and cooperating entities operating in Iraq.[16]

Attack Masking/Virtual Network. Because networked structures can so easily create and then disconnect/drop nodes, attack masking capabilities are gained. Tracing who the attacker is tied into becomes difficult if not impossible in these instances as a result of plausible deniability and inability to connect the dots. This becomes an even greater problem in cyberspace operations where information systems belonging to neutral and even allied groups can be turned against a third party. An additional danger stemming from this attribute is the creation of a 'virtual network', as in the case of a terrorist conspiracy, which pulls together nodes/cells for only one attack and then ceases to exist after that operation. This falls within the concept of 'strategic indirection' and asymmetric warfare concerns.

   Al Qaeda Example. Lashkar-e-Jhangvi (LJ), a Pakistani affiliate of Al Qaeda since 2002, uses cells of two to three young men (sometimes as many as eight), that come together for an operation and then disband and later regroup at another location. These cells are scattered across Pakistan.[17] With regard to the Internet, denial-of-service and website defacement (or even capture) are not uncommon occurrences. These activities are not done directly from the attacker's computer to the target system but instead are done through third parties (and beyond), via Internet cafes, university systems and Internet sites registered under false names. This masks the operation so that the attacker remains unknown. For example, in October 2003, Haganah (⟨http://haganah.org.il⟩) was knocked off-line by successive denial-of-service attacks by Al Qaeda-affiliated forums (mostly ⟨.com⟩s) registered to Saudi Arabians and running in Malaysia.[18]

Defensive

The defensive attribute goes beyond mechanistic notions of protection and security that are derived from four-dimensional battlespace. Instead, fifth-dimensional battlespace principles are drawn upon to create new defensive capabilities. Defense can be defined by a structure's ability to evade attack, withstand physical punishment, heal itself after taking damage (like a biological entity), limit disruption to its information channels, and keep the information it possesses safe:

   Stealth-Masking Its Members (Forces). Network structures seek to shield their nodes/cells from attack by keeping secret their true relationship to the network and/or hide their true function as that of a combatant (threat). One method of doing this is compartmentalizing peripheral and less secure segments of the networked structure away from the trusted core membership. Another method is making combatants appear to be non-combatants as in the case of a 1990s female PKK suicide bomber appearing to be pregnant (with the explosive charge strapped to her stomach). Larger strike forces using vehicle-borne improvised explosive devices (VBIEDss) can mask the threat they pose by using stolen police cars or ambulances. The International Committee of the Red Cross office in Baghdad was targeted this way in

October 2003 by Iraqi insurgents who drove a stolen ambulance packed with explosives into the compound and detonated it.

Al Qaeda Example. For Al Qaeda and Taliban personnel, a survival kit found in Pakistan urges members 'to "merge with the masses" and thus "become indistinguishable" from the rest of the people' and 'Merge completely in the environment you live in. . . there will be no personal friendship, not even with the members of your own group'.[19] These concepts are drawn from both traditional guerrilla warfare literature and direct Al Qaeda linkages to Takfir wal Hijra. The Takfir, a criminal organization based in Europe and North Africa that employs undercover strategies in its drug dealings, has become an Al Qaeda node now engaging in Islamic terrorism.[20] In actual operations Al Qaeda operatives attacked the residential compound in Riyadh, Saudi Arabia in November 2003 by disguising themselves as policemen. The assault consisted of a stand-up attack followed by suicide bombings. The 9/11 attack was also conducted by a stealth-masked force – 19 Al Qaeda operatives carrying box cutters were able to blend in as airline passengers prior to seizing control of four airliners. The USS Cole attacked in October 2000 by an Al Qaeda suicide vessel represents another example. The suicide vessel was of the type used for normal harbor operations in the port of Aden and was able to pull along side the warship without signaling its true intent.[21]

Impervious to Decapitation Strikes. Because decision making is decentralized in many network structures, no key leadership target set exists which can be subjected to a decapitation strike. No 'head of the beast' exists to cut off. This is an immensely important consideration because it means that these structures are immune to a relatively basic form of disruption. Concern exists that criminal organizations, such as drug cartels, are evolving toward these structures because of such benefits. This can be seen with the shift away from the Medellin model (central star hub) towards the Cali model (multiple star hubs) used by narcotraffickers.

Al Qaeda Example. A Pakistani *jihadi* leader in May 2004 explained that there was no necessity for operational links with Al Qaeda for action in Pakistan because the concept of Al Qaeda or 'foundation' was not, in concept, a single structure or group of structures but rather 'a loose network of likeminded people', and he indicated that the concept or reality of a fixed-base-type foundation was dissolved in 2001. Operations are conducted by cells, based on the principles of the foundation, reinforced by a network and not dependent upon any one individual or group. The effort to search for and capture or eliminate bin Laden or other known and prominent figures may have motivational value for the United States and allies, and may reveal new insights into the network operations, but it will not degrade the capability of the network to operate. Capturing or killing prominent and known Al Qaeda leaders may actually make the network stronger.[22]

Offers Protection Against Precision Fire. Network forces that have swarming and distributed sensor-to-shooter link capabilities are not required to mass on the battlefield for offensive purposes. This allows them to have a higher degree of defense against precision fire than traditional hierarchical forces that must mass in order to engage in an offensive operation. This physical dispersion of network forces does not mean that they cannot be eventually located and targeted. Rather, it means that targeting is more difficult and time consuming and high-value clusters of target sets that can be destroyed or neutralized are not provided.

Al Qaeda Example. The Gardez, Afghanistan operation which took place in February and March 2002 with its swarming of Al Qaeda and Taliban forces in assault teams of two to three members offers a good example of this defensive capability in a guerrilla setting. In a terrorism mode, the stealth-masking ability of Al Qaeda operatives, as in the USS Cole incident and the 9/11 attack, makes them invisible to detection and precision fire. Personnel moving between *jihadi* groups within Al Qaeda and linked to it also provides additional layers of protection from target acquisition and fire.[23]

Provides Redundant Information Channels. Redundancy within an organizational structure is many times viewed as being inefficient. This is not always the case. Even when a networked structure is subjected to node/cell and information channel attacks, it is far more robust than a hierarchical structure. This is because of all of the information channels its redundant web-like structure provides. As a result, more of its structure has to be destroyed or disrupted to compromise its combat effectiveness.

Al Qaeda Example. The Al Qaeda C^2 star-hub that contains its leadership and committees has multiple and redundant linkages to the vast array of Al Qaeda global network nodes.

Communications can take place by numerous means including oral messages, encrypted letters (both text and using microdots), encoded emails, and hard and cell phone communications. These information channels to the leadership hub have been severely degraded as the Al Qaeda leadership has been relentlessly pursued since 9/11. Websites and chat rooms have taken on new levels of importance as the global nodes plan and carrying out their own operations. A specific example of the robustness of these information channels is the official Al Qaeda website which is known as 'Al Neda'. The Alneda.com domain name was lost in August 2003 and since that time has been operating as a parasite (or ghost) site that is 'embedded within another website without the site owner's knowledge'.[24] Al Neda easily moves from site to site by means of online cracking tools as it is removed from the earlier sites it embeds itself into.[25] Numerous other Al Qaeda and affiliated websites and chat rooms exist and result in a complex, redundant, and, at times, largely invisible global communications infrastructure.

Self-Healing Ability: Networks are well known to be resistant to traditional forms of combat power that would greatly damage them if they were hierarchical structures. Networks also possess the ability to repair (heal) damage to their structures by creating new nodes to replace ones that have been lost. In addition, they can reroute (grow back) information channels around damaged and missing nodes.

Al Qaeda Example. Since 9/11, Al Qaeda has lost parts of its core leadership through death, capture and being forced so far underground as to become ineffective from a C^2 perspective. Thousands of fighters have also been lost in Afghanistan and numerous terrorist nodes have been broken up internationally. In response, the network has replaced leaders where needed, attempted to grow new terrorist nodes to cover ones that have been destroyed, created new linkages to like-minded *jihadi* groups, continued to recruit new members and devolved network functions. To limit damage and promote faster self-healing, Al Qaeda has also used network 'cut-outs' – smuggler-chain middlemen – to insulate sections of the network from being compromised. Damaged and captured nodes can thus be jettisoned – like a gangrenous limb – and new network extremities re-grown in their place.

Information Security. Networks can protect the information they create, store and transmit by following information security (infosec) protocols. These protocols can dictate how nodes communicate with one another and the type of form the network takes (e.g. star-hub, chain, etc.) to achieve its infosec needs.

Al Qaeda Example. A terrorist survival kit, obtained in Pakistan and used by Al Qaeda and Taliban members, provides instruction on how to maintain information security for network communications. Cell phones are to be used only as a last resort (hard-line phones are preferred) and, if used, cell phone protocols such as obtaining one under a fake name and address, turning it on only when making or expecting a call, and shutting it off and disconnecting the phone's battery are to be followed. Internet use follows protocols based on using public Internet cafes, leaving no evidence of your visit behind, never going to the same café repeatedly and not using messages that will betray your ideological commitment.[26] Forms of secret communication – common, standby and alarm – and counter-surveillance techniques are also mentioned in the *Military Studies in Jihad Against the Tyrants* manual found in the Al Qaeda safe house in Manchester, England.[27] These infosec protocols result in Al Qaeda's nodes (C^2, operations, intelligence, support) being difficult to acquire and target.

From a network structure perspective, the communication paths isolated by Valdis Krebs concerning the 9/11 Al Qaeda strike force (pilots and enforcers) portray another level of information security. The pilots for the attack did not know one another and Mohamed Atta served as the star-hub node in a C^2

role.[28] Infosec needs limited the type and direction of the information flows within this small operational strike force thus making it more difficult to compromise its mission.

Combat Multiplier

A combat multiplier as an attribute of network structures was added to this analysis because of the unique operational advantages networks possess. This attribute enhances both defensive and offensive capabilities as well as the overall functioning/behavior of these structures. What is readily apparent about networks is how 'alive' they appear to be as opposed to hierarchical based structures that are more mechanistic in nature:

Increasing Returns as the Network Expands. As they grow, network structures operate in a manner contrary to hierarchical structures. Whereas hierarchies see diminishing returns as they grow too large, networks see increasing returns and value. The best example of increasing returns can be seen with a computer connected to the Internet. One or two computers linked online have basically no value but millions of computers are a different story. Everyone recognizes that being wired to the net ten years ago had far less value than it has today because of the immense communication and information/knowledge retrieval opportunities which now exist derived from email address and website proliferation. From a conflict perspective, more nodes/cells means more sensors and more weapons (fighters) that can be brought to bear in an operational environment. It is of little wonder that thousands of throwaway gumball-size or far smaller (nano) sensors will one day be distributed over future battlefields to establish battlespace-wide sensor nets.

Al Qaeda Example. Al Qaeda possesses nodes in over 60 countries and has a much greater resource pool to draw upon for its operations than it did when it was a much smaller organization. Specialists from one section of the network can now support groups linked to other parts of the network and vice versa. As an example, Indonesian Jemaah Islamiyyah (JI) cells did not have the capability to manufacture large-scale bombs until Al Qaeda technical expertise from outside the region was provided to them.[29] Groups like JI, in return, open up new theaters of operation and sources of recruits for Al Qaeda. Chechen *jihadis* bring their own expertise, lessons learned, regional contacts and unique access to resources to the network as do Moroccans, Pakistanis, Somalis and countless other groups. For instance, the covert skills of the Moroccans (Takfir wal Hijra) are already helping to make Al Qaeda operatives more stealth-masked. Chechen access to thermobaric weapons represents another example. Kevin Kelly views 'each additional member increasing a network's value, which in turn attracts more members, initiating a spiral of benefits'.[30] This process seems to be in effect for Al Qaeda.

The marginal cost of adding these new groups to the network is almost non-existent given the fact that terrorist training manuals are now in CD form and online and each group is expected to be financially self-supporting.

Ease of Growth. The plug and play nature of these structures makes add-ons relatively simple and gives them a 'tinker toy' feel. No real impediments exist to network structure growth such as size constraints, managerial staff limitations or departmental/unit boundaries. While somewhat chaotic in nature, all that is required is information channels being extended to the new nodes/cells that are joining the network. Deeper level connections into the network of course will be moderated by issues of trust.

Al Qaeda Example. Ease of growth can be attributed to the common threads that include the network's reason for existence, requirement for struggle, social and religious obligation and a common identifiable opponent. Justifying deviations from an accepted behavior pattern can increase the recruitment pool. For example, legitimizing crime in support of the network has created a recruitment pool in Morocco, Spain and France of prisoners, drug traffickers and drug users as well as a support system for this collection of nodes and cells, which helps with the sustainability of the cell. Declaring a Western lifestyle and mannerism as an acceptable deception for *jihadis* attracted the Takfir wal Hajra sect, which espouses those traits in contrast to traditional social norms, to join the network. Takfiris are suspected in the Madrid bombing. Importing influence and tactics like suicide bombing into Pakistan has created cells within the country that include individuals with better educational backgrounds and social status, unlike recruit profiles in other regions. Suicide bombing, anathema to Pakistan's social norm, was imported when the Al Qaeda networks escaped and evaded from Afghanistan, and has now been accepted as a viable tactic.[31]

Mission Tailoring. Instead of sending a one-size-fits-all military or response force, network structures can be tailored for the mission at hand. A specific grouping of nodes/cells can be matched to the needs of the mission and then quickly assembled together to carry it out. This allows for a wide variety of threats (targets) to be dealt with while in the process conserving forces and resources that can be used in other missions or as a general operational reserve. Further, these nodes/cells can stay linked to the greater network and enjoy the benefits of virtual reach-back capabilities for support.

Al Qaeda Example. The suicide bombing of the Paradise Hotel in Mombassa and the associated, synchronized attempted shoot-down of a charter jet leaving Mombassa in November 2002 demonstrates mission tailoring and possible network reach-back capability. The attack combined detailed planning, use of a practiced and evolved tactic (suicide bombing) and use of a more advanced and uncommon technology (surface-to-air missiles). The attack was tailored for the objectives in three ways. First, the attacks were aimed at Israeli targets. Second, the attacks occurred in a location to demonstrate the global reach of Al Qaeda. Third, the use of SAMs (surface-to-air missiles) demonstrated the flexibility and variety of weapons available for use in Al Qaeda's arsenals. The network structure of Al Qaeda facilitated the tailored mission by providing assets from its diverse resource pool. These assets were allocated based upon the needs of target selection, location criteria and weapons mix.

Criminal–Warfighting Orientation. The rigid nature of hierarchical structures makes their members far more likely to follow the rules of war than the members of network structures. Conformity is partially enforced by the structure itself. While not characteristic of all network structures, criminal–warfighting is far more likely to take place in them because experimentation and entrepreneurial thinking tends to dominate. It must be accepted that the operational benefits of breaking international law (cheating) are well known. Terrorists do this on a daily basis as an archetypal form of criminal–warfighters. Older behavioral patterns and legal inhibitions are simply not important or were openly cast aside as tools of ethnic (religious) oppression enforced by the status quo on those members comprising the networked structure. Another consideration for legitimate soldiers (police) will be based on reaction time. When differences in reaction time become so critical that they will spell the difference between victory or defeat, nodal members may not wait for a judge advocate's (or other legal) ruling on the legality of a weapon or technique before using it against an opposing force.

Al Qaeda Example. The original Al Qaeda entity, with funding from larger, identifiable sources and strategic influence from a variety of internal committees, has changed into a looser affiliate network with cells and outlying social and technical networks that continue to support the overarching strategy which forms the foundation of the effort. Some of the suspected operators in the Madrid train bombing belong to the sect Takfir wal Hijra ('excommunication and exile'). This group considers crime as a method to conduct operations in support of the Al Qaeda network. Acceptable social behavior of this group includes drug addiction and trafficking, radical acts and grooming standards of the Western culture. The planning and execution of the bombing demonstrates a connection between radical Islamic doctrine and organized criminal networks. The cell or node was composed of a drug gang, students and shopkeepers. Crime committed for the cause is considered justifiable. This justification of including and recruiting criminals in prison enlarges the recruitment pool.[32] The fielding of these recruits brings a new meaning to the term 'criminal–soldiers.' In addition, Al Qaeda's use of terrorism and the willingness of its operatives to torture and maim US and other prisoners makes its style of warfighting the antitheses of the Western conduct of war.

Collective Vision. Network structures benefit from what can be termed a 'leaderless C^2' type of cognition quite similar to that of Louis Beam's views on 'leaderless resistance'. A collective vision develops either by consensus or initial design that defines the raison d'être of the network. For operational military and law enforcement purposes, this would be achieving the end state that leads to a successful mission. While the cells/nodes of the network will fight (strive) toward this vision independently, they will constantly attempt to update each other via real-time information links so that a general awareness concerning the state of the battlespace (opspace) is created for the entire network to utilize.

Al Qaeda Example. The Al Qaeda network is promoting a collective vision at the strategic level. Al Qaeda promotes the strategic vision of a 'combined 20th century theory of a unified Islamic polity with restoration of the Islamic Caliphate that, at its height, stretched from Spain to India'.[33] Within this vision Osama bin Laden has been viewed as both the potential calipah (leader of the caliphate) and the mahdi (the prophesized one).[34]

In tandem with restoration of the caliphate is the ultimate destruction of the United States and Israel and the overthrow of apostate Islamic regimes. Intermediate operational visions can also be said to exist for this network such as driving the United States out of Iraq and Saudi Arabia and targeting the Saudi oil infrastructure. These represent stepping stones toward fulfilling the strategic vision.

Adaptive Behavior. As a by-product of this general awareness, cells/nodes can then determine where to put their effort in order to best benefit the overall network. This allows for adaptive behavior to take place during operational situations. When this is combined with the greater information processing speed of the network structure, it helps to explain why they can easily outdistance hierarchical structures and get inside of their OODA loops. At higher levels of abstraction, adaptation can also take place as networks alter their collective visions to meet the new realities of the strategic environment. If required, they can easily build themselves out into mutually beneficial areas within which they have never engaged before. One example would be the alliances which have formed between Mexican drug lords and Southern California street gang members.[35]

Al Qaeda Example. Al Qaeda has morphed from an outgrowth of an office of the international Muslim brigade that opposed the Soviets in Afghanistan and trained Mujahedeen (holy warriors) in the 1980s into a tightly controlled global network based in Afghanistan (1988–2001) and then into its present form (2001–2004) of a loose collection of independent nodes and cells nodes that plan, finance and conduct their own attacks.

While the Afghani training camps were initially vital to creating Al Qaeda solidarity amongst its members, these visions are now propagated and sustained by social networks relying upon the internet – the single most important communications tool utilized by radical Islamic extremists.[36] The basis of Al Qaeda adaptability is derived from its 'losing and learning doctrine' and 'goal oriented and not rule oriented' protocols. Losing and learning focuses on accepting that 'when an operation fails and/or suffers human and matériel attrition, it is not considered a strategic loss, provided the group learns, improves a does not repeat its mistake'.[37] Goal orientation allows for the end state and not the means to that end to become paramount. If one form of attack or technique fails then others will be tried. These protocols have allowed Al Qaeda to become a network that learns.

Emergence. The synthesis of network collective vision and adaptive behavior capabilities may result in network 'emergence' (the rise of spontaneous intelligence). This concept is reminiscent of hiveminds ('the sum is greater than its parts' entities) that are described in science fiction literature. These monsters of our imagination are viewed as extremely tough adversaries and may have more in common with a post-modern threat like Al Qaeda than we ever realized.

Al Qaeda Example. Unknown

Al Qaeda can and probably should be viewed using a biological metaphor if we are to properly counter it. This idea-based creature – derived from a collective (strategic) vision of the future – has been evolving (morphing) through stages of network development for years now. It is gaining more new recruits than it is losing (killed or captured members) on a daily basis and is spreading into new population centers. No ideological counter currently exists to strategically target the Al Qaeda philosophy. Al Qaeda as an organization knows how to learn and adapt itself to new environments and it exists both in traditional humanspace and within cyberspace. It even appears to have limited self-healing ability as a robust network would be expected to possess. But has Al Qaeda given rise to a form of organizational 'spontaneous intelligence'? That question will have to remain unanswered because our knowledge and understanding of 'emergence' is still too primitive to make such a determination based on any example provided. Possibly emergence is only a biological and artificial intelligence capability and not one possessed by post-modern organizations. Still, as an insurance policy against such a potential Al Qaeda capability it would be prudent to at least consider this eventuality.

FUTURE POTENTIALS

The operational combat analysis of the Al Qaeda network offers insight into how to better understand and ultimately counter non-state threats. New questions concerning Al Qaeda network operational capability are already apparent:

- At what point in its evolutionary development did Al Qaeda gain the various speed, offensive, defensive and combat multiplier capabilities identified in this analysis? In addition, at what point did 'critical mass' for network expansion into new countries and initial 'relative superiority'[38] in the war against the United States take place?
- Which capabilities are gained sequentially (in a linear fashion) and which capabilities are gained independently (in a non-linear fashion)? Speculation concerning 'shooter-to-sensor links' as a prerequisite for 'swarming' capability exists as does 'collective vision' and 'adaptive behavior' as prerequisites for 'emergence'.
- When some capabilities are gained by sections of the Al Qaeda network do other capabilities ever become degraded or disappear? The intuitive answer would appear to be yes. All channel networks, for instance, fully eliminate the impediment of information seams. Decisions can then be made with total awareness by the entire network but by gaining this capability network Infosec has been severely degraded because any nodal penetration of the network will result in all the information that it contains being compromised.[39]
- What bearing does the organizational form (chain, star, all-channel network or hybrid) of the Al Qaeda network and sub-networks (such as assault forces) have on its capabilities? These leads to questions concerning organic organizational form vulnerabilities (such as infosec for all-channel networks) and the vulnerabilities that exist at the linkage points between organizational forms (such as the interface between a star-hub and a smuggler chain).
- What better capabilities can be identified for the speed, offensive, defensive and combat multiplier attributes used in this analysis? The original capabilities were only identified in 2001 and were subsequently reevaluated and further developed for this analysis. Which capabilities currently identified overlap with others? How can these capabilities be better modeled qualitatively and quantitatively?

In addition, new questions concerning our own analytical methods and counter-OPFOR capabilities emerge from this analysis:

- Is Al Qaeda being analyzed as a postmodern criminal-warfighting entity – as it should be – or is it still viewed by means of older conceptual lenses by military and criminal intelligence analysts and equated with earlier and less capable generations of terrorist groups?

- How can cutting edge Al Qaeda analyses, represented by the order of battle and Manwaring paradigm (Sword model) models applied to Al Qaeda in this volume, benefit from this analysis and vice-verse? How do we promote all of these forms of analysis and better integrate them with netwar concepts and actual network mapping as undertaken by Valdis Krebs and others?
- What operational capabilities of our own nascent counter-insurgency networks currently exist? How do they rank with Al Qaeda's speed, offensive, defensive and combat multiplier attributes used in this analysis?

ACKNOWLEDGEMENTS

This work is partially derived from Robert J. Bunker, 'Operational Advantages of Networked Organizational Structures in Future Conflict and War', Paper presented at 'Transnational Terrorism Panel', Towards a New Asia, 3rd Asian Security Conference, Institute for Defence Studies and Analyses (IDSA), New Delhi, India, 26–29 January 2001. Published in Jasjit Singh, ed, *Reshaping Asian Security*, Institute for Defence Studies and Analyses (IDSA), (New Delhi: Knowledge World, 2001), pp.250–60. The authors would like to thank Lisa Campbell and John Arquilla for their aid in identifying Al Qaeda operational examples in this work.

NOTES

1. For more on network structure and function and issues and dynamics see John P. Sullivan and Robert J. Bunker, 'Multilateral Counter-Insurgency Networks', in this volume.
2. See Howard Rheingold, *Smart Mobs: The Next Social Revolution* (New York: Perseus Publishing, 2002); Kevin Kelly, *New Rules for the New Economy* (New York: Penguin. 1998); John Arquilla and David Ronfeldt, *The Advent of Netwar* (Santa Monica, CA: RAND, 1996).
3. Paul L. Williams, *Al Qaeda: Brotherhood of Terror* (New York: Alpha Books, 2002), pp.6–8.
4. This four stage overview was created using information principally from Rohan Gunaratna, *Inside Al Qaeda: Global Network of Terror* (New York: Berkley Publishing Group; reissue edition, 2003); Williams; and various Internet news sources, such as CNN, for timeline accuracy.
5. These basic organizational forms have been described in John Arquilla and David Ronfeldt's netwar publications.
6. Steven Johnson, *Emergence: The Connected Lives of Ants, Brains, Cities, and Software* (New York: Scribner, 2001).
7. John Boyd, *A Discourse on Winning and Losing* (Quantico, VA: MCA Press, 1987).
8. Reuel Marc Gerecht, 'The Terrorists' Encyclopedia', *The Middle East Quarterly*, Vol.8, No.3 (Summer 2001), available at ⟨http://www.meforum.org⟩.
9. C.J. Chivers and David Rohde, 'The Jihad Files: Afghan Camps Turn Out Holy War Guerrillas and Terrorists', *The New York Times*, 18 March 2002.
10. Jay Tolson, 'Cracking Al Qaeda's Code', *US News and World Report*, 17 May 2004.
11. Sean J.A. Edwards, *Swarming on the Battlefield: Past, Present, and Future* (Santa Monica, CA: RAND, 2000), p.2. See also John Arquilla and David Ronfeldt, *Swarming & The Future of Conflict* (Santa Monica, CA: RAND, 2000).
12. 'Military Officials: Empty Streets, Media Point to Planned Iraq Attack', CNN, 3 April 2004, available at ⟨http://www.cnn.com⟩.
13. Ben Venzke, *Saudi Compound Bombings (SCB) – vl.4.* (Alexandria, VA: IntelCenter, 2003), pp.5–6.

14. Mark Bowden, *Black Hawk Down*. (New York: Penguin Putnam; 2000); Patrick D. Weadon, 'Going to War? Don't Forget the OPSEC!', *OPSEC Indicator*, Vol.Z (Fall 2000).
15. 'Al-Qaida Driving U.S. Out of Saudi Arabia: Amid Terror Threat, Ambassador Telling Americans to Get Out', *WorldNetDaily.com*, 15 May 2004.
16. Robert J. Bunker and John P. Sullivan, *Suicide Bombings in Operation Iraqi Freedom*. Land Warfare Paper 46W (Arlington, VA: Association of the US Army, September 2004).
17. Nasra Hassan, 'Al Qaeda's Understudy', *The Atlantic Monthly*, June 2004, pp.42–3.
18. Aaron Weisburd, 'Al Qaeda Attacks Blogosphere', 17 October 2003, available at ⟨http://www.freerepublic.com⟩.
19. Anwar Iqbal, 'al-Qaida's Blueprint for Terror', United Press International, 13 February 2004.
20. Sebastian Rotella, 'Jihad's Unlikely Alliance', *Los Angeles Times*, 23 May 2004, pp.A1, A18–A19.
21. 'U.S. Suspects Terrorism in Navy Ship Blast', CNN, 12 October 2000, available at ⟨http://www.cnn.com⟩.
22. Hassan.
23. Ibid., p.42.
24. Michelle Delio, 'Al Qaeda Website Refuses to Die', *Wired News*, 7 April 2003, p.1, available at ⟨http://www.wired.com⟩.
25. Ibid. pp.1–2.
26. Iqbal.
27. UK/BM-1 Translation of *Military Studies in the Jihad Against the Tyrants*. See Fifth Lesson: Means of Communication and Transportation. Posted 7 December 2001 at ⟨http://www.usdoj.gov/ag/trainingmannual.htm⟩.
28. Vladis E. Krebs, 'Mapping Networks of Terrorist Cells', *Connections*, Vol.24, No.3 (2002), pp.31–34.
29. Gunaratna, p.xxxv.
30. Kevin Kelly, *New Rules for the New Economy* (New York: Penguin Books, 1999), p.25.
31. Hassan; Rotella.
32. Rotella.
33. Brian Michael Jenkins, *Countering Al Qaeda*. MR-1620-RC (Santa Monica, CA: RAND, 2002), p.4.
34. 'A Unique Opportunity to Establish the Khilafat', ⟨http://www.ummah.net/action/km/candidates.html; and 'Warnings from Islam's "Messianic Whirlpool": Jihadists in Global Frenzy over Coming of Prophesied "Mahdi", *WorldNetDaily.com*, 29 March 2004.
35. John P. Sullivan, 'Third Generation Street Gangs: Turf, Cartels and Netwarriors', *Transnational Organized Crime*, Vol.3, No.2 (Autumn 1997), pp.95–108.
36. The Internet represents the postmodern equivalent of the printed book and provides the basis for transnational network structures to achieve collective vision.
37. Gunaratna, p.xxv.
38. William H. McRaven, *SpecOps: Case Studies in Special Operational Warfare Theory and Practice* (Novato, CA: Presidio Press, 1995).
39. Preliminary research into network organizational forms and their operational advantages and disadvantages has been conducted. Robert J. Bunker, presentation on 'Networked OPFORs: Strategic and Operational Considerations', Project O'Bannon, Event 4: Terrorist Networks: An Analysis, Marine Corps Warfighting Lab, Quantico, VA, 22–23 May2002.

'Brotherhoods' and 'Associates': Chechen Networks of Crime and Resistance

MARK GALEOTTI

Banditry and resistance are deeply ingrained within the Chechen national identity. From the seventeenth century, Chechens and the Cossack soldier-settlers who had established their fortified farms north of the Terek River had routinely clashed and raided each other, although in fairness the Cossacks were, unusually for them, more often the victims than the aggressors. The nineteenth century saw the Russian Empire make a concerted effort to bring the rest of the Caucasus region under its control, by conquest, punitive massacre and deportation. However, this was always a tenuous grip on a region eager to assert its independence given the opportunity. In 1918, for example, the fragmentation of the tsarist empire allowed the creation of a Republic of the North Caucasus Federation, which in due course fell to the Red Army in 1922. The Chechens had lost a battle, but not the war. They rebelled fiercely against Stalinist collectivization in 1929, and while the Soviet state was able to crush the main risings relatively quickly, sporadic revenge killings, sabotage and protests would continue for a decade.

Joseph Stalin did not forget the Chechens. As German forces advanced into the Caucasus during the Second World War in an effort to deny the USSR its sources of oil, there was a fear the Chechens would rise to support them. In an operation typical in its breath-taking scale and mechanical brutality, Stalin had the entire Chechen population deported in February 1944: 450,000 men, women and children were scattered across Central Asia, in the process of which over 70,000 died. Only in 1957 were the Chechens allowed to return to a homeland now settled by Russians and other peoples, and even then they were twinned with the traditionally more tractable Ingushetians in a new Chechen–Ingush Autonomous Republic.[1]

This traumatic history has touched every Chechen family, and memories still run deep. The author has met Chechen school children who can recite lists of family members who died during the years in exile or the lands lost to their families. The collapse of the USSR provided yet another opportunity, one which the Chechens were not slow to take. In local presidential elections held in 1991, Chechens overwhelmingly supported Dzhokar Dudayev, who was standing on a platform of outright independence. When new Russian President Boris Yeltsin fatefully told the constituent regions and republics of the Russian Federation to 'take as much freedom as you can swallow', the Chechens took him at his word. It became clear that Moscow's imperial instincts were still alive and well, though. Clumsy attempts to pressurize the Chechens back into the federation only served to rally them behind the inept and criminal Dudayev, culminating in the 1994–96 war, resumed in 1999 and still being fought.

Meanwhile, Chechen organized crime had become a powerful force within the wider Russian underworld, albeit not quite as omnipotent and omnipresent as Russian political myth suggested. While it became commonplace for nationalist Russian politicians (and the Kremlin) to link the guerrilla resistance in Chechnya itself with these criminal structures in the rest of the Russian Federation,[2] what has become clear is that they are two essentially separate phenomena. However, they are both structured as networks, reflecting both the challenges of modern crime and insurgency, as well as the impact of their cultural heritage.

THE BUILDING BLOCKS

As with many societies shaped by an experience of external pressure and a fragmented rural economy, traditionally Chechens have identified less with any central state and much more with their position within complex, overlapping and interlocking (if also sometimes antagonistic) networks of family, clan (*teip*), region and personal allegiance. Furthermore, the leadership structures of the *teip* closely overlapped the *virds*, hereditary Sufi religious brotherhoods. Just as the approximately 150 *teips* were broadly divided between more independent highland clans and the more settled lowland ones, so too there were considerable commonalities with other North Caucasian peoples (whom the Russians lumped together as *gortsy*, 'highlanders'), and these networks could easily cross ethnic boundaries. The process of Chechen 'state building' was, after all, hijacked by the tsarist Russian invasion and occupation of the nineteenth century, and since then the institutions of central authority were seen essentially as tools of foreign occupation. Leaders might be sought or accepted, around whom to unite in a time of crisis, but theirs was a temporary and conditional authority, subject to the will of the clans, sometimes expressed through larger unions of *teips* known as *tukhums*.[3]

When an independent Chechen state was declared in 1991, although President Dzhokar Dudayev sought the trappings of statehood, from his own flag to his mint, in practice these were largely symbolic, little more than relics of the Soviet era under new banners. This took second place to other, network-based forms of authority. Dudayev proved, after all, little more than a self-aggrandizing opportunist, who presided over a criminalization of the fledgling Chechen state. Favouritism, corruption, nepotism, clientelism and localism all flourished, and in many cases power remained in the hands of the *teips*, albeit now given official sanction. Chosen and endorsed by the Chechen National Congress – in effect a gathering of the *teips* – Dudayev was in this respect simply another of Chechnya's tradition of figurehead leaders. A case in point is the way the Chechen police force suddenly grew from the 3,000 officers it inherited from the Soviet period to 14 separate forces, accounting for some 17,000 armed officers. What had happened was that clans within Dudayev's alliance were simply given the opportunity to turn their gunmen into state law enforcement officers, albeit still responsible to their clan elders. Likewise, thanks to its ability to use the Chechen State Bank (still formally a branch of the Russian State Bank), one gang linked to several *teips* close to Dudayev was able to use false *avisos* (proof of fund documents) to defraud the Russian State Bank of perhaps $700 million.

Kinship therefore still occupies a central place in Chechen society, not only defining personal identity but also providing a practical alternative to the state in so many ways, from protection (especially through the threat of the feud) to economic opportunity (whether employment while fit or the prospect of communal support when laid low by age or illness). While families, villages and *teips* share a notionally pyramidal structure, headed by councils of male elders, in practice these are relatively fluid self-help associations. The elders' role is primarily to resolve disputes such that they do not harm the community (by causing internal conflict or opening up opportunities to rivals) and acting as intermediaries with other associations, handling everything from kidnap negotiations and disputes over herding rights to matchmaking and loan-brokering, within the framework of *adat*, customary law. The *teip* can accommodate contraction or expansion; each is made up of *gars* (branches), in turn comprising several *nekye* (constituent families), and it is not unusual for a thriving *gars* or even *nekye* to become a *teip* in its own right. It can also cope with geographic dispersion: while most *teips* remain concentrated on a particular region, urbanization, land hunger and, later, the pressures of war have led to high levels of migration. While in some cases individuals and *nekye* join other clans, it is more common for them to retain a connection to their home *teip*. Third, it can also accommodate outsiders, as it has for at least two centuries been possible for other North Caucasian *gortsy* to join a *nekye* and thus a *teip* individually (perhaps by marriage or else a form of adoption), or else as families, which either join an existing *nekye* or else are integrated into a *gars* as a *nekye* in their own right. In this way, the traditional kinship structures form flexible and inclusive networks, able to operate across geographic and even ethnic boundaries, bound by common identities and a shared moral code and able and willing to incorporate outsiders able to 'buy into' that code and identity. This became a key asset both in their resistance struggle against Moscow and also in their organized criminality.

Of course, Islam has also created networks of its own. Before the Russian invasions, Islam played a relatively minor role in Chechnya, being widespread but also relatively tolerant and low-key. Religious authority manifest through the *virds* worked alongside the *teips*, with largely overlapping memberships and objectives. However, the pressures of occupation and the ensuing hardships and Russian atrocities have served to radicalize a minority of Chechen Moslems and created new structures of identity and authority, structures which increasingly have turned to foreign inspirations and paymasters, and especially Wahhabism. The impact Islam has had upon the guerrilla movement will be discussed later, but it is important to stress that – prior to the spread of Wahhabism – in most cases religious networks appear to have rested atop or fitted within existing network linkages rather than replaced them.

Much the same is true of the increasingly structured criminal groupings that emerged in Chechnya after 1991 and, even more so, within the Chechen diaspora within Russia and the other former Soviet states. Most started as small and opportunistic groups built around kin ties, usually focused on a single charismatic, effective or authoritative individual. Many never evolved beyond that, remaining essentially bandit gangs. However, for those groups which grew and became more complex and diverse, there came a point at which they could not rely solely on kin, clan and locality to recruit appropriate members and maintain internal cohesion. Some therefore stagnated, but others moved beyond these traditional networks, acquiring new contacts, members and identities, but generally without entirely abandoning their roots.

'BRATVA': NETWORK-BASED CHECHEN CRIME[4]

There is little doubt that independent Chechnya, especially under former leader Djokar Dudayev, became thoroughly criminalized. After the first war, his successor President Aslan Maskhadov had made some efforts to combat the more overt forms of banditry and organized crime. He transferred many former guerrillas to the police and established special units devoted to combating kidnapping and thefts from oil pipelines. Although to a large extent Moscow's claims that it re-invaded in 1999 in order to combat anarchy and criminality is so much self-serving rhetoric, it is certainly true the lack of effective central control over much of the country hamstrung any efforts to re-establish law and order on the part of the independent Chechen regime.

Chechen organized crime has been strikingly unaffected by the two Chechen wars, though. In part, this reflects the extent to which a combination of Chechen tradecraft and Russian corruption permit business as usual under even the most extreme conditions, as generous bribes ease passage through the battle lines. Much the same, after all, happened in the former Yugoslavia. Indeed, a number of the belligerents are also active criminals. Many rebel warlords also maintain profitable sidelines in kidnap, banditry and drug smuggling. One, Ruslan Khaikharoyev, reportedly amassed a fortune of almost $2 million through kidnappings. Conversely, several Russian field commanders also appeared to have at the very least turned a blind eye to systematic looting, drug trafficking and even large-scale sales of military equipment to their enemies. The Russians have also turned to a convicted embezzler, former mayor of Grozny (and appointee of Dudayev's), Beslan Gantemirov, to command a mercenary militia in the war, prompting one seasoned observer to call this a war of 'crooks against terrorists'.

More importantly, though, Chechen organized crime (it tends to call itself a *bratva*, 'brotherhood', rather than *mafiya*) has outgrown Chechnya. Chechens run several of Moscow's main gangs (*Tsentralnaya, Ostankinskaya, Avtomobilnaya, Yuzhno-Portovy*), with others in St Petersburg, Yekaterinburg, and all across Russia. During the first war, Moscow was worried that Chechen gangs elsewhere in the country would become a dangerous fifth column. After all, for a while under the infamous 'Khoza' (whose real name was Nikolai Suleymanov), the Chechens had been the most active and possibly even most powerful gang alliance in Moscow following a turf war in 1988–89. Even after Khoza's death in 1994 and a renewed turf war against slavic gangs (most notably the *Solntsevo, Lyubertsy* and *Balashikha* groupings), they were still a formidable force.

Heavy-handed police actions were mounted, but there were also behind-the-scenes warnings that any terrorism would lead to a major campaign, possibly including extrajudicial reprisals. Many Chechens returned to fight for their homeland or supplied money or weapons, but the actual criminal organizations did not. To an extent, this may have been out of fear of Moscow, but largely reflected the fact that they had divorced themselves from their old land. Instead, they were living well in Russia, with no more than a sentimental attachment to Chechnya itself. Indeed, if anything they were opposed to Chechen independence, which might have led to the end of their lucrative operations in Russia.

There, they are involved in a wide range of criminal activities, especially financial crime and protection racketeering. Whereas the more successful ethnically Slav *mafiya* groupings tend to move towards creating seemingly legitimate facades and maintaining the broadest possible portfolio of business activities, the major Chechen gangs tend instead to become more specialized. In particular, they have become the 'protection racketeers' protection racketeer', acquiring networks of client gangs (who could come from any ethnic background) to whom they provide services and authority and other from whom they simply demand tribute on pain of gang warfare. In this respect, the Chechens are more true to their bandit roots and also less prone to the sort of transnational deal making at which the Russians excel.

One paradox of Chechen crime in Russia is that official and unofficial accounts alike credit it with much more activity and members than it could possibly display. Even in regions where there are very few Chechens, police reports talk of dominant Chechen gangs. To some extent this could be written off as propaganda, as Moscow demonizes the Chechens, or simple racism that lumps all North Caucasian peoples as 'Chechen'. However, it also reflects the way Chechen organized crime has in effect become a 'brand name' which can be 'franchised' to other gangs. The Chechens are so notorious for their ruthlessness and efficiency that even many businesses, which might try to resist normal *mafiya* demands for protection money, are prepared to pay up. Even the Sicilian Cosa Nostra has been taken aback by the Chechens: one Italian criminal reportedly noted that 'where we would first threaten someone, the Russians would kill him. The Chechens would kill his whole family, too.' This may be apocryphal: if anything the *bratva* prides itself on the precision with which it uses violence eschewing, for example, the car bombs so often employed by Russian gangs. However, it accurately reflects the fear the Chechens can arouse even in hardened criminals. Furthermore, given that Chechen gangs will band together to protect one of their own, only the most powerful or foolhardy rivals will try to muscle into their territory. As a result, in regions where there is not much real Chechen criminal activity, gangs made up of other North Caucasian peoples will petition the local Chechen godfather for permission to use the 'brand name' in return for a cut of their proceeds. The Chechens are exemplary in their application of the art of the franchise, especially in punishing those who harm the value of their brand name (by not living up to the reputation) or using it without permission. Criminals trying to pass themselves off without permission as 'working with the Chechens' (the usual expression to symbolize being a franchisee) tend soon to realize just how they earned their reputation. One such usurper from Irkutsk failed to turn up for a meeting with his gang in 1999 – only for each member to find a piece of him waiting for them when they returned to their respective apartments.

Chechen organized crime has also spread beyond Russia's borders, although less so than the Russians and other Slavs. Gangs are operating in the Baltic states (especially Klaipeda and Vilnius, although here they are, unusually, in decline), Romania, Germany (Frankfurt and Hamburg), Netherlands, the United States (Miami) and even, reportedly, Argentina. The Chechen community in Turkey, which has long had a reputation for dabbling in banditry, is also being transformed by an influx of newcomers with greater ambitions and ample funds at their disposal. Chechens have been identified demanding protection money from criminals in Lithuania, hijacking drugs in Turkey, selling guns in the United States and talking with the Mafia in Italy. This is thus already a transnational criminal phenomenon.

Traditional Chechen organized crime is still shaped by clans and kin groups, though, and still exists within a complex network of blood ties and enmities and connections which are rooted in their histories (such as coming from the same part of Chechnya). There is also a strong sense of division between major and lesser gangs, even if there is less of a hierarchy within these two classes as one might expect. The basic structure can thus be represented as a 'snowflake' or 'starburst', with lesser but largely autonomous groups, each with their own organization, radiating from a central gang generally dominated by a single charismatic and powerful leader. In this respect, these networks are less like the stylized pyramid of traditional organized crime, and more like the *teip*, within which there is some form of central authority, but which is essentially a federation of larger and smaller, but broadly equal *gars*.

However, the introduction of the concept of the franchise has in effect created a three-dimensional structure, as all or some of the component elements also turn out to have their own networks of franchisees, bound by the same group identity. At the same time, there is still a clear sense that any true Chechen or member of a predominantly-Chechen gangs is still better than a mere franchisee. Figure 1 offers a crude representation of this structure.

Thus, the same inclusiveness which allowed the highland *teips* to incorporate non-Chechens is also aiding the creation of multi-ethnic criminal networks. Non-Chechens, by paying tribute and also demonstrating an ability to work to the norms of the 'franchise' – analogous to observing the *adat* – can be adopted as individuals or, increasingly, gangs. Filling the roles of *gars* or *nekye*, they can aspire to a greater role within the clan, while in the mean time gaining access to the powerful reputation, resources and collective identity of the *bratva*.

FIGURE 1
CHECHEN GANG STRUCTURE

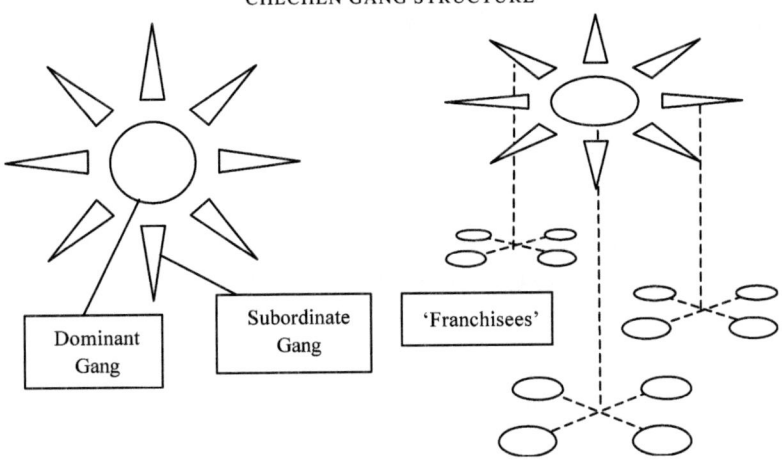

NETWAR AGAINST MOSCOW: CHECHEN RESISTANCE

Chechen resistance to Russian occupation has also shifted to an essentially network-based structure, in contrast with the more traditional, unified organized guerrilla army which successfully drove the Russians out of Grozny in 1996. To a large extent, this is a response to the massive and sustained Russian campaign, which has shattered any attempts to concentrate Chechen forces. However, it also reflects an ideological and religious schism within the resistance, which has shattered their previous coherence of command and purpose. As of writing, Chechen president-in-rebellion Maskhadov probably has control of perhaps a third of the entire rebel movement, and partial authority over another third, largely through allies of the moment, who may broadly accept his authority and yet have agendas and connections all their own. Of the rest, some are independent warlords, others extremist Islamist guerrilla groups, largely Wahhabi, including some linked to Al Qaeda.

Moscow has, for obvious political reasons, sought to link bin Laden directly with the Chechen rebellion, presenting him as the rebels' paymaster and *eminence grise*. He has been equally happy to claim the credit for the continuing war. In August 2000, for example, one of his aides declared that that he had sent 400 Arab and Afghan fighters to Chechnya, while other accounts have suggested that Al Qaeda donated $5 million or even $10 million to the rebels. However, the Islamist fraction of the rebel movement affiliated to Al Qaeda is not just a minority, it is also bitterly opposed to Maskahov for his moderate Islamic views and his apparent willingness to accept Chechen autonomy within the Russian Federation instead of outright independence. Maskhadov denounced the Wahhabis in 1997 and disbanded elements they dominated within the 'Chechen army' and since then the Islamists have tried several times to assassinate him. As a result, there have been times when Maskhadov's forces and the Russians have quietly found common cause against the extremists, such as the successful Russian operation to assassinate the most important Wahhabi warlord, Khattab, in 2002. Furthermore, the claims of support from Al Qaeda are grossly exaggerated. While there may be some credence to the assessment that there were 400 Arab and Afghan fighters within the rebel ranks in 2000, this should not be regarded as some kind of Al Qaeda foreign legion. Instead, it is more likely to include all the outsiders who came to fight in the war, motivated by individual religious commitment, anti-Russian feeling or mercenary self-interest. Some of them were undoubtedly linked or perhaps even paid by Al Qaeda, but by no means all. Furthermore, there have been other groups supporting the rebels, clearly to an extent linked with Al Qaeda but not under bin Laden's control, such as the Egyptian-based Muslim Brotherhood Organization (*Al-Iqwanul Muslamoon*), which appears to have also contributed funds and some fighters. If anything, Al Qaeda has served as the Russians' most unexpected ally, as their activities and their refusal to find common cause with the nationalists has contributed to the fragmentation of the rebel forces.

On the face of it, the structures of both the nationalist and Islamist wings of the rebel movement are very similar. Both seem to operate now as networks of semi-autonomous guerrilla units, typically no more than 50 strong, who cooperate through regional linkages with similar groups. On the one hand, this networking of the resistance is undoubtedly a weakness, and the result of military defeats. Whereas it was a military victory by the rebel army which effectively forced the Russians to begin contemplating withdrawal in the first war, there is no chance of that now. Indeed, the ferocity of the Russians' campaigns have shattered the fiction of a 'Chechen army', leaving it only able to survive in small and mobile elements. Furthermore, internecine conflicts between guerrilla factions (especially Maskhadov's nationalists and the ultra-Islamist wing) are a serious and recurring problem. As a result, the rebel forces have devolved into several networks, sometimes overlapping, sometimes cooperating, sometimes competing and warring among themselves.

The nationalists, for all they seek to retain a semblance of being an army (with 'regiments' and formal ranks in some cases), have largely devolved down to the same broad structure familiar to Chechens of the nineteenth century. Each guerrilla unit is essentially tied to a *teip*, sometimes directly by membership of that clan, other times because it is the *teip* of their leader. It is to the *teip* that they will look primarily for assistance, guidance, sanctuary and recruits. As well as assuring a degree of coherence and *esprit de corps*, this means that they are linked to the wider networking of Chechen society, and coordinated operations and transfers of material and intelligence will often he handed off through existing clan-to-clan contacts. While Maskhadov may seek to give orders, in practice they have little weight unless in reality the product of negotiations with the leaderships of appropriate *teips*. As a result, Maskhadov retains a residual authority, but even were he eliminated or persuaded to surrender, this need not have more than a temporary political impact.

On the other hand, while the Islamists operate in similar-sized and - structured units, they rarely have links with the indigenous clan structures, and when they do these are almost always essentially residual connections because of the commander's origins. If nothing else, this is a result of suspicion of the intolerance, austerity and militancy of Wahhabism, which in many ways considers the war to be less about Chechen nationhood and more about a global jihad. Thus, they have their own network, largely dominated by Wahhabist agents and religious leaders. Like the nationalist rebels, the pressure of Russians attacks has done much to weaken their central decision-making structures. Recent years have seen the dominant Islamist warlords neutralized: Salman Raduyev (who died in a Russian prison camp in 2002), Ruslan Gelayev (killed in 2004) and above all the Jordanian-born Omar ibn al-Khattab (poisoned by the Russians in 2002). So too have the key middlemen responsible for transferring funds, men and materiel to the rebels, especially Saudi-born Abu Omar Mohammed As-Seif (killed in 2001) and Zelimkhan Yandarbiyev (assassinated in Qatar in 2004). The only remaining major field commander associated with the Islamists, Shamil Basayev, remains of uncertain loyalties, and is more of an ally of the Wahhabis rather than a committed devotee of their cause. As such, although he has considerable authority within Chechnya, he is still mistrusted by the Islamists' outside ideologues and backers.

To an extent, this erosion of their central command assets within Chechnya has also led to the Islamists adopting the same diffuse structures as the nationalists, but here they run into the problem of lacking a strong clan basis to support such an existence. Instead, they have begun to rely not so much on guerrilla operations within Chechnya but terrorism within Russia. This includes numerous attacks in Moscow, including the 6 February 2004 bomb on the metro which left more than 40 dead, and also the mass hostage-taking at the Nord-Ost theatre in October 2002. This has taken their operations into the truest forms of 'netwar' fought by 'dispersed, often small groups who agree to communicate, coordinate and act in an internetted manner, often without a precise central leadership or headquarters'.[5] Indeed, these operations appear to shown little central direction at all, beyond a generic policy line which encourages attacks at particularly auspicious times. While there have been suggestions that some – especially the Nord-Ost operation, of which more below – were specifically 'commissioned', on the whole the pattern is generally reactive: likely terrorists make it known that they are willing and eager to carry out an attack (in many cases, in response to the death of a loved one at Russian hands), and at once the network swings into action to provide allies, expertise, training and materiel.

LINKS FORGED AND BROKEN

The traditional kinship structures of Chechnya have not only survived a decade of war but provided the foundations for network-based crime and resistance which have come into their own in the circumstances prevailing in the past decade. These have, however, emerged largely as separate networks rather than the unified force the Kremlin has sometimes claimed. The criminals, mindful of their own interests, have largely made a point of eschewing any connections with the rebels, even though the latter have generally seemed more eager to open a dialogue. For example, Dudayev actively sought to raise money from the Chechen criminal diaspora, by sending representatives to meet with godfathers in the town of Petrozavodsk in February 1995. However, they returned empty-handed, and a subsequent gathering of Chechen godfathers in Moscow agreed an unambiguous ban on direct transfers of money, men or weapons to the rebels. Thus, when Al Qaeda sought to procure weapons for its allies in 2000, it actually ended up paying non-Chechen criminal gangs, who smuggled the weapons into Chechnya using military supply convoys. Furthermore, the Islamists' networks are also distinct from those of both crime and the nationalist rebel rump.

That said, it is the nature of networks to expand and interconnect. There are also individuals and groups who operate at the interstices of these structures. One example would be the role of the Barayev family, long a malign force in Chechen affairs. Family leader Arbi Barayev was a rogue warlord, essentially a bandit chieftain who acted semi-autonomously under Dudayev and later, while maintaining the thin fiction of heading a wing of the Chechen forces, actually used his private army to make millions through oil smuggling, kidnappings and contract killings. While the core of his faction was still very much defined by kinship, he later began to extend his networks; smaller, local gangs were incorporated into his criminal grouping (often on a simple 'join or die' basis) and he also found himself able to work with but also play off the rival networks of Maskahdov's rebels and the growing Islamist wing. Always an uncomfortable and wilful ally of the mainstream rebels, a final break came in 1998, when Barayev tried to add the city of Gudermes to his personal fiefdom. Maskhadov's forces repelled his gunmen, after which the rebel president stripped him of his rank within the 'Chechen armed forces' and issued a formal arrest warrant, earning Barayev the distinction of being wanted by both sides. As a result, he concentrated not only on his directly criminal activities, but also offering them to the Islamists on a mercenary basis. He was reportedly promised, if not paid, $20 million from Al Qaeda for kidnapping and subsequently beheading three British and one New Zealander telecommunications workers in 1998, and was also hired to stage at least one assassination attempt on Maskhadov.

Barayev was eventually killed by Russian forces in 2001, in another operation which may have benefited from inside information and local knowledge provided through back-channels by Maskhadov's forces. Much of his criminal empire was shattered or disbanded, leaving just the central element still based on more durable kinship ties. However, the links with the extremists remained strong, fuelled now by the imperative of vendetta. Arbi's nephew, Movsar Barayev, then emerged as the ringleader (along with, reportedly, one of Arbi Barayev's widows) of the Chechen fighters who seized the Nord-Ost theatre in Moscow, an operation which led to 170 deaths when Russian security forces pumped dangerous gases into the building before staging an assault. The precise cause and motivation is still unclear, but again the most compelling picture that emerges is of a networked operation driven not only by a variety of motives but also supported by several networks. Formal sanction was given to the raid by Shamil Basayev, although apparently without Maskhadov's knowledge – indeed, it appears to have been in part an attempt to put Maskhadov's campaign in the shade, and he promptly condemned the atttack. Most practical support came from the Wahhabis; indeed, according to Dzhafarom Zufarovym, an influential Islamic leader in southern Russia, Barayev was actually hired for the mission, possibly with Al Qaeda moneys from Saudi Arabia.

Russian crime specialist Andrei Konstantinov has noted that 'to survive, the Chechen people were forced to develop their internal organizations to the highest level of all the peoples of the Caucasus'.[6] Under the pressure of struggles both within Russia's complex underworld and also amidst war at home, the Chechens are increasingly adopting flexible, network-based structures which draw upon their traditional forms of social organization, but which produce thoroughly modern criminal, guerrilla and terrorist actors. It is hard to see any of this unholy trinity imminently being defeated or dispersing of its own accord. Chechen organized crime is strongly rooted and has made the all-important leap to incorporating members and gangs from other ethnicities. If the rebels cannot win this war on the battlefield thanks to their being shattered into smaller, dispersed elements, neither does it seem likely that they can lose it, either. It is possible for a conventional army to defeat a networked, diffuse guerrilla movement. However, this requires considerable political skill, well-trained, -motivated and -disciplined troops and a successful combination of coercion and a hearts and minds campaign. The Russians appear to lack all of these beyond an appetite for widespread and often brutal coercion, which on their own does little more than ensure that the rebels continue to enjoy high levels of public support, even if largely passive rather than active. As for the Islamists and their terrorism, their networks are less deeply rooted and thinly stretched, but the cumulative anger, misery bitterness and despair of a decade of open and undeclared war has left an adequate supply of would-be martyrs and vengeance-driven men, woman and, sadly, children to maintain their operations if not for ever, at least for the foreseeable future. Just as networks are far harder to combat by an enemy, so too are they much more difficult to remove from a society once they have become entrenched. Even if Chechnya manages to win its political-military struggle for independence, it will still face another to recreate its social cohesion and traditional religious unity.

NOTES

1. Studies of Chechen history of note include Robert Bauman, 'Historical Perspective on the Conflict in Chechnia', *Low Intensity Conflict and Law Enforcement* Vol.4, No.1 (1995), pp.119–132; John P Dunlop, ad *Russia Confronts Chechnya* (Cambridge: Cambridge University Press, 1998), chs 1–2; Anatol Lieven, *Chechnya: Tombstone of Russian Power* (New Haven, CT: Yale University Press, 1998), ch.9.

2. For example, in 1996 Interior Minister Anatoly Kulikov claimed that rebel leaders planned to send fighters to Moscow to take over banks and businesses and thus precipitate a new round of turf wars: 'the goal of the looming gangster wars is the complete destabilization of Russia.' *ITAR-Tass news agency* (7 October 1996).

3. For useful assessments of Chechen society, see Sergei Arutiunov, 'Ethnicity and Conflict in the Caucasus', in Fred Wehling (ed.), *Ethnic Conflict and Russian Intervention in the Caucasus* (San Diego, CA: ISGCC, 1996); Sebastian Smith, *Allah's Mountains* (London: I.B. Tauris, 1998); Yavus Akhmadov et al., *Islam in the North Caucasus: A People Divided* (Harrisonburg, VA: William R Nelson Institute, 2001), available at ⟨http://www.jmu.edu/orgs/wrni/islam1.htm⟩; Emil Arslan Suleymanov, 'Chechen Society and Mentality', *Prague Watchdog*, 25 May 2003.

4. This section draws heavily on my earlier article 'Chechen Crime Alive and Well', published in *Jane's Intelligence Review*, March 2000, and is used with permission. The best other sources on Chechen organized crime include Mark Galeotti, 'Chechnia: The Theft of a Nation', *Boundary and Security Bulletin*, Vol.2, No.1 (1994); Andrei Zhilin, 'The Caucasian War: The Scene in Moscow', *Jamestown Foundation Prism*, 22 March 1996; Andrei Konstantinov, *Banditskii Peterburg* (St Petersburg: Folio-Press, 1997); A.L. Rudakov, *Chechenskaya mafiya* (Moscow: EKSMO-Press, 2002).

5. John Arquilla & David Ronfeldt, *The Advent of Netwar* (Santa Monica, CA: RAND, 1996) p.5.

6. Andrei Konstantinov, *Banditskii Peterburg* (St Petersburg: Folio-Press, 1997), p.155.

Multilateral Counter-Insurgency Networks

JOHN P. SULLIVAN and ROBERT J. BUNKER

Terrorism is a pervasive form of social and political violence that challenges state institutions and global security. As the 11 September 2001 ('9/11') attacks in New York and Washington, DC and the M-11 (*Eme Once*) attacks against the Madrid Metro illustrate, contemporary terrorism presents a significant challenge to global security and law enforcement institutions. Non-state actors operating across international borders, engaged in an apparent global insurgency of extremism that transects the traditional boundaries between national security and criminal enforcement, pose significant challenges to both intelligence and law enforcement agencies. Within a framework of global jihad that seeks an alternative to liberal global market-states, networked global insurgents are blending political and religious fanaticism with criminal enterprises to challenge the rule of law and exploit the seams between crime and war.

Existing security structures (domestically the police, and internationally the military and foreign intelligence services) designed to counter state-on-state threats find this new operational environment challenging at best. Preserving global and national security requires traditional organs of national security (the diplomatic, military and intelligence services) to forge new partnerships with police and public safety organizations at the state and local (sub-national) level to effectively counter these threats. Significant operational, policy and cultural challenges must be overcome to forge an effective global network of public safety, law enforcement and traditional intelligence organizations to understand and anticipate current and evolving terrorist threats.

Terrorism and fourth generation warfare (4GW)[1] are significant elements of the contemporary (postmodern) threat environment. Links between religious extremists, criminal organizations (such as narcotics traffickers) and rogue state partners complicate civil and military responses to conflict. These new adversaries, a complex opposing force (OPFOR), are diverse and linked in unfamiliar ways.[2] They include a range of actors such as Osama bin Laden's Al Qaeda and its constellation of *jihadi* networks, as well as the loose coalition of criminal actors, guerrillas and insurgents that challenge and can be expected to continue to challenge national security capabilities that were designed to operate within a nation-state framework. Outside that framework, our traditional structures have great difficulties.[3]

In this threat environment, disruption and emerging threats can be expected to be as important as – or more important than – WMD issues. Effective response to these threats demands a high degree of interoperability among all levels of responders – local, state, federal – between a variety of disciplines (law enforcement, fire service, public health and medical), and between civil and military agencies. Intelligence is an important element of forging an interagency response. To be effective, this intelligence must embrace network attributes and effectively fuse with networked operational forces.

ORGANIZATIONAL AND FUNCTIONAL BASIS OF NETWORKS

Quite a bit of information exists on social network analysis and to a lesser degree the extension and/or modification of that analysis into the realm of conflict and war. Of direct interest is the organization of networks, network roles, network reaction cycle functioning, and potentials for better efficiency based on different levels of network analysis. This research is still in its infancy and fragmentary but synergies already exist which are aiding in the creation of counter-insurgency networks.

Network (Component) Organization

John Arquilla and David Ronfeldt's typology provides a basic overview of network organization and summarizes how individual nodes link to each other:[4]

Chain: the chain or line network, as in a smuggling chain where people or goods, or information move along a line of separated contacts, and where end-to-end communication must travel through the intermediate nodes.

Star: the hub, star, or wheel network, as in a franchise or a cartel where a set of actors are tied to a central (but not hierarchical) node or actor, and must go through that node to communicate and coordinate with each other.

All-channel: the all-channel or full-matrix network, as in a collaborative network of militant peace groups where everybody is connected to everybody else.

Hybrid: there may also be hybrids of the three types, with different tasks being organized around different types of networks.

To this typology can be added Phil William's perspective on nodal 'network roles', developed for criminal network analysis, but applicable for counter-insurgency networks if slightly modified:[5]

Organizers: those core individuals and groups that provide the steering mechanism for the network.

Insulators: individuals or groups whose role is essentially to insulate the core from the danger posed by infiltration and compromise.

Communicators: individuals who ensure that communication flows effectively from one node to another across the network as a whole.

Guardians: Enforcers concerned with the security of the network who take measures to minimize vulnerability to external attack or infiltration.

Extenders: those whose role is to extend the network by recruiting new members and by negotiating with other networks regarding collaboration.

Monitors: those who ensure the effectiveness of the network and whose responsibilities include reporting weaknesses and problems to the core organizers, who can then initiate remedial action.

Linking network structures to network roles offers better insights into how networks form. In the public domain simulated modeling of notional terrorist networks has taken place[6] as has modeling concerning the 19 Al Qaeda hijackers involved in the 9/11 attack.[7] This form of analysis is typically used to identify organizers which function as command and control nodes (C^2) and to show levels of contact and trust within the network. Modeling has also been used against criminal organizations, drug cartels and militant anarchist groups by law enforcement agencies using link analysis and other tools. Not enough of this modeling, however, is taking place to better understand and improve the capability of counter-insurgency networks.[8] Much of this problem stems from lack of resources for in house studies and the information itself, which is unavailable to independent researchers because of its sensitivity.

Network (Component) Function

A network, or the components of a network, will have various functions for conflict and war. Based upon the OODA (observe-orient-decide-act) loop model[9] a basic breakdown of these functions would be as follows:

> *Observe*: sensors, scouts, intelligence (gathering)
> *Orient*: intelligence (analysis)
> *Decide*: headquarters staff (military)/officer-in-charge (police)
> *Act*: offensive, defensive, training, logistics, consequence management

Note that these represent operational functions and not network roles, which are more like military unit support functions, even though some overlap exists. This model can be used to better understand counter-insurgency network requirements and communication flows and to help with friendly force protection needs – especially as parts of the network constantly move through the loop. This model also has utility for targeting non-state opposing forces.

More efficient OODA loop functioning can also be tied into the netwar concept's five levels of analysis. The more evolved a network is in each of these areas the better it is expected to perform:[10]

> *Organizational*: learn to mix hierarchical and network forms in interagency mechanisms
> *Doctrinal*: institute doctrines, operating concepts that match network organization
> *Technological*: develop information, communication systems to serve interagency work
> *Social*: train teams to think and behave in network terms
> *Narrative*: effective 'fight for civilization' based on universal liberal values

These levels of analysis thus have a direct bearing on network issues and dynamics. In addition the primary challenge for counter-insurgency networks (counternetwar) is 'How to make the network a source of loyalty?'[11] Practical observation suggests that loyalty to the network begins to develop when an individual accepts that the network offers new mission capabilities against non-state threats. This acceptance can be derived from a convincing presentation, testimonials, independent research, a gut feeling or an immediate perceived need. That loyalty intensifies after that individual directly experiences network operational utility – during an exercise or an actual incident (operation).

Loyalty to the network can create tension with loyalty to one's hierarchy because different perspectives on cooperation exist. Networks operate as 'non-zero sum games' (everyone benefits) while hierarchies operate as 'zero-sum games' (winners and losers). As a result network nodes will share resources for the common good while stand alone nodes will hoard them for individual gain. Actual network sharing of physical resources has been observed in operational situations.

THE 'TEW' MODEL

One early effort to forge a networked response to post-modern networked threats is found in the terrorism early warning (TEW) group model. The terrorism early warning (TEW) group model was first established in Los Angeles County in 1996 to address the challenges of postmodern terrorism. The TEW follows a networked approach, integrating law enforcement, fire, health and emergency management agencies to address the intelligence needs for terrorism and critical infrastructure protection. The TEW model is based on the premise that intelligence is more than 'secret information' about an adversary. Intelligence to address contemporary threats must go beyond mere descriptions of the threat actors (opposing force, OPFOR); it must also provide a range of users (investigators, emergency responders, planners, etc.) with assessed and accurate information about the situation they are managing.

The TEW model describes this process as 'all source/all phase' fusion. For the TEW, intelligence is derived from all potential sources (classified, sensitive but unclassified, and open sources or OSINT) to provide information at all phases of a threat/response (pre-, trans- and post-incident). The TEW assumes that information germane to an event is available from local through global sources. The immediate precursor for an attack may be in the local area, across the nation, a foreign nation, in cyberspace, or in a combination of all. To achieve this local through global fusion, the TEW relies on a process known as intelligence preparation for operations (IPO).[12] IPO fuses a number of traditional intelligence processes with its own TEW process (which includes evaluating trends and potentials, capabilities and intentions, and providing an operational net assessment depending upon the current position of a threat on a notional event horizon). In short, IPO blends weather, enemy and terrain (WET), with urban IPB (intelligence preparation of the battlefield) and a variety of geospatial and geosocial tools to provide context for anticipating and understanding a suite of potential and actual threats.

The Los Angeles TEW was designed to provide the operational intelligence development of potential courses of action necessary to quickly move through the decision cycle (OODA loop), forecast the potential event horizon, and craft meaningful courses of action for interagency, inter-disciplinary response. It relies upon not only the analysis of criminal leads and sensitive sources, but also open source intelligence (OSINT) for scanning/monitoring trends and potentials that provide context for on-going assessment and to influence training and doctrinal needs. Additionally, during an actual threat period or attack, the TEW provides consequence projection (forecasting) to identify potential courses of action to the unified command structure. Essentially, the TEW is an 'all source/all phase' operations-intelligence fusion cell that fuses not only information, but a range of operational entities and intelligence disciplines to develop actionable intelligence products for achieving situational understanding.

TEW ORGANIZATION

While seeking indications and warning or during an actual event, the TEW utilizes a 'net assessment' process to determine the scope of an actual or potential event and its impact on its area of operations (operational area). Organizationally, the TEW is organized into six cells: the officer-in-charge or OIC (command), analysis/synthesis, consequence management, investigative liaison, epidemiological intelligence (epi-intel) and forensic intelligence support cells. The forensic intelligence support cell, which includes technical means and such external resources as virtual reachback, supports the others (the TEW organization is depicted in Figure 1).

The OIC (command) cell is a team that provides direction, sets intelligence requirements and is responsible for interacting with prevention and response organizations and incident command entities. The analysis/synthesis cell coordinates net assessment activities and develops the collection plan (including tasking requests for information to the various net assessment elements). The analysis/synthesis cell is also responsible for the intake of leads and reports, and developing the results of all the cells' analysis into actionable intelligence products (including advisories, alerts, warnings, and mission folders to assist response).[13] The consequence management cell assesses the law, fire and health (EMS–hospital–operational medical) consequences of the event. The investigative liaison cell coordinates with criminal investigative entities and the traditional intelligence community. the epidemiological intelligence (epi-intel) cell is responsible for real-time disease surveillance and coordination with the disease investigation. Finally, the forensic intelligence support cell exploits a range of technical means to support the TEW fusion process. These include CBRNE reconnaissance,

FIGURE 1

TEW NET ASSESSMENT ORGANIZATION

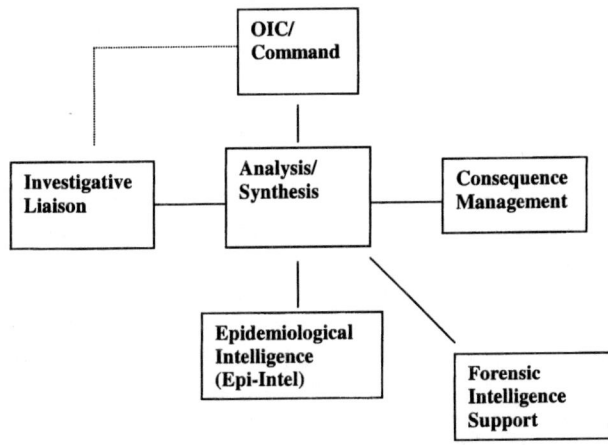

the use of sensors and detectors, geospatial tools (including mapping, imagery and GIS products), and cyber means.

The TEW model is currently expanding to other jurisdictions. At the time of this writing, there are TEWs at various levels of evolution in Orange, San Bernardino/Riverside, San Diego and Sacramento counties in California. Others also exist in Pierce County (Tacoma), Washington; Tulsa, Oklahoma; Hennepin County (Minneapolis), Minnesota; the National Capital Region (DC, VA, MD), and New Orleans, Louisiana in addition to the initial Los Angeles (LA TEW) group.

These groups are evolving into a network, sharing common organization and doctrine, in order to share threat information and support each other during critical periods. Additionally, the Memorial Institute for the Prevention of Terrorism (Oklahoma City) and the US Department of Homeland Security (Office of Domestic Preparedness) are sponsoring efforts to expand the TEW model into approximately 51 Urban Area Security Initiative (UASI) cities throughout the United States by focusing grant support for TEW initiatives.

NETWORK ISSUES AND DYNAMICS

Counter-terrorism and counter-insurgency networks are a less mature organizational form than law enforcement and military based hierarchies. As a result they are less understood and institutionalized than traditional governmental structures. In fact, from an organizational life cycle perspective these networks represent entrepreneurial (experimental) entities. Their form and functioning is still being 'worked out' and many of the potentials they offer are not fully understood.

As can be expected then counter-terrorism/counter-insurgency networks, such as the TEW, face unique challenges. It is expected that over time these challenges will be overcome and they will evolve into institutionalized structures based on common operating procedures and well defined doctrine. In the interim, various issues and dynamics currently exist:

Organizational and Bureaucratic Competition

Networked forms compete with their hierarchical predecessors. Bureaucratic inertia slows moves toward node-to-node and peer-to-peer collaboration both within and especially across disciplines (and jurisdictions). This is complicated by fiscal competition and struggles for intergovernmental primacy. While intelligence fusion groups, like the TEW, seek to serve information requirements of a number of entities to achieve a common operational advantage, some of these entities prefer concentrating (hoarding) information to bolster their organizational position.

Which Entity is in Control?

Within a networked structure, the question of which entity exerts control is unavoidable. This is as true within a single node as within a network of collaborative nodes. During exchanges between different agency personnel one of the first questions is always 'Who is in control of this group?' While this is a valid question for hierarchical [line and blocked] based structures it is an inappropriate question concerning networks.[14] Network participation is all about influence – a sharing of ideas and common visions – not control. Depending on the network organization the level of entity influence will shift. All channel networks tend to have nodes with more equal levels of influence than the star structure with more nodal influence concentrated at the hub.

Nodes which refuse to share information and ideas within a network – because of bureaucratic and cultural inhibitions – quickly get labeled as 'black holes'. These nodes suck up information and ideas but do not contribute to the common good of the network. This fosters distrust within the network. Over time those nodes lose influence within the network and risk being severely limited in their access to network information or, in extreme cases, even dropped from the network. The lack of rigid hierarchy does not mean there is no functional leadership over work processes and information assessment and sharing. Within one node, such as an individual TEW, team leaders and the OIC cell ensure coordination and interaction among cells, as well as with external entities (such as the local, state and federal agencies contributing personnel). As such, an individual TEW is a hybrid organization bridging traditional government hierarchies and network forms.

The organizational dynamics of a network (both within a networked node and among nodes) are influenced by several factors. These include measures of network connectivity and, most importantly, communications. For example, when Valdis Krebs in his paper 'Uncloaking Terrorist Networks' described Al Qaeda's 9/11 network, he identified three metrics: degrees (activity), closeness (access to other nodes), and betweeness (control over information flow).[15] In that analysis Mohammed Atta was identified as a key leader (broker of relationships and information) and the 'Hamburg cell' as a key node or hub based upon the denseness of connections within the network.[16] These central positions allow for the most important aspect of network influence: communication. Communication is essential to ensure rapid processing of information and adherence to the network's narrative vision. Communication is also essential to mitigate the tendencies toward fragmentation that occur as individual nodes become isolated and focused inward or toward other objectives.

Protocols and Rules

Defining and codifying the relations between networked actors is essential to exploiting the benefits of intelligence fusion. Information sharing to counter the evolving terrorist threat can not rely solely on top-down structures. Much of the information necessary to understand the dynamics of the threat, indeed even recognize that there is a threat, is developed from the bottom-up, as well as through multilateral exchanges of information, including indicators of potential attacks and alliances among networked criminal actors. New policy and intergovernmental instruments are needed to fully exploit lateral information-sharing and the development of distributed intelligence processing across organizational and political seams. This includes the development of mechanisms for sharing information among both intra-national and international nodes.

Specialization and Generalization

There is a tension between specialization and generalization. The TEW model fills a specialty niche, assessing and fusing interdisciplinary intelligence for counter-terrorism. Some observers prefer a model that fuses traditional intelligence for a narrower set of users (i.e., the traditional criminal and military services). These are able to focus only on criminal and military threats respectively. In reality, both types of fusion are necessary in a crime–war operational environment. Criminal and military intelligence for a range of threats including criminal enterprises of all sorts (drug cartels, gangs, organized crime, etc.) and terrorism (insurgency) need to be closely aligned with (and exploited by) the specialist TEW model for counter-terrorism intelligence fusion.

Network Scale and Degrees of Separation

Limitations exist concerning how large a network can develop because of information overload and issues of trust. Humans can only filter through so much information before they are overwhelmed. These can be seen on a daily basis concerning e-mails. E-mails serve as a means to an end but can become an end in themselves. Wading each day through thousands of e-mails generated by a network can paralyze all other activities. Intelligence and information collection, exploitation, assessment and visualization tools, such as 'intelligence bots' and other automated tools can help to lessen, but do not fully mitigate, this problem.

In regards to trust, individuals can only maintain so many relationships before they are overwhelmed with relationship maintenance. Relationship maintenance based on phone calls, e-mails and physical meetings will at some point take away from other forms of productivity. While some governmental bureaucrats are able to make a career out of attending meetings, this is the antithesis of counter-insurgency networks. The other aspect of this problem is degrees of separation influencing trust. If a network has too many degrees of separation between the various nodes, trust dissolves. If this happens the network will then begin to break apart. If ignored, hierarchical relationships can once again develop between the dropped nodal linkages and those parts of the network will be lost.

Interface with Hierarchies

Networks can interface with hierarchies in varying ways. They can develop linkages at all levels – strategic, operational and tactical – with the officer-in-charge or OIC (command) link the most prevalent for intelligence support. Tactical links are common for ground sensor and criminal intelligence needs while strategic links may be created for special facility and event access for intelligence preparation for operations.

One of the most problematic interface issues is operational tempo (OPTEMPO). Networks have far quicker reaction cycles than hierarchies because of 'their efficiency and effectiveness in procuring information'[17] This increased OPTEMPO results in the network quickly getting ahead of the hierarchy during an operation or mission. This mismatch in OPTEMPO can create communication problems because the network will be addressing problems that the hierarchy has not yet even identified. These are real life concerns that have been viewed in both exercises and actual operations. Another problem is the fact that a hierarchical based entity may refuse to work with a network. The network is viewed as too alien and/or threatening for the hierarchy's leadership and bureaucracy to interface with. As a result the fear of looking bad can become a concern of more importance for a hierarchy than mission performance.

Public–Private Network Issues

Protecting the postmodern market-state is a complex endeavor. The relationships among the variety of state and non-state actors involved are continually evolving in organizational and legal terms. Much of the critical infrastructure of modern society is privately held and operated. Private corporations and nongovernmental organizations (NGOs) provide telecommunications, information technology, energy, finance, transportation and a range of services traditionally provided by governments. (These corporate entities and NGOs are increasingly trans- and multinational in scope and nature.) The complex interdependencies among these infrastructural sectors and their relationships to governmental organizations are little understood and require a high degree of coordination among operators with sometimes divergent and sometimes convergent interests.

A counter-terrorism or counter-insurgency network will have to interoperate with a number of governmental organizations and entities at the local, state, and federal levels (for example within the US or Canada) or with a number of international or supranational entities (as in the case of the member states of the European Union). In addition, these security networks will have to interact with a number of NGOs, corporate security entities and private military and intelligence providers. Take the case of contemporary crisis and conflict management. A number of humanitarian NGOs, advocacy groups, international organizations (such as the United Nations and its various arms), military and intelligence services of multiple nation-states, and a growing number of private military companies (PMCs) operate to assess, anticipate and respond to crisis. All these diverse and diffuse entities play varying roles in understanding and containing crises and war. Peacemaking, peacekeeping, stability and support operations rely on a complex networked interaction among actors to operate. NGOs such as the International Committee of the Red Cross (ICRC), International Crisis Group, Human Rights Watch, etc. rely upon the services and co-operation of nation-states and their military organs, private security and intelligence contractors, to provide services and build global civil society. The state security services (military and police) also increasingly rely upon private contractors (PMCs and corporate intelligence services) to perform their tasks. Both mechanisms to ensure information-sharing when appropriate and safeguard information and liberties are required, The body of international law, both international criminal law and international humanitarian law (IHL) or the laws of armed conflict have not caught up to these operational realties.

MULTILATERAL COUNTER-INSURGENCY NETWORKS

Understanding and combating contemporary terrorist and insurgent networks requires diverse intelligence and security agencies to pool and aggregate their most precious resource: information. Sharing information and knowledge, and working together to develop useful information or actionable intelligence in the first place requires the development of new networked and distributed security and intelligence structures.

The networked Islamist *jihadi* networks pioneered by Osama bin Laden's Al Qaeda are increasingly being recognized as a global insurgency. These groups, or actually networks of networks, view their war as a global *intifada*. In the aftermath of the Madrid bombings, European police observed that Islamic terrorists evade detection by regrouping and recombining within the framework of loosely organized networks to evade capture and sustain operations. Yet, while the need for closer coordination and cooperation among international police and intelligence services is broadly recognized, barriers to such action are created by divergent judicial and policing systems with investigative cooperation dependent upon an informal 'sneaker net' of magistrates, prosecutors, police and intelligence officers. This is equally true in military as well as civil aspects of counter-terrorism and counter-insurgency. In Iraq insurgents are exploiting networks to recruit fighters, obtain weapons and move funds. These networks exploit criminal enterprises and linkages within the *jihadi* international to seek support from Europe, Asia and elsewhere to prosecute their local insurgency. Such cooperation is forthcoming since *jihadis* see the Iraqi theatre as only one segment of their global operational space (opspace).

While the *jihadi* international, with Al Qaeda at the vanguard, link many other networks (including notably Jemaah Islamiya and Lasker-e-Toiba) together in their quest for a new caliphate, intelligence services in traditional nation-states face several structural limitations. They are strategically limited in their ability to recognize the extent of the challenge and operationally and tactically challenged in efforts to identify, track and disrupt terrorist networks. Intelligence forums focus on sharing general threat information on regional or transnational issues, but all too often keep specific intelligence to themselves. Obviously, there is a tension between information sharing and operational security to protect sources, means, and interests. Yet, erring too much on the side of secrecy inhibits the ability to quickly and comprehensively identify and counter networked adversaries.

The networks – actually 'multi-networks' or networks of networks – challenging the nation-state are diffuse and exploit secrecy to pursue their global goals. Sometimes they appear acephalous (headless), at others they appear polycephalous (multi-headed). Frequently they employ 'swarming', a tactic where dispersed forces converge or 'swarm' to concentrate, focus, or mass their resources or effort to conduct an attack or campaign. As John Arquilla and David Ronfeldt well observed, 'it takes networks to fight networks'.[18]

The TEW model and its emerging network as described above and elsewhere[19] is an early attempt to develop a counternetwar structure to combat terrorism and insurgency. As Arquilla and Ronfeldt observed, counternetwar relies upon a blurring of offense and defense.[20] This feature is embraced by the TEW model that views prevention and response as points on the continuum of conflict, rather than separate, distinct undertakings. Combating a global insurgency requires an integrated approach. Both prevention and response are influenced by local and global factors, with local and global information requirements at various phases of operations. Such a configuration allows each TEW node to perform dynamic assessment, cutting across 'stovepipes' to configure an adaptive assessment organization that incorporates the internal (intra-node) and external (across nodes) elements necessary to identify specific threats, trends, and potentials. Configuring each node – and ultimately the entire network – to have permeable boundaries that expand capability when needed and exploit distributed subject matter expertise (exploiting the skills and capabilities of other nodes and clusters) to solve a specific problem, allows the network to become agile and adaptive. This allows each node to wield operational capability individually and across the network. Speed, adaptation, and resilience are the anticipated result.

The resulting counter-insurgency network thus will require more than linking disparate databases. It requires building and understanding relationships (individual and organizational) on a multi-lateral basis. As the web 'blog' site 'Global Guerillas' observes,[21] distributed networks have a dynamic, 'non-hierarchical' design, and are actually composed of a 'meta-matrix' of networks for a number of functions: information exchange, knowledge sharing, task completion, etc. As such, they learn and adapt at the individual node and network levels. Many networks are 'scale-free' in configuration. That is, a few nodes have a high degree of connectivity (meaning they become hubs) while others operate with a lesser degree of connectivity. These dynamics are important to consider when developing a counter-terrorism/counter-insurgency network. While individual hubs are important, and hubs with high capacity (early adapters, nodes with high throughput/bandwith, critical skills, etc.) are critical, the workload must be distributed across the network to optimize resilience. Multiple hubs, reinforced by clusters of nodes with distributed capabilities, can absorb both random failure and intentional attack. This is true both for criminal and terrorist networks and networks supporting civil society.

Networks confer many organizational advantages over hierarchies. Closing the gap conferred by these advantages requires the development of counter-terrorist/counter-insurgency networks. A dynamic and decentralized network that avoids over-centralization (a typical bureaucratic reaction to change and its challenges) ensures multilateral information exchange over one-way (usually bottom-up or top-down) information flow through bureaucratic 'stovepipes' is essential. Such a network needs to include nodes at the local level (micro-networks in themselves that integrate all necessary local actors and link with other nodes), a national network, and a broader global network of networks. Such a scalable structure must incorporate real-time information flow and distributed processing, and exploit multiple information sources and types. In such a network, all nodes are users and producers of intelligence. Information and trends from multiple nodes are assembled at individual nodes and collaboratively through node-to-node and peer-to-peer efforts. Information, analysis and intelligence are then shared across all pertinent nodes, exploiting an open architecture. Tailored and ad hoc assessment and project teams can be stood up and demobilized as the situation warrants. Speed, relevance and a common understanding of OPFOR dynamics, organization and evolution can then be assembled and disseminated to those with a need to know.

FUTURE POTENTIALS

The United States individually and the community of nations governed by the rule of law are facing a significant epochal threat. Forging an appropriate response to this evolving threat envelope is a complex and demanding task, demanding significant deliberation in order to develop a balanced approach. Yet this deliberation must occur quickly as the conflict is already in progress and promises to widen. Serious attention must be given to a revision of the entire US national security structure (as well as that of Great Britain, France, the European Union and other international structures) to break down the bureaucratic obstacles to action. Entrenched bureaucratic obstacles are in a true sense real-time barriers to effective efforts to combat terrorism and, if left untended, promise to serve as a force multiplier to the opposing force.

The global war on terrorism is the decisive conflict of the twenty-first century. Global *jihadi* networks are waging a concerted and protracted global insurgency to dominate the post-modern geopolitical landscape. This *intifada* or insurgency comes as the nation-state is negotiating an epochal shift in the organization of the state. Competing views of sovereignty are vying for prominence in the new market-state order. This 'state transition' will no longer tolerate the traditional nation-state view that crime is the purview of single states. Addressing the multinational mercenary terrorist networks of the present and of the future requires new security structures. Philip Bobbitt[22] observes that Osama bin Laden's Al Qaeda is a malignant and mutated version of the market-state. As such, Al Qaeda and its kin are more than stateless gangs. These new networked adversaries possess standing armies, treasury and revenue sources (even if derived from criminal enterprises), a bureaucracy or 'civil' service, intelligence collection and analysis organs, welfare systems, and the ability to make alliances (with state and non-state entities). They also promulgate law and policy, and declare war. As such, the Al Qaeda network and others like it are virtual states. These virtual states are non-territorial market-states (although they sometimes hold and control territory) and through insurgency seek to hold or influence more.

Dark or malevolent networks are only one side of the equation. Technology and its impact on social organization are making networks an element of civil society as well. Transnational networks are starting to emerge to counter these threats. The interdependence of contemporary society increasingly relies upon 'networked civil society' to address interdependent issues such as transnational organized crime, terrorism, human rights, environment, finance and trade. As such, the globalization of justice and security is in its early stages.[23] Mechanisms to understand and counter the cross-cutting threats of global insurgency, terrorism, and fourth generation warfare to states, regions and economic actors are starting to be formed. A global counter-terrorism and counter-insurgency network (or networks) are necessary to preserve both national and global security during this tumultuous phase.

ACKNOWLEDGEMENTS

This work is partially derived from John P. Sullivan, 'Networked All-Source Fusion for Intelligence and Law Enforcement Counter-terrorism Response', paper presented to 'Integrating Intelligence and Law Enforcement for Homeland Security', Intelligence Studies Section of the International Studies Association (ISA), 2004 ISA Annual Convention, Montreal, Quebec, Canada, 18 March 2004. Specific observations on the operational capacity and practices of existing counter-terrorism and insurgency efforts and nascent networks are withheld for operational security (OPSEC) purposes.

NOTES

1. Fourth generation warfare (4GW) describes an operational environment where a variety of non-state actors go beyond terrorism (which is a tactic) to challenge the nation-state. See for example, G.I. Wilson, John P. Sullivan and Hal Kempfer, 'Fourth Generation Warfare: It's Here, And We Need New Intelligence-gathering Techniques for Dealing with It', *Armed Forces Journal International*, October 2002, pp.56–62.
2. One early analysis of the potential convergence of narcotics enterprises, terrorists and other networked actors was discussed in Robert J. Bunker and John P. Sullivan, 'Cartel Evolution: Potentials and Consequences', *Transnational Organized Crime*, Vol.4, No.2, Summer 1998, pp.55–74.
3. See Robert J. Bunker, *Five-Dimensional (Cyber) Warfighting: Can the Army After Next be Defeated Through Complex Concepts and Technologies?* (Carlisle, PA: US Army War College, Strategic Studies Institute, 1998) for a cogent discussion of the complexities of the evolving threat environment.
4. John Arquilla and David Ronfeldt, 'The Advent of Netwar (Revisited)', in John Arquilla and David Ronfeldt (eds), *Networks and Netwars: The Future of Terror, Crime, and Militancy* (Santa Monica, CA: RAND, 2001), pp.7–8.

5. The category of 'crossovers' was deleted. 'Insulators' were retained but their utility is questionable. Phil Williams, 'Transnational Criminal Networks', in John Arquilla and David Ronfeldt (eds), *Networks and Netwars: The Future of Terror, Crime, and Militancy* (Santa Monica, CA: RAND, 2001), pp.82–4.
6. Richard Rothberg, 'From the Whole Cloth: Making up the terrorist network', *Connections*, Vol.24, No.3 (2002), pp.36–42.
7. Vladis E. Krebs, 'Mapping Networks of Terrorist Cells', *Connections*, Vol.24, No.3 (2002), pp.31–4.
8. Resources exist on the US military side. FBE Delta noted decrees in decision making, mission timeline, shooter effectiveness, assets scrambled and leaders. *Fleet Battle Experiment Delta Quick Look Report, An Assessment of IT-21 Warfigting Value-Added, 1 Mar 99.*
9. See John R. Boyd, *The Essence of Winning and Losing*, 28 June 1995, available at ⟨http://www.au.af.mil/au.awc⟩ and John R. Boyd, Lecture, US Naval Institute Seminar, Washington, DC, September 1996.
10. John Arquilla and David Ronfeldt, *The Advent of Netwar* (Santa Monica, CA: RAND, 1996), p.33 and the narrative level of analysis in Table 1 of Arquilla and Ronfeldt's essay in this volume.
11. Arquilla and Ronfeldt, *The Advent of Netwar*, p.33.
12. See Matt Begert and Dan Lindsay, 'Intelligence Preparation for Operations', in Robert J. Bunker (ed.), *Non-State Threats and Future Wars* (London: Frank Cass, 2003), pp.133–43.
13. Mission Folders are incident-specific tools to assist incident commanders; they include real-time threat information and estimates, technical information and potential courses of action.
14. See Table 1 concerning the differences between these organizational forms, in Barry Wellman, 'The Rise (and Possible Fall) of Networked Individualism', *Connections*, Vol.24, No.3 (2002), pp.30–32.
15. Valdis E. Krebs, 'Uncloaking Terrorist Networks', FirstMonday, Vol.7, No.4, (April 2002), available at ⟨www.firstmonday.dk/issues/issue7_4/krebs⟩.
16. Ibid.
17. Phil Williams, 'The Nature of Drug-Trafficking Networks', *Current History* Vol.97, No.618 (April 1998), p.156.
18. Arquilla and Ronfeldt, 'The Advent of Netwar (Revisited)', p.15.
19. For additional information on the prospects for the TEW model to serve as a counternetwar structure see John P. Sullivan, 'Networked Force Structure and C⁴I', in Robert J. Bunker (ed.), *Non-State Threats and Future Wars* (London: Frank Cass, 2003), pp.144–58.
20. Arquilla and Ronfeldt, 'The Advent of Netwar (Revisited)', p.12.
21. 'Global Guerrillas' is one of the many emerging web 'blog' sites seeking to understand and navigate the changing, networked dynamics of post-modern conflict. The site carries the kicker 'The next generation of terrorism. How it will develop and how it will be fought.' See ⟨http://globalguerillas.typepad.com⟩.
22. Philip Bobbitt (like others) argues that an epochal shift in the organization of states is underway. Bobbitt posits that the new state form supplanting the nation-state is the market-state. Within that analysis, he sees terrorist networks (with Al Qaeda being an early example) as a malevolent form of market-state. See Philip Bobbitt, *The Shield of Achilles: War, Peace, and the Course of History* (New York: Anchor Books, 2002), esp. pp.820–21.
23. See Anne-Marie Slaughter, *A New World Order* (Princeton, NJ: Princeton University Press, 2004).

Selected Bibliography

Al Qaeda, *Declaration of War Against the Americans Occupying the Land of the Two Holy Places.*
   Access via ⟨http://www.Pbs.org/newshour/terrorism/international/fatwa_1996.html⟩.
   This fatwa was originally published in a London based newspaper, *Al Quds Al Arabi*,
   (August 1996).
Al Qaeda, *Military Studies in the Jihad Against the Tyrants.* UK/BM-1 Translation (Posted 7
   December 2001) at ⟨http://www.usdoj.gov/ag/trainingmannual.htm⟩.
Alexander, Yonah, 'Terrorism in the Twenty-First Century: Threats and Response', *DePaul
   Business Law Journal* (2000).
Allenby, Braden R., 'Environmental Security: Concept and Implementation', *International
   Political Science Review* (2000).
Akhmadov, Yavus et al, *Islam in the North Caucasus: A People Divided* (Harrisonburg: William R
   Nelson Institute, 2001). Access via ⟨http://www.jmu.edu/orgs/wrni/islam1.htm⟩.
Anderson, Sean K., 'Warnings versus Alarms: Terrorist Threat Analysis Applied to the Iranian
   State-Run Media', *Studies in Conflict and Terrorism*, Vol.21 (Fall 1998), pp.277–303.
Arquilla, John and David Ronfeldt, *The Advent of Netwar* (Santa Monica, CA: RAND, 1996).
Arquilla, John and David Ronfeldt, *Swarming & The Future of Conflict* (Santa Monica, CA:
   RAND, 2000).
Arquilla, John and David Ronfeldt, eds *Networks and Netwars: The Future of Terror, Crime, and
   Militancy* (Santa Monica, CA: RAND, 2001).
Arutiunov, Sergei, 'Ethnicity and Conflict in the Caucasus', in Fred Wehling (ed.), *Ethnic Conflict
   and Russian Intervention in the Caucasus* (San Diego, CA: ISGCC, 1996).
Avruch, Kevin, *Culture and Conflict Resolution* (Washington, DC: United States Institute of
   Peace, 1998).
Barabási, Albert-László, *Linked: The New Science of Networks* (Cambridge, MA: Perseus
   Publishing, 2002).
Bauman, Robert, 'Historical Perspective on the Conflict in Chechnia', *Low Intensity Conflict &
   Law Enforcement*, Vol.4, No.1 (1995).
Begert, Matt and Dan Lindsay, 'Intelligence Preparation for Operations', in Robert J. Bunker (ed.),
   Non-State Threats and Future Wars (London: Frank Cass, 2003), pp.133–143.
Bergen, Peter L., *Holy War, Inc., Insider the Secret World of Osama bin Laden* (New York, NY:
   The Free Press, 2001).
Biddle, Stephen, *Afghanistan and the Future of Warfare: Implications for Army and Defense
   Policy* (Carlisle Barracks, PA: Strategic Studies Institute, 2002).
Bobbitt, Philip, *The Shield of Achilles: War, Peace, and the Course of History* (New York: Anchor
   Books, 2002).
Bollier, David, *The Rise of Netpolitik* (Washington, DC: The Aspen Institute, 2003).
Boutros-Ghali, Boutros, *An Agenda for Peace* (New York: United Nations, 1992).
Boutros-Ghali, Boutros 'Global Leadership After the Cold War', *Foreign Affairs* (March–April
   1996).
Bowden, Mark, *Black Hawk Down* (New York: Penguin Putnam, 2000).
Boyd, John R., *The Essence of Winning and Losing* (28 June 1995). Access via ⟨www.au.af.mil/
   au.awc⟩.
Buchanan, Mark, *Nexus: Small Worlds and the Groundbreaking Science of Networks* (New York:
   Norton and Company, 2002).
Bull, Hedley, *The Anarchical Society: A Study of Order in World Politics* (London: Macmillan,
   1977).
Bunker, Robert J., 'Epochal Change: War Over Social and Political Organization', *Parameters*,
   Vol.27, No.2 (Summer 1997), pp. 15–24.
Bunker, Robert J., *Five Dimensional (Cyber) Warfighting: Can the Army After Next be Defeated
   Through Complex Concepts and Technologies?* (Carlisle Barracks, PA: Strategic Studies
   Institute, US Army War College, 1998).

Bunker, Robert J., 'Operational Advantages of Networked Organizational Structures in Future Conflict and War', in Jasjit Singh (ed.), *Reshaping Asian Security* Institute for Defence Studies and Analyses (IDSA), (New Dehli, India: Knowledge World, 2001), pp.250–260.

Bunker, Robert J., Presentation on 'Networked OPFORs: Strategic and Operational Considerations', Project O'Bannon, Event 4: Terrorist Networks: An Analysis, Quantico, VA: Marine Corps Warfighting Lab, 22–23 May 2002.

Bunker, Robert J., 'Battlespace Dynamics, Information Warfare to Netwar, and Bond-Relationship Targeting', in Robert J. Bunker (ed.), *Non-State Threats and Future War* (London: Frank Cass, 2003), pp.97–107.

Bunker, Robert J. and John P. Sullivan, 'Cartel Evolution: Potentials and Consequences', *Transnational Organized Crime*, Vol.4, No.2 (Summer 1998), pp.54–74.

Bunker, Robert J. and John P. Sullivan, *Suicide Bombings in Operation Iraqi Freedom*, Candidate Land Warfare Paper (Arlington, VA: Association of the US Army, 2004).

Capra, Fritjof, *The Hidden Connections* (New York: Doubleday, 2002).

Carley, Kathleen M., Jeffrey Reminga and Natasha Kanmeva, 'Destabilizing Terrorist Networks', *NAACSOS Conference Proceedings*, (Pittsburgh, PA, 2003). Access via ⟨http://www.casos. ece.cmu.edu/casos_working_paper/Carley-NAACSOS-03.pdf⟩.

Carré, John le, *The Constant Gardener* (New York: Charles Scribner's Sons, 2001).

Chase, Robert S., Emily B. Hill and Paul Kennedy, 'Pivotal States and U.S. Strategy', *Foreign Affairs* (January–February 1996), pp.33–51.

Clausewitz, Carl von, in Michael Howard (ed.), *On War*, trans. Peter Paret (Princeton, NJ: Princeton University Press, 1976).

Corr, Edwin G. and Max G. Manwaring, 'Some Final Thoughts', in Max G. Manwaring and Anthony James Joes (eds), *Beyond Declaring Victory and Coming Home* (Westport, CT: Praeger, 2000), pp.248–252.

Creveld, Martin van, *The Transformation of War* (New York: The Free Press, 1991).

Davis, Mike, 'Planet of Slums', *Harpers Magazine* (June 2004).

Defense Science Board, *Final Report of the Defense Science Board Task Force on Globalization and Security* (1999).

Department of the Army, FM 30-5, *Combat Intelligence* (October 1973).

Dorff, Robert H., 'Strategy, Grand Strategy, and the Search for Strategy', in Max G. Manwaring, Edwin G. Corr and Robert H. Dorff (eds), *The Search for Security: A U.S. Grand Strategy for the Twenty-First Century* (Westport, CT: Praeger, 2003), pp.131–137.

Dunlop, John P., *Russia Confronts Chechnya* (Cambridge: Cambridge University Press, 1998).

Edwards, Sean J.A., *Swarming on the Battlefield: Past, Present, and Future* (Santa Monica, CA: RAND, 2000).

Esty, Daniel C., et al., 'The State Failure Projects: Early Warning Research for U.S. Foreign Policy Planning', in: John L. Davies and Ted Robert Gurr (eds), *Preventive Measures: Building Risk Assessment and Crisis Early Warning Systems* (New York: Rowman & Littlefield, 1998), pp.27–38.

Falkenrath, Richard A., Robert D. Newman and Bradley A. Thayer, *America's Achilles Heel Nuclear, Biological, and Chemical Terrorism and Covert Attack* (Cambridge, MA: MIT Press, 2001).

Finch, Raymond C., III, 'A Face of Future Battle: Chechen Fighter Shamil Basayev', *Military Review* (June–July 1997). Access via ⟨http://fmso.leavenworth.army.mil/fmsopubs/issues/ shamil/shamil.htm⟩.

Galeotti, Mark, 'Chechnia: The Theft of a Nation', *Boundary & Security Bulletin*, Vol.2, No.1 (1994).

Galeotti, Mark, 'Chechen Crime Alive and Well', *Jane's Intelligence Review* (March 2000).

Garfinkel, Simson L., 'Leaderless Resistance Today', *First Monday*, Vol.8, No.3 (March 2003). Access via ⟨http://firstmonday.org/issues/issue8_3/garfinkel/index.html⟩.

Gelb, Leslie H., 'Quelling the Teacup Wars', *Foreign Affairs* (November–December 1994), pp.5–6.

Gerard Oag, Graham, *Pre-empting Maritime Terrorism in Southeast Asia* (Institute of South East Asian Studies: 29 November 2002). Access via ⟨http://www.iseas.edu.sg/viewpoint/ggonov02.pdf⟩.

Gerecht, Reuel Marc, 'The Terrorists' Encyclopedia', *The Middle East Quarterly*, Vol.8, No.3, (Summer 2001). Access via: ⟨www.meforum.org⟩.

Giap, Vo Nguyen, 'The Factors of Success', *People's War, People's Army* (New York: Frederick A. Praeger, 1962), pp.36–37.

Gilpin, Robert, *War & Change in World Politics* (Cambridge, MA: Cambridge University Press, 1993).

Global Guerillas Website. John Robb, webmaster. Access via ⟨http://www.globalguerillas. typepad.com⟩.

Godson, Roy and William J., Olson, 'International Organized Crime', *Society* (January–February 1995), pp.18–29.

Griffin, Roger, ed., *Fascism* (New York: Oxford University Press, 1996).

Gross, Bertram, *Friendly Fascism: The New Face of Power in America* (South End Press: Boston, MA, 1980).

Gunaratna, Rohan, *Inside Al Qaeda: Global Network of Terror* (Hurst & Co.: London, 2002).

Ted Gurr, 'A Causal Model of Civil Strife: A Comparative Analysis Using New Indices', *American Political Science Review*, Vol.62 (4 December 1968).

Hassan, Nasra, 'Al Qaeda's Understudy', *The Atlantic Monthly*, June 2004, pp.42–43.

Herman, Arthur, *The Idea of Decline in Western History* (New York: The Free Press, 1997).

Hobsbawm, Eric J., *Bandits*, revised ed. (New York: The New Press, 2000).

Hobsbawm, Eric J., *Primitive Rebels: Studies in Archaic Forms of Social Movement in the 19th & 20th Centuries*, 3rd ed. (Manchester: Manchester University Press, 1971).

Hoffman, Bruce, *Inside Terrorism* (London: Victor Gollancz, 1998).

Hoffman, Nicolas von, 'Contract Killers: How Privatizing the U.S. Military Subverts Public Oversight', *Harpers Magazine*, June 2004, pp.79–80.

Homer-Dixon, Thomas F., *Environment, Scarcity, and Violence* (Princeton, NJ: Princeton University Press, 1999).

Howard, Michael, et al., *The Laws of War: Constraints on Warfare in the Western World* (New Haven, CT: Yale University Press, 1994).

Jenkins, Brian, 'International Terrorism: A New Mode of Conflict', in David Carlton and Carlo Schaerf (eds), *International Terrorism and World Security* (Los Angeles, CA: Crescent Publications, 1975).

Jenkins, Brian M., *Will Terrorists Go Nuclear?*, P-5521 (Santa Monica, CA: RAND, 1975).

Jenkins, Brian M., *Countering al Qaeda*, MR-1620-RC (Santa Monica, CA: RAND, 2002).

Jenkins, Brian M., 'Redefining the Enemy: The World Has Changed, But Our Mindset Has Not', *Rand Review*, Spring 2004.

Johnson, James Turner, *Just War Tradition and the Restraint of War* (Princeton, NJ: Princeton University Press, 1981).

Johnson, Steven, *Emergence: The Connected Lives of Ants, Brains, Cities, and Software* (New York: Scribner, 2001).

Jordan, Amos A., William J. Taylor, Jr and Lawrence J. Korb, *American National Security: Policy and Process*, 3rd ed. (Baltimore, MD: The Johns Hopkins University Press, 1988).

Jordan, David C., *Drug Politics: Dirty Money and Democracies* (Norman, OK: University of Oklahoma Press, 1999).

Kalathil, Shanthi and Taylor C. Boas, *Open Networks, Closed Regimes: The Impact of the Internet on Authoritarian Rule* (Washington, DC: Carnegie Endowment for International Peace, 2003).

Kaplan, Robert D., 'The Coming Anarchy', *Atlantic Monthly*, February 1994.

Kaplan, Robert D., *The Coming Anarchy* (New York: Random House, 2000).

Kearney, A.T., 'Measuring Globalization: Economic Reversals, Forward Momentum', *Foreign Policy*, Vol.54 (March–April 2004).

Kelly, Kevin, *New Rules for the New Economy* (New York: Penguin Group, 1998).

Konstantinov, Andrei, *Banditskii Peterburg* (St Petersburg: Folio-Press, 1997).

Krebs, Vladis E., 'Mapping Networks of Terrorist Cells', *Connections*, Vol.24, No.3 (2002), pp.31–34.

Krebs, Valdis E., 'Uncloaking Terrorist Networks', *First Monday*, Vol.7, No.4 (April 2002). Access via ⟨http://www.firstmonday.dk/issues/issue7_4/krebs⟩.

Krebs, Vladis E. and Jume Holley, *OpportuniTies: Sustainable Communities through Network Building* (2002). Access via ⟨www.orgnet.com/OpportuniTies.pdf⟩.

Laquer, Walter, 'Post-Modern Terrorism', *Foreign Affairs* (September–October 1996).

Laquer, Walter, *The New Terrorism* (Oxford: Oxford University Press, 1999).

Lewis, Bernard, *The Crisis of Islam, Unholy War and Unholy Terror* (New York: Modern Library, 2003).

Liang, Qiao and Wang Xiangsui, *Unrestricted Warfare* (Beijing: PLA Literature and Arts Publishing House, 1999).

Liddell-Hart, B.H., *Strategy*, 2nd rev. ed. (New York: Signet, 1974).

Luikart, Kenneth A., 'Transforming Homeland Security – Intelligence Indications and Warning', *Air and Space Power Journal* (Summer 2003).

Mackinlay, John, 'Beyond the Logjam: A Doctrine for Complex Emergencies', in Max G. Manwaring and John T., Fishel (eds), *Toward Responsibility in the New World Disorder: Challenges and Lessons of Peace Operations* (London: Frank Cass, 1998).

Mackinlay, John, 'War Lords', *Defense and International Security* (April 1998), pp.24–32.

Mair, Stefan, 'The New World of Privatized Violence', *International Politik und Gesellschaft* (February 2003). Access via ⟨http://fesportal.fes.de/pls/portal30/docs/FOLDER/IPG/IPG2-2003/ARTMAIR.HTM⟩.

Manwaring, Max G. and John T. Fishel 'Insurgency and Counter-Insurgency: Toward a New Analytical Approach', *Small Wars & Insurgencies*, Vol.3, No.3 (Winter 1992), pp.272–310.

Markle Foundation Task Force on National Security in the Information Age, *Protecting America's Freedom in the Information Age* (New York: Markle Foundation, 2002). Access via ⟨http://www.markletaskforce.org/⟩.

Mathews, Jessica, 'Power Shift', *Foreign Affairs* (January–February 1997).

Monge, Peter and Noshir Contractor, *Theories of Communication Networks* (New York: Oxford University Press, 2003).

Montake, Simon, 'Pirates Ahead!', *Christian Science Monitor*, 18 March 2004. Access via ⟨http://www.csmonitor.com/2004/0318/p13s02-woap.html⟩.

Morgenthau, Hans J., *Politics Among Nations: The Struggle for Power and Peace*, rev. Kenneth W. Thompson (McGraw Hill, New York, 1985).

Mylroie, Laurie, 'Iraq and the Clinton Presidency', *Journal of Counterterrorism & Homeland Security*, Vol.8, No.2 (2002), pp.10–15.

Mylroie, Laurie 'Going after Iraq', *Journal of Counterterrorism & Homeland Security*, Vol.8, No.4 (2002), pp.10–13.

Nisbet, Robert, *History of the Idea of Progress* (New Brunswick, NJ: Transaction Publishers, 1994).

Nye, Joseph S., Jr, *The Paradox of American Power* (Oxford: Oxford University Press, 2002).

Olson, William J., 'International Organized Crime: The Silent Threat to Sovereignty', *The Fletcher Forum of World Affairs*, Summer–Fall 1997, pp.66–80.

Payne, Stanley G., *A History of Fascism, 1914–1945* (Madison, WI: The University of Wisconsin Press, 1995).

Pennell, C.R., ed., *Bandits at Sea: A Pirates Reader* (New York: New York University Press, 2001).

Peters, Ralph, 'The New Warrior Class', *Parameters*, Summer 1994, pp.16–26.

Pizarro, Eduardo and Ana Maria Bejarano, 'Colombia: A Failing State?', *ReVista: Harvard Review of Latin America*, Spring 2003, pp.1–6.

Post, Jerrold M., 'It's Us Against Them: The Group Dynamics of Political Terrorism', *Terrorism*, Vol.10, No.1 (1987).

Post, Jerrold M., 'Rewarding Fire with Fire: Effects of Retaliation on Terrorist Group Dynamics', *Terrorism*, Vol.10 (1987), pp.23–36.

Rapoport, David, 'Fear and Trembling: Terrorism in Three Religious Traditions', *American Political Science Review*, Vol.78, No.3 (1984).

Raufer, Xavier, 'Gray Areas: A New Security Threat', *Political Warfare: Intelligence, Activities, Measures and Intelligence Report 20* (Spring 1992).

Rheingold, Howard, *Smart Mobs: The Next Social Revolution* (New York: Perseus Publishing, 2002).

Rich, Paul B., 'Warlordism, Complex Emergencies and the Search for a Doctrine of Humanitarian Intervention', in D.S., Gordon and F.H., Toase (eds), *Aspects of Peacekeeping* (London: Frank Cass, 2001), pp.253–273.

Risse, Thomas, 'Transnational Actors and World Politics', in Walter Carlsnaes et al. (eds), *Handbook of International Relations* (London: Sage Publications, 2002).

Ronfeldt, David, 'Social Science at 190 MPH on NASCAR's Biggest Superspeedways', *First Monday* (February 2000). Access via ⟨http://firstmonday.org/issues/issue5_2/index.html⟩.

Rothberg, Richard, 'From the Whole Cloth: Making Up the Terrorist Network', *Connections*, Vol.24, No.(3) (2002), pp.36–42.

Rudakov, A.L., *Chechenskaya mafiya* (Moscow: EKSMO-Press, 2002).

Schmid, Alex P. and Janny de Graaf, *Violence As Communication: Insurgent Terrorism and the Western News Media* (London and Beverly Hills, CA: Sage Publications, 1982).

Shawcross, William, *Deliver Us from Evil: Warlords, Peacekeepers, and a World of Endless Conflict* (New York: Simon & Schuster, 2000).

Shultz, Richard H. and Andreas Vogt, 'It's War! Fighting Post-11 September Global Terrorism through a Doctrine of Preemption', *Terrorism and Political Violence*, Vol.15, No.1 (Spring 2003).

Singer, P.W., 'War, Profit, and the Vacuum of Law: Privatized Military Firms and International Law', *Columbia Journal of International Law* (2004).

Slaughter, Anne-Marie, *A New World Order* (Princeton, NJ: Princeton University Press, 2004).

Smith, Sebastian, *Allah's Mountains* (London: I.B. Tauris, 1998).

Starhawk, *Webs of Power: Notes from the Global Uprising* (Gabriola Island, BC: New Society Publishers, 2002).

Steele, Robert David, *The New Craft of Intelligence: Personal, Public, & Political* (Oakton, VA: OSS International Press, 2002).

Stern, Jessica, *Terror in the Name of God: Why Religious Militants Kill* (New York: Ecco Press, 2003).

Sullivan, John P., 'Networked Force Structure and C⁴I', in Robert J. Bunker (ed.), *Non-State Threats and Future Wars* (London: Frank Cass, 2003), pp.144–155.

Sun, Tzu, *The Art of War* trans. Samuel B. Griffith (London: Oxford University Press, 1963).

Toffler, Alvin, *Power Shift* (New York: Bantam, 1990).

Toffler, Alvin and Heidi, Toffler, *War and Anti-War: Survival at the Dawn of the 21st Century* (New York: Little, Brown and Company, 1993).

Venzke, Ben, *Saudi Compound Bombings (SCB) – v1.4* (Alexandria, VA: IntelCenter, 2003). Access via ⟨www.intelcenter.org⟩.

Venzke, Ben, *al Qaeda Wave Attack Assessment v. 1.0* (Alexandria, VA: IntelCenter, 2003). Access via ⟨www.intelcenter.org⟩.

Walzer, Michael, *Just and Unjust Wars* (New York: Basic Books, 1977).

Wechsler, William F., 'Strangling the Hydra: Targeting Al Qaeda's Finances', in James F. Hoge, Jr and Gideon Rose (eds), *How Did This Happen: Terrorism and the New War* (New York: Council on Foreign Relations, 2001).

Weigley, Russell F., 'The Evolution of Strategic Thought', in B. Thomas Trent and James E., Harf (eds), *National Security Affairs: Theoretical Perspectives and Contemporary Issues* (New Brunswick, NJ: Transaction Books, 1982).

Weinberger, David, *Small Pieces Loosely Joined: A Unified Theory of the Web* (Cambridge, MA: Perseus Publishing, 2002).

Wellman, Barry, 'The Rise (and Possible Fall) of Networked Individualism', *Connections*, Vol.24, No.3 (2002), pp.30–32.

Williams, Paul L., *Al Qaeda: Brotherhood of Terror* (New York: Alpha Books, 2002).

Williams, Phil, 'The Nature of Drug-Trafficking Networks', *Current History* (April 1998).

Williams, Phil, 'Transnational Criminal Networks', in John Arquilla and David Ronfeldt (eds), *Networks and Netwars: The Future of Terror, Crime, and Militancy* (Santa Monica, CA: RAND, 2001).

Wilson, G.I., John P. Sullivan and Hal Kempfer, 'Fourth Generation Warfare: It's Here, And We Need New Intelligence-gathering Techniques for Dealing with It', *Armed Forces Journal International*, October 2002, pp.56–62.

Wilson, John, *Karachi: A Terror Capital in the Making* (New Delhi: Rupa & Co., 2003).

Zhilin, Andrei, 'The Caucasian War: The Scene in Moscow', *Jamestown Foundation Prism*, 22 March 1996.

INDEX

4GW 29–30, 80, 115–16, 132, 184, 197n
11 September 2001 (9/11) 1, 101, 115,
122, 123, 183; and globalization 40–1,
42, 50; information security 161–2;
modeling 185; narrative dimension 14;
network 191; organizational
dimensions xxiv–xxv; stealth-making
159; US counterattack 149

Abadan, Iran 123
abstention 102, 103, 107, 108
Abu Ghraib 79
Abu Sayyaf Group (ASG) xvii
accountability 57–65
Adams, Gerry 104, 108, 109, 110, 111,
113
adaptive behavior 152, 165–6, 167
adat 172, 176
Adid, Mohammed Farah 156
Afghanistan 9, 13, 14, 23, 72, 77;
Al Qaeda 61, 86, 117, 121, 139, 148–
9, 165–6
Al-Ansar xiii
Al Ansari, Mustafa Abdul Kader 157
Al-Iqwanul Muslamoon 178
al-Khattab, Omar ibn 179
Al Neda 160
Al Qaeda xii, xiii, 1, 74, 101–2, 184,
196; 9/11 115, 191; adaptation 69–70;
Afghanistan 61; Chechnya 177, 178,
180; cultural pedigree xvii; evolution
148–50; future potentials 167–8; as
global revolutionary 125–7; and
globalization 41, 47, 51, 56, 64;
hegemonic warfare 116; insurgency

72; leadership 5, 107, 111, 114;
Manwaring paradigm 117, 118, 119;
networks 5, 6, 8, 9–10, 84, 86, 194;
operational combat analysis 151–66;
order-of-battle 129–30, 131, 132–44;
organization 13, 14; poetry xvi; and
warlords 77
Al-Qurashi, Ubeid xiii
al-Sadr, Moktada 77
al Zawahiri, Ayman 119
Algeria 72
all-channel networks 185
ambiguity 32
American Border Patrol (ABP) xv
anger 104
anomalies 143–4
anti-colonialism 48
Arab street 90, 98
Arafat, Yasir 53, 55
Argentina 73
armed struggle 102, 103, 107, 108, 110
Arquilla, John 52, 70, 147, 156, 184–5,
194, 195
Arroyo, Gloria Macapagal 11
As-Seif, Abu Omar Mohammed 179
Asahara, Shoko 50
asymmetric warfare 29–30, 80, 115–16,
132, 184, 197n
asymmetry 29–30
Atta, Mohammed 50, 161–2, 191
attack masking 152, 157–8
attention 52
attrition war 29
Aum Shinrikyo 50, 51, 56
Australia 14